Introduction

There is a long history in every sentence, every word·we speak has a tremendous history, every metaphor is full of historical symbolism. —Carl Jung, *Dream Analysis*, 1958

The words of a living language are like creatures: they are alive. Each word has a physical character, a look and a personality, an ancestry, an expectation of life and death, a hope of posterity. —Morris Bishop, *The American Heritage Dictionary of the English Language*, 1969

For the most part our words came deviously, making their way by winding paths through the minds of generations of men, even burrowing like moles through the dark subconsciousness. —John Moore, *You English Words*, 1961

In an often cynical world where attention spans seem best suited to YouTube videos and where much of the populace is seemingly obsessed with the low-brow goings-on of Britney or Lindsay or Paris, one amazing fact rises above the muck: it's amazingly rare to meet a person who isn't in some way interested in words and language. From slang-slinging youngsters to crossword-solving oldsters, from inveterate punsters to intrepid neologists, some aspect of language appeals to each person.

Is there one slice of the language pie that everyone likes? Probably not. People are just too complex to like any one thing universally. However, in my own admittedly limited experience (I haven't met every person in the world), I have yet to come across a person who doesn't appreciate a good story about the origins of a word or phrase. Tell a person how an Egyptian god, salt, and camel dung were once combined linguistically to produce the word *ammonia*, and he'll beg for more. Explain how there's an honest-to-goodness saint behind the decidedly unsaintly word *tawdry*, and you'll start to gather a crowd. Explain how the unlikely word duo of *supercilious* and *eyebrow* are actually closely related, and you'll be the hit of the party (at least until they serve the cake).

You'll find these stories and hundreds more here in *The Complete Idiot's Guide to Weird Word Origins*. (Including the story of how the word *weird* is related to the word *fate*. Weird!) From *A1* to *zydeco*, this book gives you the histories and mysteries, the unexpected twists and surprising turns, behind nearly 600 words and phrases. Why do magicians say *abracadabra?* Why do we eat crow and humble pie? Who put the pigeon in *pigeonhole*, the goat in *scapegoat*, and the dog in *underdog?* You'll find the answers to these questions and many more in the pages that follow.

Before you get started, here are a couple of housekeeping notes about the otherwise oh-so-simple text:

- **Pointers to related words.** One of the fascinating things about word origins is that a single root word can sprout many different lexical plants, so many of the words in the book are related. So if I use a word that's defined somewhere else in the book, I'll format it in small caps, like this: SMALL CAPS.

- **Handling gender pronouns.** Whenever I talk about a generic person in this book, I almost always refer to that person as *he* or *him.* This is nothing more or less than laziness on my part because in a book such as this that's not written linearly (that is, I didn't start with the As and work my way methodically to the Zs), it's just too hard to alternate gender (which is my preferred way of handling gender pronouns). Why not just use genderless (genderful?) constructions such as *his/her* or *s/he?* Don't be silly.

- **Sidebars.** Finally, you'll see tons of extra doodads called *sidebars* positioned on many of the book's pages. These asides are designed to supply you with extra information that I couldn't resist adding. Here's what they look like:

Snappy Title

Sidebars provide extra details, fascinating asides, linguistic diversions, and other TIDBITS. (Ooh, look, there's one of the word pointers that I just talked about.)

Acknowledgments

She was a copy editor, possessed of the rare capacity to sit all day in a small cubicle, like a monk in a cell, and read with an almost penitential rigor. —David Leavitt, *Lost Language of Cranes*

Foreword

As a lexicographer, I am often asked (usually at a party, while I have a drink in one hand and a canapé in the other, and without a dictionary in sight) where a particular word came from. "It's such an interesting word," my interlocutor says. "Where is it from? What's its story?"

Most people, when they ask about a word's history, want to be told that the word comes from an acronym (preferably one that involves kings and unspeakable acts) or, at the very least, that their word, the one that caught their eye, the one they've been *meaning* to look up forever, is the *only* word in the entire English language known to come from Etruscan.

Unfortunately, the stories behind most words are usually straightforward (and "straightforward," in etymological terms, is another way of saying "boring"). Most words haven't lived daring lives of adventure and excitement: most words have just gone on, year in and year out, meaning much the same thing as they did the year before. Word enthusiasts are often disappointed both in how many words' histories are unknown, and in how many of the histories that are known read like the minutes of a particularly dull school board meeting, instead of like beach-thriller novels.

But even when a word's story is known, and is exciting (as the ones in this book are), what does it really tell us? Etymology is to words as genealogy is to people: knowing that your great-grandfather captained a whaling ship is fascinating, but it doesn't mean that *you* know port from starboard. By the same token, knowing that *aloof* comes from the nautical phrase "a luff," meaning "to steer a boat to windward," won't necessarily add any tang of salt air to your use of the word ... but it may just give you a feeling of deep and abiding satisfaction. Knowledge, in this case, is its own reward.

If you, too, feel that little thrill whenever you discover the hidden past of a favorite word, this book is certain to yield many little "aha!" moments of pleasure at the connections between words and languages, and to give you some rip-roaring good stories about your language's ancestors to tell.

—Erin McKean, editor, *VERBATIM: The Language Quarterly*

The editors of the world are, to me, both eyebrow-archingly inspiring and head-scratchingly awesome. They're smart, dedicated, and possessed of the seemingly impossible ability to see both the forest and the trees at the same time. I admire editors not only because they have that admirable quality of being right almost all the time, but also because they have the uncanny ability to track down the most subtle of grammatical gaffes and logical errors. In short, I'm pro-editors because editors make me look like a pro. For this book, the wonderful people who made me look like a much better writer than I am include development editor Lynn Northrup and copy editor Michael Dietsch. Special thanks, as well, are due to acquisitions editor Michele Wells, who was silly enough to ask me to write this book in the first place.

Trademarks

All terms mentioned in this book that are known to be or are suspected of being trademarks or service marks have been appropriately capitalized. Alpha Books and Penguin Group (USA) Inc. cannot attest to the accuracy of this information. Use of a term in this book should not be regarded as affecting the validity of any trademark or service mark.

A1

You use this adjective to describe something that's truly top-notch or first class (you know, something like "This is an A1 book!"). You may also see it written as *A-1* or *A 1*, and you may hear folks describe something as *A number 1*. All these variations come from the eighteenth century when an Englishman named Edward Lloyd (whose name lives on as the founder of the famous insurer Lloyd's of London) began publishing Lloyd's Register, an annual list of ships and their equipment. Yes, people actually read that kind of thing back in those days. Anyway, each ship was given a two-part rating: the first part referred to the ship itself, and a rating of A meant that the ship's hull was brand-spanking new or fully restored; the second part referred to the ship's equipment, and a rating of 1 meant that the ship was fully stocked with the latest gear ("well and sufficiently found" in the quaint and indecipherable prose of the day). The worst rating given by Lloyd's Register was C3, but (not all that surprisingly) that designation never took off as a synonym for something not very good ("Britney's new album is C3!").

abracadabra

If you're a magician who's a bit on the old-fashioned side, you can use the word *abracadabra* right before you perform a trick as a way of ensuring the "success" of the trick. The rest of us can use the word to refer to any kind of nonsense or BALDERDASH. (Not surprisingly, a search of the literature reveals that the phrase "legal abracadabra" is quite common.) The traditional explanation for the origin of this curious word (no one knows exactly where it came from) is that the two "abra" parts are based on the first letters of the Hebrew words *ab* ("father"), *ben* ("son"), and *ruach acadosch* ("holy spirit"). Another good guess is that it comes from the Chaldean phrase *abbada ka dabra,* which means, curiously, "perish like the word." Abracadabra doesn't show up in English until 1696, but it's much older than that, first appearing in a second-century Latin poem by the Roman physician Quintus Severus Sammonicus (they don't make names like *that* anymore!). It's thought that abracadabra was used as a kind of charm, but only if it appeared in the following form:

A B R A C A D A B R A
A B R A C A D A B R
A B R A C A D A B
A B R A C A D A
A B R A C A D
A B R A C A
A B R A C
A B R A
A B R
A B
A

Write it like that on a piece of parchment or inscribe it on a handy amulet, suspend it around your neck, and you'd soon be rid of your toothache or fever or whatever. Take two abracadabras and call me in the morning …

accomplice

See COMPLICITY.

adultery

You may be surprised to hear that there's no adult in adultery. That's because the word *adultery,* "extramarital sex," goes back to the Latin term *adulterare,* "to pollute, corrupt, or defile." (This in turn comes from *alterare,* "to alter.") Having relations with someone outside of one's marriage was seen as defiling—or adulterating—the marriage vows, and the verb eventually turned into the noun adultery. There's no adolescent in adultery, either, but there is an adult, because that word traces back to the Latin *adultus,* a form of the verb *adolescere,* "to grow up," which was the source of the word *adolescent.*

algorithm   **3**

aegis

The word *aegis* (it's pronounced *EEjis*) means "protection, support, or patronage." For example, *They returned to their homes under the aegis of the U.N. peacekeeping force* or *The charity ball was held under the aegis of the Chamber of Commerce*. Things are always "under" the aegis because the word comes from Greek mythology, where it represented the shield of Zeus himself.

algebra

See ALGORITHM.

algorithm

This term will be familiar to anyone who has taken Computer Science 101 (remember flow charts?); it refers to some logical sequence of steps that leads to the solution of a problem. The idea is to then translate those steps into programming code so that a computer can be dragooned into performing the grunt work of producing the actual solution. What term could be more high-tech? Strange, then, that the word wasn't coined at IBM in the 1950s, Microsoft in the 1980s, or somewhere in Silicon Valley in the 1990s. No, this word's pedigree goes way back to the *ninth century!* Back in 830, an Arab astronomer named Mohamed ibn Musa al-Khwarizmi wrote an important book on mathematics that, through various translations (and a few hundred years), brought Arabic numerals to the attention of Europe, thus blessedly ending the dominance of Roman numerals (the Super Bowl notwithstanding). The use of Arabic numbers and the decimal system was named after al-Khwarizmi, and became known as *algorism*, which turned into *algorithm*. By the way, the name of al-Khwarizmi's mathematics treatise was (take a deep breath) *Al-Kitab Almukhtamar fi Hisab al-Jabr w'al Muqabala* (this translates roughly as *The Compendious Book on Calculation by Completion and Balancing*), and it provided the math geeks of the day with techniques for manipulating equations. The *al-Jabr* portion of the title eventually turned into the word *algebra*.

all over but the shouting

When someone tells you that "it's all over but the shouting," you know he's telling you that although some situation or event is not yet done, the outcome or result of that situation is clear. And yet when the end does come, there's often no shouting at all. What's up with that? It turns out that there *used* to be shouting—lots of it. In England way back in the day, towns would make major decisions by a kind of live referendum. All the folks would gather in the town square or perhaps the village green and debate the matter at hand. They would then come to a decision based on a voice vote, and because of this, these gatherings were known as *shoutings*. If, before the gathering, the outcome of the vote was known or obvious, then the situation was said to be *all over but* (or *bar*) *the shouting*.

allure

An alluring person is one who is highly attractive and enticing. The verb *allure* made its way into English by way of the French verb *aleurrer*, "to bait." It was originally used by falconers and referred to a device or bait to lure the birds into returning, from which we get the current sense of "enticing." I suppose this means that the person doing the alluring must have to watch the other person like a hawk!

aloof

The word *aloof* means "detached, distant," and we use those terms metaphorically. That is, the person isn't literally distant, just emotionally or socially distant. However, at one time aloof really did refer to something that was literally distant. Back in the mid-sixteenth century, sailing captains would ask their helmsmen to keep the ship's bow to the wind to avoid being blown toward the lee shore. In the sailing lingo of the day, *luff* referred to either the windward direction or to the windward side of the ship. So to steer with the bow to the wind meant to steer in the direction of the windward side. To make this so, the captain would give the order to "steer aluff," where the word *aluff* is a combination of the prefix *a-*, meaning (in this case) "in the direction of" and *luff*. A hundred years or so later, *aluff* had become *aloof*, but it still referred to steering the bow of a ship into the wind. Remember that the goal of steering aloof was to keep some distance between the ship and the shore, so it didn't take long before aloof also came to mean "at some distance; apart." The current sense of being emotionally detached or distant followed in quick order, so that by 1602, William Shakespeare, in his play *Hamlet*, had the character Laertes say "I stand aloof, and will no reconcilement."

Amazon

These days, this word refers to the world's second longest river, the world's largest (online) retailer, or a physically imposing woman who is both strong and strong-willed. This last meaning fits well with the origins of the word *Amazon*, which refers to a mythical race of all-female warriors who lived around Scythia (which would be where Ukraine sits today). The Greek historian Herodotus described them as particularly fierce fighters and called them *Androktones*, or "men-killers." Homer mentions the Amazons in *The Iliad* and says that they "fight like men." The origin of the word *Amazon* is disputed, but the most interesting idea is that it combines the prefix *a*, meaning "without," and the Greek term *mazos*, meaning "breast." (The latter gave us the now-obsolete word *mazology*, the study of mammals—now called mammalogy—one characteristic of which is the existence of mammary glands, that is to say, breasts.) This harkens to the legendary tendency for your average Amazon warrior to have her right breast removed so that it wouldn't get in the way when wielding a bow and arrow. Now *that's* dedication!

The Amazin' Amazon

If the Amazon is the second-longest river in the world, what's the longest? That distinction belongs to the Nile River, which at 4,160 miles (that's 6,695 kilometers in metric-speak) is just a bit longer than the Amazon's 4,049 miles (6,516 kilometers). Or is it? A recent (Summer 2007) report by a team of Brazilian scientists upped the length of the Amazon to 4,225 miles (6,800 kilometers), making it (assuming the report is confirmed) the new champ.

ambulance

You may know that the verb *ambulate* means "to walk," and the adverb *ambulatory* means "of or relating to walking." Both terms came our way from the Latin word *ambulare*, "to walk." By now you may be scratching your head because the word *ambulance* is mighty close to *ambulate* and *ambulatory*, but it's a vehicle, for Pete's sake! The thing has no legs! Ah, but it once did, in a manner of speaking. It used to be that in a war, if you got injured on the battlefield, your peers simply left you there until darkness fell and it was safe to drag you out for medical ministrations (assuming you were still alive to benefit from them). In the early nineteenth century, the French decided this wasn't a great state of affairs. Their solution was to trick out a wagon or cart with basic medical supplies. They could quickly run the wagon onto the battlefield, pick up a wounded soldier, and tend to his injuries while getting him the heck out of there. The French saw this as a kind of moving hospital, so they named the wagon a *hôpital ambulant*, or "walking hospital." During the Crimean War in the mid-nineteenth century, the British took note of these *hôpitals ambulant* and borrowed the idea. They eventually dropped the *hôpital* part, and the wagons became known as just *ambulances*.

ammonia

The gas ammonia is composed of three parts hydrogen and one part nitrogen, but linguistically it's composed of an Egyptian deity, salt, and camel dung! Let me explain: ancient Egyptian mythology included a primordial god named Amun ("the hidden one"), who was variously represented as a ram or as a man with a ram's head. The Greeks worshipped the same god under the named Ammon. Near this god's temple, devotees would for some reason heat camel dung (or perhaps camel urine) and sea salt to produce a substance called *sal ammoniac*, "salt of Ammon." In 1782, a Swedish chemist with nothing better to do combined sal ammoniac with an alkali to create a new gas, which he dubbed *ammonia*.

antediluvian

If you want to describe something as old, you might call it *aged*, *archaic*, *antiquated*, or even *ancient*. However, if you want to describe something that's *really* old—and since you seem to like adjectives that begin with the letter *a*—then I suggest the word *antediluvian*, "extremely old." How old are we talking here? Well, since this term comes from the Latin *antediluvium*, which combines *ante-*, "before," and *diluvium*, "deluge," then we're talking about, literally, before the Biblical Flood. Now *that* is old.

antimacassar

In Virtues nothing earthly could surpass her Save thine "incomparable Oil," *Macassar!* This sarcastic bit of verse was penned by none other than Lord Byron (in his 1819 poem *Don Juan*), and he's talking about a product called Macassar Oil, which first appeared earlier in that century. Macassar Oil was an unguent for the hair that claimed to remove "impurities," provide hair with a "beautiful gloss and scent," hold curls in place, and even cure baldness. The manufacturers claimed it was made from oils imported from a place called Macassar, a port on the Indonesian island that we now call Sulawesi. This is unlikely, but no matter: the product was a rousing success and before long few heads remained unoiled. That was bad news for the sofas and chairs of the day, because they soon became covered in oily stains. To fight back, housewives covered their furniture with decorative cloths that served to protect the fabric from the onslaught of Macassar Oil, so they become known as *antimacassars*.

April

See SEPTEMBER.

Aprium

See PLUOT.

arsenic hour

As most moms and dads know (assuming they have the time to find out these things), the arsenic hour is the hectic time of day after the parents arrive home from work and before dinner is served. This phrase also has a huge number of synonyms: *witching hour, sour hour, hurricane hour, granny hour, scotch hour, sherry hour,* and *suicide hour.* Clearly there's a deep well of black humor that's the source of these terms. Arsenic? Suicide? This forces those of us who are childless to wonder just what on Earth is going on out there! In neological circles, the presence of a large number of synonyms for something usually means not only that that something is an extremely common phenomenon, but also that it doesn't have an official name. (The sociological term for arsenic hour is the forgettable and far too understated *transition time*). Given the apparent intensity of the experience, people feel a need to label it somehow, so they come up with "X hour" constructions modeled, no doubt, on phrases such as *rush hour* and, ironically, *happy hour.* It's likely, too, that there's some influence here from the 1863 Henry Wadsworth Longfellow poem, *The Children's Hour:*

> Between the dark and the daylight,
> When the night is beginning to lower,
> Comes a pause in the day's occupations,
> That is known as the Children's Hour.

assassin

In the days of Omar Khayyam (he of the Rubaiyat fame), a band of malcontents roamed the Elburz Mountains, not far from the Caspian Sea. The leader of these bandits was an old school friend of Omar's, a man named Hasan Sabah, whose notoriety earned him the nickname Old Man of the Mountains. That notoriety was earned in rather ghastly fashion: from time to time, he and his followers would set upon and kill members of the government, religious figures, and other local VIPs. To get themselves stoked for these murderous missions, the rebels would eat copious amounts of the drug hashish. In the Arabic of the day, a person who ate a lot of hashish (or who was addicted to it) was called a *hashishiyun*, and that name soon stuck to this band of whacked-out executioners. Over time, the word *hashishiyun* came to refer to anyone who is hired (or feels a strong need) to kill a public figure, and the word itself morphed into our modern word *assassin*. It gives a whole new meaning to the phrase "stone-cold killer."

August

See SEPTEMBER.

average

This solid mathematical term is actually founded upon the not-so-solid sea. Its origins lie in the French word *avarie* and the Spanish equivalent *averia*, which both originally referred to a duty or tax charged to imported goods. The word became the abstract noun *average* in English by tacking on the suffix *-age* (a common linguistic process that has given us words such as *breakage*, *postage*, and *wreckage*). Over time, the meaning of the word *average* changed to any unexpected expenses incurred while shipping goods, and then to the expenses arising from damage or loss to goods shipped at sea. The owners of the cargo, the operators of the ship, and the insurers of both would figure out a way to distribute these expenses equitably among themselves. Eventually this idea of an equal distribution attached itself to the mathematical idea of the arithmetic mean, and our main sense of average was born.

backgammon

If you love whiling away the hours playing the subtle-but-fun game of *backgammon*, as I do, then you know that one of the central strategies of the game is to land on an opponent's single checker, which sends that checker back to the bar to start all over again. That idea of sending a checker back is where the "back" part of *backgammon* comes from. The "gammon" part comes from the Middle English word *gamen*, "game." So backgammon is literally the "back-game." Feel free to use this story to distract your opponent the next time you play.

baker's dozen

Way back in the thirteenth century, Britain's King Henry III passed a law (or, really, revived an old law, but I pedantically digress) called the Assize of Bread and Ale (an *assize* is a statute or decree) that regulated the price of bread. Any miscreant baker who tried to sell a too-small loaf could be subject to a stiff fine, or could even be pilloried or whipped. Harsh! Bakers, most of whom (in my experience) have at least the standard complement of gray matter, had no desire to incur any of these punishments, but they realized that baking loaves to an exact weight is tough. It was always possible that a loaf or three could be a bit under the prescribed weight. So they hedged their bread bets by adding something extra to each purchase. This extra tidbit was called the *inbread* or the *vantage loaf.* If you were just buying a loaf, the baker would slip you a small chunk of bread as well; if you were buying a dozen loaves, then the paranoid baker would often give you a whole other loaf, just to be safe. It was this large-order premium that gave us the phrase *baker's dozen*, which means "thirteen."

balderdash

Writing in *The Baltimore Evening Sun* in 1921, H. L. Mencken, the great editor and satirist, described President Warren G. Harding's writing style: "It is rumble and bumble. It is flap and doodle. It is balder and dash." That last sentence is, of course, a play on the word *balderdash*, "nonsense." The origins of this fun word aren't certain, but most of the people who research this kind of thing for a living think that it comes from combining the dialect term *balder*, "to use coarse language" (which in turn comes from the Dutch term *balderen*, "to roar, thunder"), and the verb *dash*, "to smash something to pieces; to throw something violently." See also ABRACADABRA.

bandwagon

To *jump* (or *hop*) *on the bandwagon* means to join a popular movement. It's used for all kinds of rages and crazes nowadays, but it was first popularized in political campaigns. A hundred years or so ago, politicians running for office would literally put a musical band on a wagon and ride around a town to advertise their candidacy and whip up enthusiasm. Local officials who wanted to show their support for the candidate would jump onto the moving bandwagon.

bankrupt

To go belly-up, financially speaking, is usually bad news for the bank, a fact reflected in the origins of the word *bankrupt*. This term comes from the Italian phrase *banca rotta*, which means "broken bench." The *banca* (bench) in question was a money-dealer's table, and this word *banca* led to our modern word *bank*. The bench is broken because the poor sap undergoing financial ruin has in a very real sense "broken" his relationship with the bank. This idea is also the source of related phrases such as *to go broke* and *to break the bank*.

bellwether

A *bellwether* is something that acts as an indicator of a future trend, but to understand the origins of the word, you need to give some thought to a castrated male sheep. Wait, work with me here. An old word for such a sheep is *wether*. In the old days, a shepherd would hang a bell around the oldest wether in the flock, and the other sheep would then follow this "bellwether" wherever he went (these are, after all, sheep we're talking about). Over time, the word *bellwether* became associated with anything that acted as a leading indicator of some future trend.

between the devil and the deep blue sea

If you're *between the devil and the deep blue sea*, you face a difficult decision where the choices on both sides are equally dangerous or unpleasant. It would be reasonable to assume that the devil in question is old Satan himself, but he's involved in this story only tangentially. The real devil is a seam between the planks on the hull of a wooden ship, which an old edition of Funk and Wagnall's dictionary defines, unhelpfully, as "a seam between the garboard-strake and the keel." All the seams on a wooden ship must be caulked to keep out water, and certain ones were apparently very hard to get to (must be that darn garboard-strake!). In fact, the sailors of those days would often describe those seams as being "the devil to get at," and so the difficult-to-reach seams became known as *devils*. A particularly tough job would be having to caulk one of these seams mid-voyage. Out there in the middle of the ocean, the poor seaman would literally be "between the devil and the deep blue sea." This old nautical saying later found a place among landlubbers facing an equally difficult (although in most cases a certainly less dangerous) dilemma.

Damned if You Do ...

If you're between the devil and the deep blue sea, you could also say that you're on the *horns of a dilemma*. No, those aren't the devil's horns, but something even more figurative. In the philosophical discipline known as *rhetoric*, a *dilemma* is a form or argument in which you give your adversary a choice of two equally unpleasant alternatives. The classic example is the question "Do you still beat your wife?" where it doesn't matter whether you answer yes or no. In a rare moment of philosophical near-whimsy, this was pictured as presenting the two horns of a bull to your opponent, and if you dodge one, you'll still be impaled on the other. So a dilemma was also known as a *horned argument* or a *horned syllogism*, and eventually the choice itself became known as being on the *horns of a dilemma*.

bigwig

If you want to refer to an important person, but you want to do so with a dash of humor or perhaps a pinch of contempt, look no farther than the word *bigwig*. If you've seen any period movies that take place in eighteenth-century Europe, you've no doubt noticed that all but the poorest men of the day wore wigs. Why this should be so is something I'll leave to the hair historians (although I'm thinking the fact that dandruff shampoo hadn't been invented yet is a major clue). As with most goods, there was a wig hierarchy, with short, cheap hairpieces at the bottom and long, luxurious wigs at the top. In general, the longer the wig, the more expensive it was and so, by association, the more important was the person under the wig. This association was heightened by Louis XIV, king of France, whose midlife crisis involved wearing immensely long wigs, a fashion soon copied by the sycophants and other hangers-on at the royal court. It eventually became customary for only nobles, judges, and clergy to wear long wigs, and by the end of the eighteenth century, people had started referring to these gentleman mockingly as *big wigs*, then *big-wigs*, and eventually *bigwigs*.

billion

> A billion here, a billion there, and pretty soon you're talking real money. —Everett Dirksen

If you live in North America, you're no doubt accustomed to thinking of a billion as a thousand millions, but if you live in Britain, you're more likely to think of a billion as a million millions, instead. Who's right? In the language game, on a fundamental level the only true sense of "right" we have to go by is popular usage; that is, the more people who use a word in a certain way, the more "right" that sense becomes. So, from that point of view, the "thousand millions" sense of *billion* is "right" because even some Brits are starting to use it. It may be an inevitable change, but it's a shame nonetheless, because it destroys the etymological roots of the word *billion* (not to mention words such as *trillion* and *quadrillion*, as you'll soon see). The word *billion* is actually a blend of the prefix *bi-* and the word *million*. In this case, though, the *bi-* prefix refers to the second power—a number squared, that is multiplied by itself—which is to say a million millions. Similarly, a *trillion* is supposed to be the third power of a million: a million million millions, or a billion millions, or the number 1 followed by 18 zeroes. The same process also gives us *quadrillion* (the fourth power of a million), *quintillion* (the fifth power of a million), *sextillion* (the sixth power of a million), *septillion* (the seventh power of a million), *octillion* (the eighth power of a million), and *nonillion* (the ninth power of a million). This eminently logical numbering scheme was created by the French mathematician Nicolas Chuquet (it's sometimes called the "Chuquet system"), and is still followed to some extent in Britain. Elsewhere, however, the numbers are all smaller by a factor of a thousand, making the prefixes (*bi-*, *tri-*, *quad-*, and so on) all but meaningless. The *Oxford English Dictionary* (*OED*) quite rightly calls this "an entire perversion of the nomenclature of Chuquet."

bistro

This is a small, informal restaurant. There are several explanations floating around about the origin of this word. One story is that, after the defeat of Napoleon in 1815, Russian soldiers hanging out in Paris would go into restaurants and shout "Vee-stra, vee-stra!" which is Russian for "Hurry, hurry!" The French took up the word as *bistro* and associated it with small restaurants where you could get a meal quickly.

blacklist

If you're on someone's *blacklist*, that's not a good thing, because it means that person disapproves of you, suspects you of some wrongdoing, or just wants to exclude you from something. However, that's not as bad as being on the original blacklist, which was maintained by Charles II of England. That list consisted of the 58 judges and other officials responsible for executing his father, Charles I, in 1649. When Charles II got the throne back in 1660, 20 of those on the blacklist escaped, but of the rest he put 13 to death and had the remaining 25 sentenced to life in prison. Ever since this notorious episode, we've used *blacklist* as a noun to refer to people we suspect or disapprove of.

Black and White

In case you're wondering, yes there is such as thing as a *whitelist*, a list of acceptable people or things. People use it as the opposite of a blacklist, and the term *whitelist* (as the phrase *white list*) entered the language around 1900. In modern computing parlance, a whitelist is a list of names, e-mail addresses, website addresses, or programs that are deemed to be spam- or virus-free.

B

blackmail

An old legend has it that the word *blackmail*, "a payment extorted by intimidation," originally referred to the chain-mail armor of errant knights, which some mysterious force would turn black as punishment for the knight's misdeeds. Interesting in a King Arthurish way, but pure hogwash, of course. The *mail* we're dealing with here isn't chain mail, but an obsolete form of the word that in Scotland once meant "rent." Farmers would pay the local chieftains and landowners mail in the form of silver coins, which were known as *white money.* By the sixteenth century, however, the usual mail wasn't good enough for the greedy chiefs, and they started demanding extra protection money from their tenant farmers who, if they refused to pay, would find their crops destroyed, or worse. The word *black* has long been associated with dark, negative things, and to those poor farmers, few things were as dark and negative as these extorted sums, so they starting referring to it as *blackmail.*

bleachers

You might not think that laundry hanging on an outdoor clothesline would have anything in common with baseball, but I urge you not to bet any money on the lack of a connection. First, you may know that the verb *bleach* means "to whiten clothing or linens by washing them and then hanging them to dry in the sun." This image of linens spending hours in the sun must have popped into the brain of some wit watching a daytime baseball game, because he looked at the folks sitting in the sun in the outfield stands and figured they resembled a bunch of clothes getting bleached. Each person then became a *bleacher,* and before you know it the stands themselves were called *bleachers.*

bling-bling

One of hip-hop's most popular slang terms is *bling-bling*, which originally referred to the massive amounts of showy jewelry worn by some rappers, but now it's the hip-hop equivalent of *glitz*, a flashy, possibly even tasteless, display of wealth. It was coined by rapper B.G. in his 1999 hit single, "Bling, Bling." Soon after, the cover of *Newsweek*'s October 9, 2000, issue screamed, "Welcome to the Bling Bling Generation." In the article, B.G. explains how he came up with the phrase:

> I was just thinking how I like to get my shine on when I go out. You know, I've been through a lot. Life is hard growing up in the projects and seeing all kind of things kids shouldn't see. So now that I got myself out of that situation and doing well, I'm going "bling-bling" because I deserve to.

blog

See WEBLOG.

blue-pencil

This verb means "to shorten the manuscript or make it more concise." It comes from the blue lead pencils that editors once used to mark corrections, particularly deletions.

bluestocking

You use this term to refer to a woman with pretentious literary interests. The story behind this curious word is that around 1750, a Mrs. Elizabeth Montagu, who looked down on the less-refined entertainments of the day, organized a series of get-togethers in which the object was literary conversation. Although most of the attendees were women, one regular was a man named Benjamin Stillingfleet who, rather than wearing the black silk stockings that were considered fashionable and proper at the time, wore "vulgar" blue worsted stockings. The gatherings were soon mockingly nicknamed the Blue Stocking Society, and the short form *bluestocking* has been applied to the literarily pretentious ever since.

blurb

This term refers to "comments or notes about the book that appear on the book's dust jacket." This fun word was coined in 1907 by the humorist Gelett Burgess. Burgess was presenting copies of his book *Are You a Bromide?* to members of the American Booksellers Association. As a special treat, Burgess created a special dust jacket that showed a woman named Miss Belinda Blurb singing the praises of the book. The term *blurb* caught on a few years later, and Burgess later described the blurb as "a sound like a publisher ... abounding in agile adjectives and adverbs, attesting that this book is the 'sensation of the year.'" (A recent coinage is *blurb whore*, a writer who provides flattering comments about a book or movie in exchange for meals, travel, or some other perk.) Mr. Burgess is also famous for coining a word that never caught on but certainly deserved to: *tintiddle*, "a witty retort, thought of too late." See also BROMIDE.

bogus

If you don't mind sounding a bit surfer-dudish, you might describe something that's fake, deceitful, or useful as *bogus*. Dudes use the word as an adjective, and so have the rest of us for most of the word's 150 years in the language. However, when *bogus* first laid claim to some English ground, it was a noun; specifically, a machine for counterfeiting coins. For example, an article in the November 2, 1827, edition of the *Painesville (Ohio) Telegraph* refers to "The eight or ten boguses which have been for some time in operation." This type of machine was also called a *bogus press*. The noun version of the word *bogus* also eventually referred to any counterfeit coin. However, by the mid-eighteenth century, the connotations of the bogus machine gave birth to *bogus*, the adjective, meaning (of course) "counterfeit" and then more generally "fictitious, spurious." That's all well and good (if I do say so myself), but where did the noun *bogus* come from? No one knows for a fact, but a tantalizing clue comes from a Dr. S. Willard, who told the *OED* of one Eber D. Howe, one-time editor of the aforementioned *Painesville (Ohio) Telegraph*, that when the first coin counterfeiting machine was discovered, people thought it was awfully mysterious-looking, so people called it a "bogus." Dr. Willard suggests this is a shortened form of *tantrabogus*, a dialect term applied to anything that was unusual in appearance. Dr. Willard relates a similar word, *tantrabobs*, as being a synonym for the devil. Therefore, *bogus* may be derived from *bogey* and *bogy*, which both mean "devil; goblin." Of course, all of this speculation may just be bogus. (You *knew* I was going to end with that, didn't you?)

book

Authors sometimes jokingly refer to themselves as "tree-killers" because of the great numbers of trees that go into the making of their books. However, from a historical point of view, they could also get away with calling themselves "tree-makers." That's because the word *book* can be traced back to Anglo-Saxon times when scribblers used to scribble on chunks of bark from the beech tree. Their name for this tree was *boc*, and eventually that also became their name for the slabs of beech bark–based writings that they would bind together. That word eventually changed to *book* and stuck around even when the beech-bark slabs were replaced by printed pages.

boot

The verb *boot* means "to turn on a computer." (The similar verb *reboot* means "to restart a running computer," by pressing the machine's restart button or, more likely these days, by selecting the operating system's Restart command.) The verb *boot* comes from the phrase *bootstrap loader*, a tiny program used to start a computer. In the earliest machines, the bootstrap loader code was entered into the computer by hand using a series of toggle switches on the front panel. (And you thought Windows was hard to use!) Later machines read the bootstrap loader from punch cards or paper tape, while nowadays the code resides permanently in a chip inside the computer. In all cases, though, the bootstrap loader's job is to initialize the computer to the point where it can launch a slightly more complex program that would get the computer ready for its regular duties. This program then calls yet another program that loads the computer's operating system. This convoluted process enables the computer to initialize itself and get up and running into some kind of useful state. In other words, the computer *pulls itself up by its own bootstraps*, hence the name *bootstrap loader* for the computer's startup code. These days, the verbs *boot* and *reboot* have broken free of the shackles of computerdom and are roaming at will in the real world. In particular, you often see the verb *reboot* in nondigital contexts, where it means "to make a fresh start."

bootlegger

These days, tall boots that come up to the knees and even higher have a deservedly kinky connotation, and are definitely a women-only fashion statement. However, in days or yore, men would often wear tall boots as a matter of course. In the seventeenth century, the leg of a tall boot was called, no surprises here, the *boot-leg* and then later the *bootleg*. In late 1800s, it was illegal in many places in the United States to traffic in alcohol. Some dedicated liquor salesmen got around that by smuggling bottles inside their bootlegs, and these fellows soon became known as *bootleggers*. So although we normally associate bootleggers with Prohibition in the 1920s, the term *bootlegger* was in use as early as 1889. On a more modern note, smugglers still ply their sly trade these days, of course, and they've given rise to two recent bootlegger-related coinages: a *buttlegger* is a person who smuggles cigarettes, and a *bitlegger* is a person who illegally copies software or digital music.

bowdlerize

If you *bowdlerize* a manuscript, it means that you remove obscene or otherwise objectionable material from the text, particularly if those expurgations are excessively prudish. This comes from Dr. Thomas Bowdler, who in 1818 published *The Family Shakespeare* in which he had expunged from the works of William Shakespeare all those words that, as he put it, "cannot with propriety be read aloud in a family."

That Cheeky Dr. Johnson

My favorite expurgation story concerns the great lexicographer Dr. Samuel Johnson. After he had published his famous dictionary, two prudish ladies approached him and thanked him for leaving out "all naughty words." Dr. Johnson, ever the wag, replied "What! My dears! Then you have been looking for them?"

boycott

In Ireland in the late nineteenth century, much of the land was owned by Englishmen who rented out chunks of their properties to poor tenant farmers. These absentee landlords hired managers to watch over their estates, collect rents, and evict those who couldn't pay. One such manager was a former soldier named Charles Cunningham Boycott, who was employed by the Earl of Erne to manage his estates at Lough Mask House in Connaught. Meanwhile, a fiery Irish populist named Charles Parnell had created the Irish Land League with a mandate to reform how Ireland's land was held. On September 19, 1880, Parnell spoke to some citizens in Connaught and urged them to protest the recent evictions of tenant farmers. In particular, he urged the people to ostracize the evictors:

> When a man takes a farm from which another has been evicted, you must show him on the roadside when you meet him, you must show him at the shop counter, you must show him in the fair and at the market place and even in the house of worship, by leaving him severely alone, by putting him in a sort of moral Coventry, by isolating him from the rest of his kind as if he were a leper of old.

The stubborn Boycott refused to knuckle under to such pressure, and when he tried to evict yet another farmer, his remaining tenants forced Boycott's workers to leave him, he was refused service in all the local shops, his mail wasn't delivered, and he was booed and jeered whenever he showed his face in public. The idea of refusing to deal with someone or something as a protest or punishment soon took hold, and the name Boycott was attached to such a protest with amazing speed. For example, on November 20, 1880, just two months after Parnell's rabble-rousing speech, the *Times of London* reported that "The people of New Pallas have resolved to 'Boycott' them and refused to supply them with food or drink." The word *boycott* even spread throughout Europe and added itself to the lexicons of France (*boycotter*), German (*boycottiren*), and Dutch (*boycotten*), among others. In case you're wondering, yes there is such a thing as a *girlcott*—it's a boycott that includes only female participants. The most famous example is the great tennis player Billie Jean King's frequent calls for a "girlcott" of the Wimbledon tennis tournament because she feels that the women players don't get a large enough share of the prize money.

brand

The word *brand* has a curious and yet somehow inevitable history. It's an ancient word (it appears in *Beowulf* as *bronde*) that came into English from the Germanic term *brandoz*, a shortening of a phrase that meant "burn word." It originally referred to a piece of wood burning at one end, or a flaming torch. By the mid-sixteenth century, *brand* had come to mean a mark made by burning with a hot iron, usually to identify a criminal, but before long it meant a mark of ownership burned into the hides of cattle, horses, and other animals. In the early nineteenth century, the manufacturers of some goods started burning their names onto casks, wood, metal, and other materials, and these trademarks became known as *brands*. By the late 1800s, companies looking to differentiate themselves in the marketplace started adding logos and other design flourishes to their packages. Some products, such as Campbell's Soup and Quaker Oats, went a step further and used their logos, designs, and advertising to create a feeling—such as comfort or folksiness—about the product in the mind of the consumer. The modern concept of the *brand* was born.

brass tacks

See GET DOWN TO BRASS TACKS.

bridal

There's not many a bride who drinks ale at her wedding (the wedding dress on your average bride would burst after the first glug or two), but if one did, she'd have history and a bit of etymology on her side. That's because the word *bridal*, "relating to the bride in a wedding," comes from the phrase *bride-ale*, "a wedding festival." An *ale*, you see, once upon a time referred to a festival—or a *merry-meeting*, as they used to say (and I wish they still did)—particularly one where the partygoers' main activity was drinking ale. Besides bride-ales, beer-swillers of yore also used to imbibe at *bed-ales*, *church-ales*, *clear-ales*, *dirge-ales*, *help-ales*, and *soul-ales*, and even *Mary-ales* (a festival in honor of the Virgin Mary). Ale drinkers, apparently, have no shortage of excuses to hoist a few.

bridezilla

The *bridezilla* is a bride-to-be who, while planning her wedding, becomes exceptionally selfish, greedy, and obnoxious. This word is a combination of *bride* and *Godzilla*, the fictional mutant dinosaur created by U.S. hydrogen bomb testing in the Pacific that, in numerous films in the 1950s and '60s, would wade onto land and destroy everything in its path. The bridal version of this monster is created by the maniacal need to have "the perfect day" and she'll walk over anyone and everything to get it.

Brobdingnagian

This sizable adjective means immense or enormous. It comes from Brobdingnag, a country in *Gulliver's Travels* by Jonathan Swift, where everything was enormous. For example, the place had "corn rising at least forty feet … a hedge of at least one hundred and twenty feet high, and the trees so lofty that I could make no computation of their altitude." It's the adjective of choice when more prosaic modifiers such as *huge*, *colossal*, and *mammoth* just won't cut the verbal mustard. The opposite, of course, is *Lilliputian*, another word that comes from a place name in *Gulliver's Travels*: Lilliput, populated with "human Creatures not six Inches high." See also YAHOO.

broccoflower

See PLUOT.

bromide

A *bromide* is an unoriginal, trite, or commonplace saying or remark. It is, in other words, something that might put you to sleep in short order. That's apropos because the word *bromide* used to refer to a dose of potassium bromide, which was used as a sedative in the nineteenth century. In his 1906 book *Are You a Bromide?*, the humorist Gelett Burgess (whom, as the coiner of the word BLURB, you met earlier) called people who used hackneyed phrases *bromides*, and the meaning eventually transferred to the phrases rather than the people who use them. (In case you're wondering, the *bromo* part of the upset-stomach medicine Bromo-Seltzer comes from the earlier sense of *bromide*.)

Bronx cheer

See RASPBERRY.

buff

You probably know that a *buff* is someone who's an enthusiast or has exceptional knowledge about a particular topic. For example, we have *Star Trek* buffs who learn Klingon, and *Star Wars* buffs who dedicate their lives to eradicating the memory of Jar Jar Binks. I don't know if there are any buffalo buffs, but that would be fitting since the two words are related. In the early twentieth century, volunteer firemen in New York City would in the winter wear *buff coats*, so called because they were made from buffalo hide. Because of these distinctive coats, the firemen were known as the Buffs. Within a few years the term *buff* was being applied to any person who was a friend or admirer of the Buffs, and then more generally to any person who was "an enthusiast about going to fires," as one Webster's dictionary put it. By the 1930s it had taken on the more general "enthusiast" sense.

bug

I'm talking here about the computer version of a bug: "a flaw in the logic or syntax of a software program." There's a popular and appealing tale of how the word *bug* came about. Apparently, an early computer pioneer named Grace Hopper was working on a machine called the Mark II in 1947. While investigating a glitch, she found a moth among the vacuum tubes, so from then on glitches were called bugs. Appealing, yes, but is it the real history of the term? Not quite. In fact, engineers had already been referring to mechanical defects as "bugs" for at least 60 years before Ms. Hopper's discovery.

The First Bug

As proof of the antiquity of this sense of the word *bug*, the OED offers the following quotation from an 1889 edition of the *Pall Mall Gazette*:

"Mr. Edison, I was informed, had been up the two previous nights discovering 'a bug' in his phonograph—an expression for solving a difficulty, and implying that some imaginary insect has secreted itself inside and is causing all the trouble."

bully pulpit

A *bully pulpit* is a public position of prominence, such as political office, that gives the holder a large audience. The "bully" in bully pulpit has nothing to do with the cruel thugs who terrorize schoolyard playgrounds. Instead, this bully is an archaic word that means "wonderful; splendid." Bully pulpit was coined by former U.S. President Teddy Roosevelt, who used the phrase to describe the presidency.

bungalow

Whether or not you've ever been to India, if you live in a bungalow then you've been there at least linguistically. That's because the word *bungalow* comes to us from the Hindi term *bangla*, "a one-story house," which in turn comes from the adjective *bangla*, meaning "in the style of or belonging to Bengal." Folks in Britain's India Office took up the word in the late seventeenth century, and it entered English as *bungale*, then *bungalo*, and finally *bungalow* in the mid-nineteenth century.

bunk

You may recall a classic scene in a *Seinfeld* episode where Jerry, George, and Elaine engage in a bit of seat-of-the-pants linguistics:

> JERRY: I thought the whole dream of dating a doctor was debunked.
>
> ELAINE: No, it's not debunked, it's totally bunk.
>
> JERRY: Wait, isn't bunk bad? Like, "that's a lot of bunk."
>
> GEORGE: No, something is bunk and then you debunk it.
>
> JERRY: What?
>
> ELAINE: Huh?
>
> GEORGE: I think.

Indeed. In any case, the verb *debunk* means "to remove or refute nonsense," and it combines the suffix *de-*, "remove" and the word *bunk*, "nonsense." The latter is our real concern here, and I can tell you first off that *bunk* is actually short for *bunkum*, which also means "nonsense."

This longer word is a variation on the name *Buncombe*, a county in North Carolina. No, it's not a county full of nonsense-spewers (as far as I know, anyway), but it did have one memorable prattler. Back in 1820, Congress was coming to the end of a long and tedious debate on the Missouri Compromise, and the House members finally called for a vote. Before they could get things started, a congressman named Felix Walker, whose district included Buncombe County, rose to speak. And boy, did he speak. He went on and on about nothing much in particular, ignoring the increasingly vocal objections of his peers. He stated flatly that the people of his district wanted no less of him, and that he was expected "to make a speech for Buncombe." The word *buncombe* soon became synonymous with political claptrap, and then it took on nonsensical talk of all kinds.

buttonhole

Sometimes new words are created simply by a person (or a bunch of people) making a "mistake." (I use quotation marks here because this is a natural process that goes on all the time, so it shouldn't have a fully negative stigma attached to it.) One kind of error that results in new words is mishearing an existing word. For example, the verb *to buttonhole*, "to detain a person in conversation and not allow them to escape," was originally *button-hold*, as though the accosting conversationalist had taken hold of a button on the victim's coat or shirt to prevent that person from leaving. See also PEA.

The Terrible Under Toad

One of my favorite words creating via mishearing (albeit in a literary setting, in this case) is *undertoad*. This word comes from the phrase *Under Toad*, which was coined by John Irving in his 1976 book *The World According to Garp*. In the book, the youngest child, Walt, is constantly being warned to "watch out for the undertow" while playing in the surf, but he mishears the word as "Under Toad":

"Garp ... realized that all these years Walt had been dreading a giant *toad*, lurking offshore, waiting to suck him under and drag him out to sea. The terrible Under Toad."

You see this word in print on occasion, where it's used to mean "anxiety characterized by an overarching fear of the unknown in general and one's personal mortality in particular."

caboodle

See KIT AND CABOODLE.

cahoots

If you're in *cahoots* with someone, it means you're collaborating with that person as part of a conspiracy or for some other villainous purpose that requires a gang of some sort. So what exactly are you in when you're "in" cahoots? You might actually be in a cabin, of all things, because it's likely that the word *cahoots* comes from the French word *cahute*, "cabin; hut." The idea being that if you're in league with some people who are up to no good, then back in the day you'd do your conspiring in a cabin. This theory gets a bit of a boost by the fact that *cahoots* started off as the singular *cahoot*. For example, here's an early nineteenth-century citation from *Chronicles of Pineville:*

> Pete Hopkins aint no better than he should be, and I wouldn't swar he wasn't in *cahoot* with the devil.

The earliest known use of the plural *cahoots* is from 1862, but no one knows why the "s" was tacked on. I should also mention a second theory about the origins of *cahoots*. Some authorities believe it comes from the French term *cohort*, "company; band," which was certainly the source of the English word *cohort*, "colleague; accomplice."

cakewalk

Eating cake is one of the easiest tasks I know (no matter how much I've stuffed myself beforehand), so walking around with a cake would therefore be quite hard (one has to avoid the temptation to dig in and, of course, there's the whole drooling problem). So you may be surprised that *cakewalk* means "something easy." However, the original cakewalk had nothing to do with carrying a cake during a stroll. Instead, it's an old African American tradition whereby couples would compete to see which could walk with the most style and grace. The winning couple's prize? You guessed it: a cake. Not that this was at all easy, mind you. One journalist of the day described "cake-walking" as "a graceful motion, conducted upon the toes and ball of the foot." The sense of a cakewalk as being something easy came about when people began using the term humorously. That is, if something that is normally quite difficult turned out to be easy in a particular instance, people would call it a "cakewalk" compared to what normally occurs. While we're in cakewalk mode, I would be remiss if I didn't also mention that this is where the expression *takes the cake* comes from. Obviously, the winners of the cakewalk would, literally, take the cake, so for a while this phrase referred to something that was the best. Before too long, however, people began using the expression ironically to refer to things that were egregiously unbelievable or incredible.

callous

You use this adjective for an individual who feels little or no emotion and has no sympathy for others. The original ancestor of *callous* was the Latin word *callum*, meaning "hard skin," from which we get the notion of a callous person being hardened emotionally. (This hardness is also reflected in a couple of synonyms: *hard-boiled*—used almost exclusively to describe private detectives in crime novels—and *hard-hearted*.) As you may have guessed by now, the Latin term *callum* was also the source of the noun *callus*, "a hard thickened part of the skin." You may also have guessed that it's very easy to confuse callous and callus, so be careful when using either word.

canapé

This appetizer is a small cracker or piece of toast covered with some kind of savory. Unfortunately, it's a little *un*savory to consider that this word's origins are mosquito related! It goes back to the Greek word *konopion*, "a mosquito net," which turned into the English word *canopy*, "a curtain that encloses a bed or sofa." The French call the enclosed sofa a *canapé*, and the inventor of the above dish thought the cracker or toast acted as a kind of sofa for the topping, so—voilà!—the *canapé* was born.

canary

"Among these islands is Ninguariae, so named from its perpetual snow, and wrapped in cloud; and next to it one named Canariae, from its multitude of dogs of a huge size." This excerpt comes not from some antiquated travel guide, but from Pliny the Elder's massive encyclopedia, *Naturalis Historiae* (Natural History), written around 77 C.E. Here he's retelling the story of an expedition by Juba II, king of Numidia, to a group of islands northwest of Africa. Juba was particularly struck by one island that was populated by large dogs. In Latin, the word *canis* means "dog," and the adjective *canarius* means "relating to dogs." So Juba named the place *Canariae insulae*, "Isle of Dogs." This island was famous at the time for these dogs, but it also had lots of small, green birds that some Europeans took a fancy to in the sixteenth century. They brought a few back home and named them (in English) *Canary birds*, because, of course, they came from the Canary Islands. Over time, the birds became quite popular (and quite yellow, thanks to the efforts of domestic breeders), and now we use the word *canary* exclusively to refer to the bird, and the word's canine roots (like the dogs themselves) are but dust in the wind.

candidate

If you're the least bit cynical about politicians, you'll no doubt be surprised to learn that the word *candidate* comes from the Latin word *candidatus*, which means "clothed in white." What's up with *that?* The story is that, in ancient Rome, people who aspired to political office wore white togas to symbolize the purity of their motives (insert snort here). The same Latin root—*candere*, "white; glistening"—also gave us *candid*, "open and sincere," and *candor*, "honesty and sincerity of expression."

cappuccino

See ESPRESSO.

cat got your tongue?

If someone doesn't say something for a while, particularly if you're expecting some kind of response or comment from that person, you might retort with something like, "What's the matter? Cat got your tongue?" The evocative phrase *cat got your tongue* feels very old, but it's actually only been around for about a century, with the earliest known use coming in 1911. No one's quite certain of its origins, but it probably comes from the habit cats have of grabbing things like birds, mice, and fuzzy toys, and taking them somewhere to play with them. So if a person doesn't speak when expected, it's as though some nearby cat has made off with the person's tongue.

catch-22

A catch-22 is a situation in which the desired outcome is impossible to achieve because the rules that govern the situation always work against the solution. A common catch-22 situation is when young workers can't get a job unless they have experience, but they can't get experience unless they get a job. Catch-22 comes from Joseph Heller's 1961 novel *Catch-22*, which covers the antics of bomber pilots in World War II. Heller explains catch-22 in the following passage:

> There was only one catch and that was Catch-22, which specified that a concern for one's safety in the face of dangers that were real and immediate was the process of a rational mind. Orr was crazy and could be grounded. All he had to do was ask; and as soon as he did, he would no longer be crazy and would have to fly more missions. Orr would be crazy to fly more missions and sane if he didn't, but if he was sane he had to fly them. If he flew them he was crazy and didn't have to; but if he didn't want to he was sane and had to.

celebutard

A *celebutard* is a celebrity who is or is perceived to be unintelligent. This fine coinage combines *celebutante* and *retard* to form a most useful insult in this age of people who are famous only for being famous. The word *celebutante* was coined in 1939 and is itself a blend of *celebrity* and *debutante*; it refers to a person who is a famous socialite.

chafe

See CHAUFFEUR.

chauffeur

You know that a chauffeur is a person paid to drive someone else's car, but you might not know that it would be really appropriate if that car was a Firebird, a Spitfire, or just any old hotrod. That's because this word comes to us from the French term *chauffeur*, or "stoker." What's a stoker, you ask? It's a person whose job it was to build up (or *stoke up*) the fire that created the steam that powered the original automobiles back in the day. (Think: Stanley Steamer.) That French word came from the verb *chauffer*, which means "to heat" and just happens to also be the source of the English word *chafe*, which originally referred to rubbing something to keep it warm (such as your hands on a cold day), but now more often refers to causing friction or irritation by rubbing, or to causing someone to become annoyed or irritated (presumably because he's being rubbed the wrong way).

cheap

If you describe something as *cheap*, you probably mean that the thing doesn't cost much or that it costs less that you might expect. (Other meanings of *cheap*—"of poor quality," "not worth much," "undeserving of respect"—we'll give a nod to, but pass by in silence.) However, the word *cheap* was a paid-up member of the language for hundreds of years before that sense of the word found favor. Prior to that, the word *cheap*—spelled variously as *ceap*, *ceape*, *chep*, and *chype*—meant simply "buying and selling" or "a market." The original here was the Old English word *céap*, "buying and selling." By about the fourteenth century, shoppers were describing markets as either *good cheap*—a buyer's market, usually one with low prices—or *dear cheap*—a seller's market, usually with high prices. Humans are natural bargain-hunters, of course, so the *good cheap* phrase was much more popular than *dear cheap*. So much so, that by the early sixteenth century, the thrifty had shortened *good cheap* to just *cheap*, and we've used that word to mean "inexpensive" ever since. (You may be wondering about the word *cheapskate*, "a stingy or ungenerous person." The *cheap* part you now know all about, but the *skate* part goes back to the late nineteenth century, when it started life as a slang term for a mean or contemptible person. Add "cheap" into the mix, and you've got one unpleasant person there.)

chew the fat

If you *chew the fat* with someone, you have yourself a good old-fashioned chinwag, or perhaps you spin a yarn for that person. There is, fortunately, no actual fat involved, although there used to be. In the nineteenth century, sailors would often have to make do with salt pork when their regular supplies ran out. That's some tough eating, particularly the fat, so it's no wonder those old tars would grumble and complain when faced with another meal of salted pork bellies. From this idea of literally chewing the fat and complaining about it, the phrase *chew the fat* at first meant "to complain or grumble about something." The modern sense of "to chat; to tell a story," came later when people would get together and swap tales while chewing on a piece of beef jerky or something similar.

chip on his shoulder

If you say that a person is walking around with a *chip on his shoulder*, it means that the guy is acting overly sensitive or defiant thanks to some feeling of inferiority. So what's up with the chip? It's figurative now, but it used to be all too literal. For example, check out this citation from the May 20, 1830, edition of the *Long Island Telegraph*:

> When two churlish boys were determined to fight, a chip would be placed on the shoulder of one, and the other demanded to knock it off at his peril.

This is what people used to do back in those rougher days: put an actual wood chip on one shoulder and dare anyone to knock it off. Fortunately, by the late nineteenth century that spoiling-for-a-real-fight sense of the phrase gave way to the more general (and less dangerous) sense of someone who is belligerent and quick to take offence.

chow

I hate to be the bearer of bad (and quite distasteful) news, but there seems to be a link between the word *chow*, slang for "food," and Chow, the dog breed. *Chow* is actually short for *chow chow*, and it entered the language as a bit of Pidgin English used by Chinese laborers in the nineteenth century, who used the phrase to mean "food." It probably came from the Mandarin word *ch'ao*, "to fry or cook." The *OED* tells us that this sense of *chow* is "supposed to be due to the use of the chow ('the edible dog of China') as food by poor Chinese." Yuck.

How Now, Brown Chow?

The *OED* thinks *chow*-as-food and *Chow*-as-dog are related, but lots of language authorities don't buy it. One theory is that when those Chinese laborers used the phrase *chow chow*, they were really referring to a kind of sweet jam or preserve made of ginger and orange peel. Similarly, many linguists think the name of the dog breed comes from the Chinese *Chou* dynasty. Fingers crossed!

claim jumper

See KANGAROO COURT.

club-sandwich generation

See SANDWICH GENERATION.

codswallop

This fun word means nonsense, rubbish, or drivel. However, no one has any idea where the word came from. The tale most often told concerns a gentleman named Hiram C. Codd, who sold bottled lemonade in England in the 1870s. In those days, *wallop* was a slang term for an alcoholic drink, especially beer, so "Codd's wallop" became a sarcastic reference to any weak drink and then to anything of little or no value. Of course, it's entirely possible that this story is itself just a load of codswallop!

coin

See MONEY.

complicity

We don't often associate crime with laundry (with the act of money laundering being the obvious exception, I guess), but the word *complicity* (which means "involvement in an illegal act") is close. This word comes from the Latin *complex* or *complicem*, "closely connected," which combines *com-*, "together," and *plic*, "to fold." Like laundry. Sort of. Anyway, this same root sprouted another word, *complice*, which means "an associate in crime," and that later became our word *accomplice*. Strangely, no one knows why or how the *ac-* prefix got tacked onto the front.

comptroller

You'll occasionally stumble upon the word *comptroller* (for example, the comptroller general of the United States) and may be tempted to pronounce it *komp·TROH·lur*. Don't! It's pronounced exactly the same as *controller*, and it means the same thing as well. Why does comptroller even exist, in that case? To answer that, you first need to know that controller comes from a combination of the Latin *contra*, "counter," and *rotulus*, "roll." That is, the original controllers kept a "counter-roll" to double-check the accounting. However, *contra* became *compte* in French, and some overly zealous scribe thought controller ought to be spelled comptroller.

court

Anyone who has visited a courtroom is well aware of the motley collection of lawyers, plaintiffs, defendants, and hangers-on that always congregate there. It's much like a farmyard with its motley collection of animals. Too much of a metaphorical stretch, you say? Perhaps, but it's not all that much of a linguistic stretch. That's because the word *court*, "the room in which law cases are heard," goes back to the Latin word *cohors*, meaning "farmyard." It eventually became the French word *court*, which meant "the king's lands or residence." Since this is where the king also made judicial decisions, *court* eventually came to mean what it does today.

cowabunga

The August 20, 1995, edition of *The New York Times* included a photo of massive waves in the waters near Queens, New York, a temporary phenomenon caused by Hurricane Felix. Even more interesting was the photo's caption: "Cowabunga!" That this bit of teen slang—it's used to express astonishment, exuberance, or enthusiasm—would make it into the august *Times* is delightful all by itself, but it's clear that someone at the paper knew a bit about the history of the word. That's because *cowabunga* isn't just a catchphrase used by Bart Simpson (of the animated TV show *The Simpsons*) or before him the *Teenage Mutant Ninja Turtles*. Way back in the 1960s, in the surfing-themed TV show *Gidget*, one of the characters would yell "Cowabunga!" as he ran with his surfboard into the water. This was a reflection of the surfing slang of the day, when surfers would routinely scream "Cowabunga!" at the start of a particularly tasty ride or gnarly wave. Hence the caption in the *Times*. However, *cowabunga* is a bit older than that, and in fact originated with the popular children's program *The Howdy Doody Show* in the mid-1950s. One of the main characters of the show was Chief Thunderthud, and he used the word *kawabunga* to mean "bad things." (The opposite term was *kawagoopa*, "good things," but that didn't make a dent in the culture, which is some sort of sign of the times.) The word *cowabunga* was made up out of thin air by Eddie Kean, a writer for *The Howdy Doody Show*, and talk about a coinage with legs! It's more popular than ever 50 years later, and it's never gone out of style as a catchphrase in any decade: *The Howdy Doody Show* (1950s); surfer culture and *Gidget* (1960s); the children's educational TV show *Sesame Street* (1970s); *Teenage Mutant Ninja Turtles* (1980s and 1990s); and *The Simpsons* (1990s and 2000s).

cranky

A person who is *cranky* is ill-tempered, nasty, crotchety, and right-angled. Okay, your average cranky person isn't right-angled, but that's what the word *cranky* once meant. It was used for centuries (since at least the year 1000) to describe handles or treadles bent at a right angle, usually to be used to turn something. This came from the Old English word *cranc*, "to curl oneself into a ball, particularly because of a battle-field injury." The central idea of something being bent instead of straight eventually caused people to start using *cranky* to refer to people who were weak or sick. Before long folks applied this metaphor to people's mental state. For example, Charles Dickens in his novel *The Old Curiosity Shop* has the character Mr. Swiveller (great Dickensian name!) say, "That his friend appeared to be rather 'cranky' in point of temper."

crocodile tears

"In that contre ... ben gret plentee of Cokadrilles ... Theise Serpentes slen men, and thei eten hem wepynge." (In that country ... be a great plenty of crocodiles ... These serpents slay men, and then eat them, weeping.) The quotation (with my translation after it) comes from Sir John Maundeville's book *The Voyage and Travels of Sir John Maundeville*, published around 1400. Subsequent scholarship showed that much of this book is a fake, pure and simple. However, the book was tremendously popular in its day, and the idea of a crocodile weeping while gnawing on some hapless human who'd crossed its path took hold and can be found in many literary works, including Shakespeare's. However, people eventually realized that, no, crocodiles don't weep while eating (humans or anything else), so the tears reported by Maundeville and taken up by other authors were false. In 1563, one author wrote, "I begin to fear, lest his humility ... be a counterfeit humility, and his tears crocodile tears." Ever since, we've used the phrase *crocodile tears* to refer to any display of false sadness or insincere grief.

The Tears of the Croc

Not so fast on the whole "crocodiles don't cry" theory. In October 2007, a University of Florida zoologist named Kent Vliet announced that he had indeed seen crocodiles tearing up while eating. It appeared to be a physiological response (not, obviously, sadness or remorse), but the tears were real nonetheless. Perhaps previous researchers just never got close enough to see the tears!

Croesus

A *Croesus* (pronounced *KREE·sus*) is a wealthy man, although you more often hear the person described as *rich as Croesus*. It comes from

Croesus, King of Lydia, who was reputedly very wealthy indeed. So was Midas, the mythic king of Phrygia who was given the power to turn anything into gold with a simple touch. That's why people who can make pots of money are said to have the *Midas touch* or the *golden touch*.

cubicle

If you've been working so hard lately that you feel as though you're practically *living* in your cubicle, that's at least a linguistically appropriate feeling. That's because the word *cubicle* comes from the Latin term *cubiculum*, which roughly translates as "bedroom." That was how *cubicle* was used in English until around the sixteenth century. About 300 years later, cubicles resurfaced as small sleeping areas that were separated using wooden partitions that didn't quite reach the ceiling. The office cubicle as we know it today was the brainchild of a fellow named Harold Probst, who worked for the Herman Miller company in the 1960s. Before Mr. Probst came along, offices were arranged *bullpen*-style, with desks out in the open in regimented rows, the workers arranged like so many galley slaves. Probst saw much wrong with this design, including what he memorably called the "idiot salutation problem": the constant interruptions caused by every Tom, Dick, and Harriet saying "Hello" to you as they walked by. His solution was to use panels and tall storage units to give each worker his or her own private area, and thus the modern cubicle was born. (Later, someone asked Probst if he thought of himself as the "Father of the Cubicle." He answered, "My God, that's about as interesting as being the father of the Pet Rock.")

More Cubicle Coinages

We live in a syllable-cutting society, so it's not surprising that the three-syllable *cubicle* is often chopped down to the one-syllable *cube*. Those with a more sardonic view rarely let a few extra syllables get in the way of a word that hits just the right note of disdainful mockery, which explains the popularity of Douglas Coupland's famous coinage from his book, *Generation X*: the *veal-fattening pen*.

cuckoo egg

This phrase refers to an MP3 song file that contains either a song different than what its name suggests, or a short sample of the song followed by noises or an anti-Napster message. It comes from the bizarre actions of the cuckoo bird, which lays an egg and then leaves it in the nest of another bird species. The egg is incubated and hatched by the other bird, which even feeds the resulting chick as if it were her own. The cuckoo chick will even go so far as to forcibly remove the other chicks from the nest, leaving itself as the sole beneficiary of the food provided by the mother bird.

culprit

You may think that the word *culprit*, "a person accused or guilty of a crime," is related to *culpable*, "relating to someone or something that's guilty and deserving of blame or punishment." If so, you're right but probably not in the way you think. Hundreds of years ago, after a prisoner had pleaded "not guilty," the Clerk of the Crown would then say, "*Culpable: prest d'averrer nostre bille,*" a French phrase that means, "Guilty: ready to prove our charge." (In those days, court proceedings were conducted in French.) This would be recorded in short form as *cul. prit.* (*prit* being a variation of *prest*). Later, when French was no longer used, people thought *cul. prit.* referred to the prisoner, and so the word *culprit* passed into the language by, as the *OED* cheekily puts it, the "fortuitous or ignorant" combining of these two words.

curmudgeon

The quintessential grump is the *curmudgeon*, a bad-tempered, gruff, and stubborn person. He's usually old (and almost always a he), but I've met many a middle-aged curmudgeon in my day (and the occasional female one, too). In any case, this word's a major linguistic mystery in that no one has the faintest idea where it came from, other than the fact that it landed on two feet in the language in 1577. Some folks think it might be somehow related to the word *cur*, a mongrel dog, which certainly seems like a promising start.

Oh, Evil Heart!

The word *curmudgeon* was the source of one of the most embarrassing gaffes in the history of lexicography (dictionary making). In his famous dictionary published in 1775, Samuel Johnson claimed that curmudgeon was "a vicious manner of pronouncing *coeur méchant,* Fr. an unknown correspondent." That is, he thought the word was from the French words *coeur,* "heart," and *méchant,* "evil." Crucially, he used "Fr." as a short form of "from," so he was saying he got this from an anonymous source. A later lexicographer, John Ash, thought "Fr." meant "French," so he wrote "from the French *coeur,* unknown, and *méchant,* correspondent." D'oh! Incidentally, Johnson's explanation was wrong, and the origins of the word *curmudgeon* remain a mystery.

cut and run

In recent years, people have been using this phrase to mean something like "to cut one's losses and withdraw from the field of battle." Used mostly with reference to abandoning the wars in Iraq and Afghanistan, when used this way the phrase has the stink of cowardice about it. However, the actual meaning of the phrase—"to hurry off; to leave without delay"—contains nary a whiff of the poltroon. It's actually a nautical term, and it refers to a sailing tactic whereby the crew, instead of taking the time to hoist the anchor back into the boat, would simply cut the anchor cable so that they could make sail instantly.

cyberspace

When you're online, you're said to be in *cyberspace,* the virtual terrain created by computers connected to the Internet. Cyberspace is a metaphor that's used to describe the "place" where e-mail and chat conversations are held, where web-based stores and libraries are located, and along which you "travel" to visit websites from other parts of the (real) world. The *cyber-* prefix comes from the Greek word *kuberman,* "a person who steers a ship." (See also GOVERNOR.) *Cyber-* came into English in the 1940s when mathematician Norbert Weiner used *cybernetics* as the name for his theories related to communication and control in machines and animals. The word *cyberspace* was coined by the writer William Gibson in his 1984 novel *Neuromancer.* He envisioned a future dystopia that contained a virtual world (sometimes called the "matrix") where people could "jack in" to communicate with each other and manipulate data as though they were physical objects. He defined cyberspace as a "consensual hallucination experienced daily by billions of legitimate operators" and as a "graphic representation of data abstracted from the banks of every computer in the human system." Sounds about right.

daisy

The daisy is one of the prettiest flowers, and one of the most interesting since it closes its rays (the white florets that extend out from the yellow disc in the center) at night and opens them again in the morning. The opening of the rays to reveal the disc is reminiscent of an eye opening, and that how the word *daisy* originated: it comes from the Old English phrase *daeges eage*, "day's eye." It first appears in English around the year 1000, and gradually morphed from *daeges eage* to *dayes-eye* to *daysy*, to the modern spelling *daisy* (which first appeared around the middle of the fifteenth century).

dandelion

If you're into gardening, you might want to get yourself a good, sturdy pair of gloves for the next time you decide to do some weeding. That's because you might come across a dandelion or two, and that can be dangerous, if only etymologically. The danger lies in the origin of the word *dandelion*, which comes from the French phrase *dent de lion*, and before that the Latin phrase *dens leonis*, both of which mean "lion's tooth." Fortunately, there are no actual teeth involved, but rather the shape of the plant's leaves is reminiscent of the tooth of a lion. The term entered English first as *dent de lion* in the early sixteenth century, but by the end of the seventeenth century the anglicized version *dandelion* had taken root. If you simply can't get enough of lion-related word histories, see also PANTS.

None for Me, Thanks

You can be thankful that we didn't take up the *other* word that the French use for dandelions: *pissenlit*, which literally means "wet-the-bed"! The French believe that dandelions are a powerful diuretic, and if you eat too much dandelion salad (yes, dandelions are supposed to be quite tasty) at dinner, there may be, uh, trouble overnight.

D

dead ringer

It must be said that although the Internet is a wonderful invention full of interesting tidbits and fascinating facts, it's been a real pain in the you-know-what for those of us in the language game. That's because the Internet, through e-mails created and forwarded by dopes, and through websites maintained by people who have no earthly idea what they're talking about, etymological zombies have been given a new and larger space to roam. These zombies are the cute but patently untrue stories told about the origins of certain words and phrases. One of the most persistent of these zombies is the story of the "origin" of the phrase *dead ringer*, "a person who looks exactly like someone else." In medieval Britain (so the bogus story goes), people were so worried about accidentally being taken for dead and buried alive in a coffin that they took to inserting strings in their coffins, and those strings were attached to bells above ground. So if you woke up one day 6 feet under, no worries: just ring the bell and you'll be topside in no time. Wait, it gets better: apparently this happened often enough that people would see these previously "dead" people on the street and assume it was just a look-alike. Somehow these people became known as dead-ringers. It's all CODSWALLOP, of course, and it doesn't even make sense! So what's the *real* story? In the seventeenth century, *to ring the changes* meant to go through all the ways that a series of bells could be wrung. This phrase later meant "to try every possible way of doing something," and later became a con game in which the swindler confuses the mark by constantly changing his money to the point where the swindler ends up with more and the mark with less. From here the phrase became part of nineteenth-century criminal slang where it meant "to change bad money for good" (what we call *money laundering* today). That was eventually shorted to *ring*, and the good money being substituted for the bad eventually became known as the *ringer*. From there, the word *ringer* came to refer to something of higher quality surreptitiously substituted for something of lower quality. Since the ringer must look like the original, when you add the adjective *dead*, "complete; total," you get *dead ringer*, "a look-alike."

deadline

> I love deadlines. I especially like the whooshing sound they make as they go flying by. —Douglas Adams

Any freelance writer will tell you that the secret to getting more work from a client is to meet that client's deadlines the first time (and each time) you work for them. Not that this is a life-and-death situation by any means, although there was once a day when it was. The notion of the *deadline*, "a time by which a task must be completed," entered the language around 1920, but the word's origins go back to the U.S. Civil War, specifically to a notorious Confederate prison called Andersonville. There the prison authorities drew a line inside the prison grounds, 17 feet from the wall. The prisoners were told that if anyone crossed that line, the guards would assume that person was trying to reach the wall to escape, and the guards were ordered to shoot and kill that prisoner, no questions asked. Not surprisingly, that line became known as the *dead line*, a phrase that first appeared in 1864. Newspaper editors have long given their reporters a time by which their stories were due. If the story was late the editor would probably, in the press vernacular still in use to this day, "kill" the story. So the time by which a story was due became a kind of journalistic dead line, and we've used *deadline* in that sense ever since.

deadpan

If you do something or say something *deadpan*, it means that you do it without emotion and without any expression on your face. You are, in a sense, acting, and that's appropriate because the word *deadpan* was originally actors' lingo for delivering a line without expression. Back in the 1920s, when the term first appeared (as the phrase *dead pan*), the word *pan* was a slang term for "face." So delivering a line *dead pan* meant saying the line with a "dead" (that is, expressionless) face.

December

See SEPTEMBER.

deep six

When you *deep six* something, you reject, dispose of, cancel, or abandon that thing. You might think this must be somehow related to *six feet under,* "dead and buried," which entered the language in the 1940s. It's actually a bit older than that, and we need to go back to the days when ships determined the depth of the water without benefit of sonar. Instead, a sailor would drop into the water a lead-weighted line marked in FATHOMS. When he saw the depth was 6 fathoms (36 feet), he'd shout out "by the deep six." What's the significance of 6 fathoms? It's the minimum depth at which a burial at sea can take place. So we have a strong association between the phrase *deep six* and death, and indeed *deep six* entered the language in the 1920s as a synonym for death. However, by the 1940s the phrase had taken on the more figurative sense that we use today.

Six Down

One of my favorite new words (the earliest citation I know of comes from 1986) is the adjectival phrase *six down,* which describes a crossword puzzle constructor or fan who has passed away. For example, National Public Radio's Liane Hansen, speaking in 1997, said that "Eugene Moleska [the long-time crossword editor of *The New York Times*] became six down on August 3, 1993."

devil-may-care

If someone has a *devil-may-care* attitude, it means that person behaves in a wildly reckless, careless, or raffish manner. The adjective comes from the old phrase "Devil may care!," which such people used to say when scolded for their behavior. The idea behind it was as though they were saying "The devil may care (about my terrible behavior, presumably because I'll go to hell for it, and so the Devil gets a new recruit), but I don't."

Devil's advocate

As you may know, an *advocate* is a person who speaks or argues in favor of something. A *Devil's advocate* is a person who criticizes or argues against something purely for the sake of argument or to provoke a discussion. This comes from the name given to the Roman Catholic official who is appointed to argue against someone's beatification or canonization. Now *there* is a job you wouldn't want to bring home every night!

digital

You'd think computers would have taken us away from counting things using our fingers. However, that's not the case, at least from a linguistic point of view. That's because the word *digital*, "having to do with numbers," goes back to the Latin word *digitus*, "finger." The story here seems to be that the Roman numerals (I, III, III, and so on) were called "digits" because they resembled human fingers, and we've used "digit" to refer to numbers ever since.

dine

See JEJUNE.

dog days

In most of the world, the intense heat, haze, and humidity of late July and early August are fit for neither man nor beast, particularly dogs, whose panting tongues nearly reach the ground on these sweltering days. So you might jump to the conclusion that we call this time of year the *dog days* because our poor dogs seem to suffer the most during this time. Well, no, you're not even close, I'm afraid. The real 411 here is that during the summer the ancient Egyptians were on the lookout for the brightest star in the sky. When that star rose at the same time as the Sun (what astronomers call the *heliacal* rising of the star), they knew that the Nile would soon overflow its banks and so the land around the river would be fertile again. The Greeks kept an eye on this star, too, and they gave it the name *Seirios*, "burning," because it arrives at the hottest time of year. (We now call the star *Sirius*.) The Greeks also plugged the star into their mythology, and decided that it worked well as the hunter Orion's hound. The Romans thought all this was fine by them, so they took the Greek word for "dog," *kyon*, and used it to name the star *canicula*, "small dog" (they named the constellation that contains the star *Canis Major*, "Greater Dog"). The time of year when this Dog-star (as it's also called) rose with the Sun became known as the *dies caniculares*, or the "dog days."

dog that caught the car

This great idiom refers to a person who has reached his or her goal but doesn't know what to do next. It's based on the strange habit that some dogs have of chasing cars that are passing by on a nearby road. What on Earth would one of these crazed canines do if it actually *caught* a car? This idiom is also seen as the *dog that caught the truck* and the *dog that caught the bus*.

dog's breakfast

Today's modern dog is most often a pampered beast with designer clothes to wear, doggie daycares to hang out in, and their own celebrities to carry them everywhere they go. Alas, life hasn't always been so good for your average pooch: sleeping outside or in some crummy shed; working for a living herding or hunting or whatever; and acting as the family garbage disposal, with breakfast most often consisting of whatever scraps were leftover from last night's dinner. The thoroughly unpleasant prospect of such a meal is the source of the phrase *dog's breakfast*, "a mess," which entered the language in the 1930s and refers not just to an unpalatable meal, but in a figurative sense to anything that's sloppy, disordered, or chaotic. (Some people prefer to use the phrase *dog's dinner*, instead.) By the way, it's this older sense of a dog having a hard life that's the source of the phrase *it's a dog's life* (which has been around since the sixteenth century), meaning that life or some situation is difficult or miserable.

More Dogged Investigating

The word *dog* seems to be one of those rare words that's both very old (it dates to at least 1050) and without an ancestor in any other language. The original term was *docga*, which some Old English speaker coined as the name for some powerful breed of dog, now long forgotten. Within a few hundred years the term had generalized to refer to any type of dog. Dog terms that *do* have a pedigree in another language are *hound* (from the Teutonic *hund*) and *canine* (from the Latin *canis*).

doubting Thomas

See SKEPTIC.

drawn and quartered

> I went out to Charing Cross, to see Major-general Harrison hanged, drawn, and quartered ... he looking as cheerful as any man could do in that condition. —*The Diary of Samuel Pepys*, October 13, 1660

These days, if you've been *drawn and quartered* (or, particularly in Britain, *hanged, drawn, and quartered*), it means you've been treated terribly in some fashion. However, no matter how shabbily you've been abused, it doesn't compare a jot to the treatment that originated this phrase. Back in the seventeenth and eighteenth centuries (and even well in the nineteenth), anyone convicted of high treason would be punished in the most horrible fashion you can imagine. To give you some idea, here's the text that the judge would typically read to the convicted prisoners:

> That you, and each of you, [the condemned prisoners' names would be inserted here], be taken to the place from whence you came, and from thence you are to be drawn on hurdles to the place of execution, where you are to be hanged by the neck, but not until you are dead; for while you are still living, your bodies are to be taken down, your bowels torn out, and burnt before your faces; your heads are to be then cut off, and your bodies divided each into four quarters, and your heads and quarters to be then at the King's disposal; and may the Almighty God have mercy on your souls.

Ouch! The word *drawn* here means "dragged," and a *hurdle* (in case you're wondering) was in those days a kind of sled used to transport those convicted of high treason to be *half hanged*, "hanged until not quite dead." So it appears the longer phrase should really be *drawn, hanged, and quartered*, but they don't ask my opinion on these things. Note, too, that the *OED* has a 1655 citation that refers to some convicts being "hanged, bowelled, and quartered for treason."

drink the Kool-Aid

This newish verb means "to become a firm believer in something; to accept an argument or philosophy wholeheartedly or blindly." The phrase comes from the 1978 "Jonestown massacre" in which members of the Peoples Temple cult committed suicide by drinking cyanide-laced Kool-Aid. (Some folks say the drink of choice was actually Flav-R-Aid, but "drink the Flav-R-Aid" doesn't have quite the same ring to it.)

drive-in

In 1923, the owner of a Sacramento A&W had a light-bulb-over-the-head moment and hired waiters to run mugs of frothy root beer out to customers waiting in cars. By 1930, the word *drive-in* had entered the lexicon and the it-could-only-happen-in-America notion of getting served and eating in one's car became a bona fide fad. Only a few drive-in restaurants still exist but, happily, the "waiters" in these establishments are still called *carhops*, a term that dates from 1937.

dumb

Words from other languages often influence existing English words. For example, the word *dumb* originally meant "lacking the power of speech," but now it's usually taken to mean "stupid" (except in phrases such as *struck dumb* and *deaf, dumb, and blind*). This change was caused by the German word *dumm*, which means "stupid." Enough German immigrants used this word (for example, *dummkopf*, which means, literally, "stupid head") that it became associated with *dumb* and the "stupid" sense took over.

dunce

Some words have careers equivalent to human riches-to-rags stories, and *dunce* is one of them. In this case, you know that *dunce* refers to a person who is unintelligent, dull-witted, and incapable of learning. However, the word's origins lie in the rarefied heights of scholarship and intellectual acumen! Our story begins with a fellow named John Duns Scotus, a Scottish scholastic theologian who was known as the "Subtle Doctor." He was highly educated with a sharp mind, and he wrote many books on theology, logic, and philosophy, which were used as textbooks throughout Britain (indeed, throughout Europe), even for many decades after he died in 1308. The followers of his theology were called *Duns men*, then *Dunsmen*, and finally *Dunses* by the middle of the sixteenth century. Around that same time, however, church reformers attacked Duns's theological principles as being too complex. The Dunses fought back by railing against the "new learning." Their obstinacy earned them a reputation of being stuck in the old ways, and they were ridiculed as "hair-splitters," "egregious blockheads," and "barking curs." By around 1577, the name of one of the sharpest minds in theological scholarship was now associated with minds of the completely opposite character:

> But now in our age it is growne to be a common proverbe in derision, to call such a person as is senselesse or without learning a Duns, which is as much as a foole.

By the early seventeenth century, the name *Duns* had transformed into the noun *dunce*, and the fall was complete.

earmark

If you *earmark* something, you designate that thing for a particular purpose. This is true even if the thing being earmarked has no ears. What gives? The tale here is that the things originally being marked most definitely had ears. I'm thinking of sheep, cattle, and other farm animals which, back in the sixteenth century, were subjected to the indignity of having notches cut in their ears. These notches were unique to each farm, so they served as signs of ownership and were called *eare markes*. By the late sixteenth century, the phrase *eare marke* had been generalized to mean any mark of ownership or identifying mark, and by early in the seventeenth century, the verb *eare-marke*, meaning "to mark as one's own," had taken root. There things stood for quite a while, until the late nineteenth century, when people starting putting identifying marks on their checks, a process some wag called *ear-marking*. From there, it was a short hop to using *earmark* to refer to setting aside money for a particular purpose, and by the 1920s, the verb had taken on the more general sense that we use today.

earwig

You may be familiar with an insect called an earwig, which is a common garden pest. As far as I know it doesn't have any ears to speak of, so what's up with the name *earwig*? The original was the Old English term *éarwicga*, which combines *éar* "ear," and *wicga*, "wiggle," a variation on the verb *wriggle*. The rather ghastly notion behind all this is that people at one time thought this insect would wriggle it way into a person's ear and use its large pincers to penetrate into the brain. Not only did people worry about this back in the day, but they even had a cure for it, as given here by Philemon Holland's 1601 translation of Pliny's *Natural History*:

> If an earwig ... be gotten into the eare ... spit into the same, and it will come forth anon.

Try telling them *that* in the emergency ward!

easel

An *easel* is a frame or structure that holds an artist's canvas while he dabs away with one eye closed. The easel, in a sense, carries the burden of the canvas, making a kind of inanimate beast of burden. I stretched that particular metaphor beyond the breaking point to illustrate the origin of the word *easel*, which lies in the Dutch word *ezel*, an ass (that's a donkey to you). Someone with a particularly fertile (or warped) imagination took a look at a frame used to support a painting and thought, "My word, that looks an awful lot like a certain horselike quadruped! Let's call it an *easel* from now on!" Someone else (or, who knows, perhaps the same person) looked at the four-legged frame that carpenters use for sawing wood and thought it resembled a horse; hence the word *sawhorse* was born.

eat crow

If you're forced to *eat crow*, it means you have to admit an error or do something humiliating. The phrase was originally *eat boiled crow* and dates from the 1870s (although the *OED* has a charming citation from the December 1, 1851, edition of the *San Francisco Picayune*: "I kin eat a crow, but I'll be darned if I hanker after it"). The source of this phrase is probably no more complicated than the idea that crow's meat would be singularly unpalatable, given the crow's omnivorous and often disgusting diet. However, there's a terrific story about the origins of the phrase, and though it's sadly unproven, it's too good not to relate it here. It seems (so the story goes) that during a ceasefire in the War of 1812, an American soldier out hunting for food crossed into British territory and shot a crow. A British officer happened by, somehow took the American's gun, and forced the fellow to eat some of the crow. Satisfied, he warned the soldier not to cross British lines again, returned his gun, and promptly had it pointed right back at him, with the American wanting the Brit to eat some of the crow as payback. When the British officer later complained about all this, the American soldier was called to account, asked if he knew the British officer, and replied "Yes, I dined with him yesterday." It's a great story, for sure, but I'm not going to tell you that it's true, otherwise I might be forced to eat … well, you know.

eat humble pie

When we're forced to apologize or admit an error, we seem to do a lot of eating, at least figuratively. We're forced to EAT CROW, as you've seen, but we may also have to *eat our words* or *eat humble pie*. This last phrase seems straightforward linguistically: eating humble pie is just a metaphorical way of saying we need a shot of humility, right? Not so fast, my friend. The phrase *eat humble pie* actually has a fairly meandering and unexpected history that involves errors, puns, and the innards of a deer. Yes, you read that right: the innards of a deer. Apparently, long ago people would remove a deer's liver, heart, and entrails, cook them in some way, and then eat the result. Yum. These innards were known as *numbles*, from the Latin *lumbulus* (itself from *lumbus*, meaning "loin"). Numbles were eaten as early as the fourteenth century, but sometime in the fifteenth century, people started hearing a phrase such as "a numbles" and assuming the person was really saying "an umbles," and from then on we used the word *umbles* to refer to a deer's edible innards. One gastronomic variation here was the *umble pie*, which was just what you'd expect: the umbles baked into a pie, which was apparently quite good. In a diary entry dated July 8, 1663, Samuel Pepys writes that "Mrs. Turner came in, and did bring us an umble pie hot out of her oven, extraordinary good." Most of the time, however, the umble pie was made for servants and others in the lower classes (the upper classes would be eating the actual meat of the deer). So umble pie had a whiff of the low about it, and to eat it was something of a humiliation if you weren't used to that kind of thing. Sometime in the mid-seventeenth century, it's assumed that some wag recognized the humiliating aspects associated with eating umble pie, and the near-identity of the words *umble* and *humble*, and coined a pun: to *eat humble pie* meant to apologize humbly or to submit to humiliation. Another possibility is that because in some British dialects the "h" is routinely dropped, someone heard "umble pie" and thought the term was really "humble pie."

eavesdropper

You probably know that to *eavesdrop* means "to secretly listen in on a conversation," but what can this unsavory act possibly have to do with eaves or drops? There *is* a connection, but to see it we need to go back to the dim mists of the English language, back in the ninth century. Even as early as that, people talked about a house having *yfesdrype*, which later became *eavesdrip*. Both terms at first referred to the water that drips off the eaves of a house during a rainstorm. The word later changed to *eavesdrop*, and it came to mean the area on which rainwater tended to fall off the eaves of a house. Your typical eaves only extend a small amount past the walls, so this eavesdrop area would be fairly close to the house. If this area also happened to be near an open window or door, then it would be an ideal spot to stand and listen in on a conversation within the house. By the fifteenth century, some crooks were doing just that, and these wrongdoers were called *eavesdroppers*. Writing in one of very first law dictionaries—with the wonderful title of *Les termes de la ley; or Certain difficult and obscure words and terms of the common laws and statutes of this realm now in use, expounded and explained*— John Rastell defined these new miscreants as follows:

> Eavesdroppers are such as stand under walls or windows by night or day to hear news, and to carry them to others, to make strife and debate amongst their neighbours.

By the eighteenth century, the word had generalized to refer to anyone who listened secretly to a conversation, even without the possibility of getting wet.

Ebonics

Black English is also known as *Ebonics*, a word that combines *ebony* ("black") and *phonics*. The term became a lexical celebrity thanks to a hubbub at a school board, of all places. On December 18, 1996, the board members of the Oakland Unified School District voted unanimously to give Black English official status as a second language. The board's reasoning was simple: Black English was a dominant vernacular since the district's student population was 53 percent black. Those students who spoke Black English needed instruction on how to "decode" their native dialect into standard English, which would better prepare them for life outside of school. From the response this decision generated, you'd have thought the board members had voted in favor of regular torture sessions. Parents, pundits, and even leaders of the black community such as Jesse Jackson, Maya Angelou, and Spike Lee condemned the move. (Sample headline: "The Ebonic Plague.") The usual criticism was that Black English was a "lazy," "inferior," slang dialect and that for black kids to get ahead in this world they needed to learn only standard English. (Note that the school board caused much of its own grief by claiming that Black English was "genetically based," a foolish and indefensible notion that pleased no one.) The critics, in this case, could not have been more wrong. There is nothing inferior about Black English, those who speak it aren't being even remotely lazy, and it's certainly not slang. Black English is recognized by the vast majority of linguists as a legitimate language with its own grammar, phrasing, and lexicon.

Alabonics to Zionics

The infamy of Ebonics (it was voted "most controversial" word for 1996 by the American Dialect Society) has given the world's wags a new reason to live: coming up with humorous constructions using the *-onics* suffix, which roughly translates as "the language, dialect, or speech patterns of." Examples are legion and run the gamut from *Alabonics* (the dialect used in Alabama) to Moronics (the speech patterns of stupid people) to Zionics (the language of Jewish Americans). Among the more popular of these terms were the "white English" corollary to Ebonics: *Ivoronics* (ivory plus *phonics*), and *Bubbonics*—*bubba* (slang for a southern male, especially an uneducated "good ol' boy" or redneck) plus *phonics*—the speech patterns of the U.S. South.

egregious

Egregious, "conspicuously or outrageously bad," comes from the Latin *egregius,* "outstanding," which combines *e-,* "out of," and *gregis,* "the herd." That is, the original meaning of this word described a person or thing that was of superior quality, that was literally chosen from the herd. This is totally opposite to what the word means now, which shows you that the paths taken by words aren't always straight lines!

enormous

If you enjoy applying your carpentry skills in the service of building really large wooden objects, then you can safely describe those objects as enormous. That's because the word *enormous* comes to us via the Latin term *enormis*, which is a marriage of the prefix *e-*, "out," and the noun *norma*, "a carpenter's square." Weird! A Latin variant of *norma* is *normalis*, which means "right-angled," and that's the meaning the word *normal* had when it first entered English around the mid-seventeenth century. Meanwhile, the word *enormous* shouldered its way into English in the early sixteenth century and its original meaning was "deviating from the ordinary rule; unusual." (As, say, a carpentry project would turn out of you didn't bother to use your square.) This unusualness became applied to things that were larger than usual as early as 1544, but it didn't seem to settle into the language until about the mid-seventeenth century.

epicure

This term refers to a person with sophisticated tastes, especially when it comes to food and wine. The word comes from a Greek philosopher named Epicurus, who lived from 341 to 270 B.C.E. He believed that pleasure was the highest aim of human life, but he viewed pleasure as the absence of pain and difficulty. This meant that one must practice self-restraint and moderation and forego such obviously painful activities as marriage, children, and dealing with other people! His followers eventually twisted this philosophy into self-gratification and lazy indulgence, but the word gradually took on its current meaning over the past 400 years or so.

espresso

Since this book was to a large extent fueled by excessive quantities of espresso, I'd be remiss if I didn't talk about the word *espresso* itself. It's short for the Italian phrase *caffé espresso*, which literally means "pressed-out coffee." Pressed-out? That describes the technique used to make espresso on older machines: you pull down a handle that forces hot water at high pressure through the ground coffee. (This is why brewing a single serving—a *shot*—of espresso is often called *pulling a shot*.) Lots of people use the word *expresso*, instead, and that variation is accepted by lots of dictionaries, so don't let anyone tell you it's wrong. In fact, you can tell them that not only is it correct culturally, but it's also correct etymologically. That's because both the Italian *espresso* and the English *express* (in the sense of "to press or squeeze") originate with the Latin word *exprimere*, "to press out."

Thank You, Brother Marco

I'm not brave enough to drink my espresso straight up. Instead, I use my espresso machine to steam some milk and I add that to my shot, creating one of the world's most wonderful drinks: the cappuccino. The word *cappuccino* comes from the Capuchin monks, who were noted for wearing a robe that included a sharp-pointed hood, called a *capuche*. Legend has it that a monk named Marco d'Aviano invented the cappuccino in Vienna when the Turkish army broke off its siege of that city and left behind sacks of coffee so bitter that the monks had to cut it with milk to drink it. The resulting beverage was about the same color as the monk's brown robes, too, so that may also have had something to do with the name.

extempore

See OFF THE CUFF.

Falloween

See HALLOWEEN.

farrago

A *farrago* is a medley or a confused mixture of things, and so it's often fodder for ridicule or derision. That's apropos because the word comes to us from the Latin term *farrāgo*, "mixed fodder for cattle."

fathom

> Full fathom five thy father lies;
> Of his bones are coral made;
> Those are pearls that were his eyes:
> Nothing of him that doth fade,
> But doth suffer a sea-change
> Into something rich and strange.

With that song, the "airy spirit" Ariel leads the shipwrecked Ferdinand to dry land, and the action begins in Shakespeare's 1611 play *The Tempest*. By that time, the word *fathom*, "a sea depth of 6 feet," had been in the language for hundreds of years. Strangely, its linguistic forebear was the Old English word *faethm*, which meant "embracing arms." Hunh? Perhaps even stranger, the British Parliament allegedly once defined a *fathom* as "the length of a swain's arms around the object of his affections" (a *swain* is a lover). By the sixteenth century, a *fathom* was more generally defined as the length created when one stretches one's arms out to their fullest extent. Obviously this length would vary considerably depending on who was doing the stretching, so by

Shakespeare's day the length of the fathom had become set at 6 feet. See also DEEP SIX.

feisty

A *feisty* person is one who's plucky, excitable, or spirited, sometimes aggressively so. This is, as you know, a book about weird word origins, and they don't come any weirder than the origins of the word *feisty*, which began its career as the West Germanic term *fist*, "to break wind"! Didn't see *that* coming, did you? It entered English in the mid-fifteenth century as the verb and as a noun that meant "breaking wind" and stayed that way for a while. Witness this memorable stanza from the 1667 poem *Scarronides* by Charles Cotton:

> With that he whistled out most mainly,
> You might have heard his Fist as plainly
> From one side of the Skie to th' other,
> As you and I hear one another.

A bit earlier (in the sixteenth century) people in England started describing certain dogs as *fisting hounds*. These were invariably small lapdogs, and you can imagine that when one broke wind (as dogs are wont to do), it wouldn't be a pleasant thing. Eventually the word *fist* became associated with these small dogs themselves, and when the word crossed the Atlantic to take up residence in the United States, the pronunciation had changed so that *fist* now rhymed with *heist*. The meaning also broadened slightly to refer to any small, aggressive dog that barked constantly, and eventually the spelling settled on *feist*. The spiritedly aggressive nature of a feist was also a trait seen in certain humans, so by the end of the nineteenth century, folks were describing such people as *feisty*. (Although now that you know the true origins of the word, you might think twice before applying this adjective to anyone you admire.)

More Breaking News

If you can stand just a bit more information related to breaking wind, I can tell you that the verb *fizzle*, "to fail after a strong start; to make a hissing sound," originally meant "to break wind without noise." It comes from the word *fise*, a variation on the verb *fist* that I talked about with regard to FEISTY.

filibuster

The word *filibuster* (an exceptionally long speech designed to delay or obstruct legislative action) has a strange history that would probably take a filibuster or two to describe. The condensed version is that it comes from the Dutch word *vrijbuiter*, "freebooter," which is another name for a pirate (*vrijbuit* literally means "free booty"). This word then passed into French (*flibustier*) and Spanish (*filibustero*) before arriving on English shores as *filibuster*, and it referred to any marauding pirate who sought to encourage revolutions in Central America. It was the obstructionist warfare of these pirates that gave politicians a good word for the obstructionist verbal warfare waged by some of their colleagues.

flibbertigibbet

A *flibbertigibbet* is a silly, irresponsible, flighty person, especially one who chatters constantly. In Anne Tyler's book *The Accidental Tourist*, Muriel Pritchett (if you didn't read the book, she was Geena Davis's character in the movie) spent most of her time rambling on aimlessly, and she used flibbertigibbet to describe herself (accurately!). Proving its versatility, this word has also appeared in Shakespeare's *King Lear* ("the foul fiend Flibbertigibbet") as well as in the lyrics to the song "How Do You Solve a Problem Like Maria?" from *The Sound of Music* ("A flibbertigibbet, a will-o'-the-wisp, a clown").

The origin of this word is obscure, but the *OED* speculates that it's an imitation of the sound of idle, trivial chatter. That makes it *onomatopoeic*, which describes a word formed from the imitation of the sound associated with the thing or action it refers to. *Onomatopoeia* (the process) is also responsible for two other terms that deal with idle chatter: *babble* and *yadda-yadda-yadda*.

Listen Up!

Onomatopoeia means, literally, "name-making," but it refers to the specific process of creating words from the sounds associated with things. (This is also called *echoism*.) The letter Z seems to figure in many of these coinages: *buzz, fizz, sizzle, whizz, zap, zing, zither, zip, zoom.* Animals are popular onomatopoeic targets: *bow-wow* (dog), *bleat* (sheep), *cheep* (bird), *clip-clop* (horse), *coo* (pigeon), *gobble* (turkey), *purr* (cat), and *quack* (duck). Not that these are necessarily accurate interpretations. In fact, it's amazing how varied these kinds of words are from culture to culture. In French, a dog's "bow-wow" is *oua-oua* (pronounced "wah-wah"); in Italian, it's *bu-bu* and in Rumanian, *ham-ham;* Vietnamese dogs *gau-gau,* and Turkish ones *hov-hov;* Tagalog dogs *aw-aw,* Japanese hounds *wau-wau,* and Indonesian breeds *gong-gong.*

F

fluffer

A *fluffer*—also called a *house fluffer*—is a decorator who recommends improvements and renovations designed to maximize a house's sale price. The word *fluffer* comes from the idea of fluffing a pillow or cushion to make it look fresh and neat. So in general a fluffer would be a person who makes things neat and tidy. And, indeed, the London Underground has employed "fluffers" since at least the 1950s. These women (they're almost always women) walk the tracks in the early morning hours, sweeping debris from the rails as they go. House fluffers are a much newer breed who take the fluffed-up pillow idea and extend it to the entire house. They're also known as *stagers* and *resale decorators.*

fly by the seat of your pants

In the early days of flying, aviators didn't have the huge range of instruments that they do today, so they'd often have to rely on training, instinct, and experience to get to their destination in one piece. This was also true later on when planes with some instrumentation flew during fog or dark when those instruments became useless. In some cases flying this way meant that the pilot had to pay attention to the "feel" of the aircraft, including the vibrations and G forces that he could detect through the cockpit seat. Thus it was said that such a pilot could *fly by the seat of his pants.* That phrase was adopted into broader use, and we now use it anytime someone performs an action by relying only on instinct, experience, and training.

focus

When you focus on something, either mentally or with a camera, do you feel hot? Probably not (although I guess it depends on what exactly you're focusing), but there's plenty of heat behind the word *focus*. That's because its linguistic origin is the Latin word *focus*, meaning "hearth, fireplace." It would seem we have a ways to travel here, but the journey's not as far as you think. In the seventeenth century, scientists studying optics noticed that light rays reflected or refracted through a lens would converge on a point. In particular, if that point happened to lie on a piece of paper or something similar, the material would burn. Scientists called this "burning point" the *focus*, because (one supposes) it's a kind of fireplace in miniature. This led to the more general idea of concentrating on a particular point, from which people began to use *focus* to refer to putting your attention on a particular thing or to the sharpness of an image.

fogey

For a definition of the word *fogey*, you can't do better than the one that appears in the *OED*: "A disrespectful appellation for a man advanced in life; esp. one with antiquated notions, an old-fashioned fellow, one 'behind the times'." It's a "disrespectful appellation" indeed, but where does it come from? The best guess is that it's a variation on the word *foggy* which, in this case, refers not to misty weather, but to a sense prevalent in Scotland in the seventeenth and eighteenth century: "mossy; covered with moss." The proverbial rolling stone gathers no moss as you know (Rolling Stones guitarist Keith Richards may be the exception), and older people don't "roll" as much as they once did, so they may get more "mossy" as they age. There's also another sense of *foggy* that means "flabby; corpulent," and that may also be the source of *fogey* (since most people tend to put on quite a bit of weight when they're older). For another take on the elderly, see GEEZER.

football

KING LEAR	Do you bandy looks with me, you Rascal?
	Strikes Oswald
OSWALD	I'll not be strucken my Lord.
KENT	Nor tript neither, you base Foot-ball player.
	Trips Oswald.

This bit of physical comedy from Shakespeare's 1605 play *King Lear* is noted for the strange appearance of the phrase *Foot-ball player*. The Bard wasn't talking about soccer (what everyone in the world outside of North America calls *football*) and of course he wasn't referring to the National Football League. The *football* in question here was a rough and often bloody game where a melee of young men would attempt to kick an inflated leather ball into a rival team's zone. This was at first performed outdoors, and the zones could be a mile or more apart. In the twelfth century the game was first played on a field, and it was given the name *fut balle*.

fork over

In the nineteenth century, the word *fork* meant "finger" in the criminal argot of the day. This probably came from the idea of a pickpocket using his fingers to "snag" wallets and watches and whatever else. (The word *fork* was also a synonym for "pickpocket.") So if your average hoodlum back then had to hand over something to someone, he might well say that he had to "fork over" (or "fork out") the item. The phrase found its way into polite society (helped no doubt by its appearance in Charles Dickens's 1865 novel *Our Mutual Friend*), and we non-criminals have used it mean "hand over; give up" ever since.

Presumably for "Duking" It Out?

The fanciful notion of fingers as "forks" is also the source of the phrase that means "fingers" in Cockney rhyming slang: Duke of Yorks (= forks = fingers). If you haven't the faintest idea what I'm talking about and think, in fact, that I've gone barking mad, hold that thought until you read my entry for RASPBERRY, which has a sidebar that explains this rhyming slang business.

fourth estate

Ever wonder why the press as a whole is sometimes called the *fourth estate?* To find the reason, you must travel to Britain, where the three *estates of the realm* are the Lords Spiritual (senior bishops who sit in the House of Lords), the Lords Temporal (peers who sit in the House of Lords), and the elected members of the House of Commons. A story has it that a British parliamentarian from the eighteenth century named Edmund Burke once pointed to the reporters' gallery and called them "a Fourth Estate more important far than they all."

49er

See KANGAROO COURT.

Frankenfood

It's not often that we can trace the origin of a word to a specific person, thus assuring the neologist of linguistic fame (if not fortune). Who wouldn't want to go down in history as the coiner of a word that has found a permanent place in the lexicon? Consider, then, professor Paul Lewis, of Newton Center, Massachusetts, who wrote the following letter to the editor, which appeared in the June 16, 1992, edition of *The New York Times:*

> To the Editor:
>
> "Tomatoes May Be Dangerous to Your Health" (Op-Ed, June 1) by Sheldon Krimsky is right to question the decision of the Food and Drug Administration to exempt genetically engineered crops from case-by-case review. Ever since Mary Shelley's baron rolled

his improved human out of the lab, scientists have been bringing just such good things to life. If they want to sell us Frankenfood, perhaps it's time to gather the villagers, light some torches and head to the castle.

The cheeky and evocative coinage *Frankenfood* caught on almost immediately. By the end of the summer of 1992, it had appeared in the *Boston Globe*, the *Los Angeles Times*, and *Newsday*. Now the word is ensconced in at least three major dictionaries.

Schmoozeoisie

Professor Lewis was so pleased with the success of his new word, that he tried to foist another upon the world: *schmoozeoisie*, the class of people who make their living by talking. Alas, this blend of *schmooze*, "to talk persuasively to someone, especially for personal gain," and *bourgeoisie*, "the affluent middle class," was too clever by half, and resides now in the lexical Dead Letter Office.

freelance

The word *freelance* was coined in 1820 by Sir Walter Scott in *Ivanhoe:*

> I offered Richard the service of my Free Lances, and he refused them—I will lead them to Hull, seize on shipping, and embark for Flanders; thanks to the bustling times, a man of action will always find employment.

He was talking about mercenary knights of the Middle Ages who, in "bustling times" would sell their warrior skills to the highest bidder. By the end of the nineteenth century, the word had come to mean a self-employed journalist or writer. Nowadays it refers to anyone who is self-employed.

frienemy

A *frienemy* (or *frenemy*) is a friend who acts like an enemy; a fair-weather or untrustworthy friend. This just-so blend of *friend* and *enemy* was coined by singer/songwriter Gregg Alexander of New Radicals and first appeared in his 1998 song, "You Get What You Give," a catchy tune if there ever was one. The rap group Arsonists also used the word (as "Frienemies") as the title of a song on their album "As the World Burns," released August 24, 1999, and the word also made an appearance on the HBO show *Sex and the City*.

fussbudget

Fussbudget is a wonderful old word for a person who worries a lot, particularly about trivial things. A *fuss*, as you know, is a commotion or bustle, especially one that's a bit over the top. No one's quite sure where the word came from, but the *OED* speculates that it might come from "the sound of something sputtering or bubbling, or expressive of the action of 'puffing and blowing'." Why not? So the "fuss" part of *fussbudget* makes sense since this worrywart makes a fuss by constantly fretting over trivial matters. The "budget" side seems like a tougher lexical nut to crack because we normally associate the word *budget* with some kind of formal or informal plan for spending money. Does the fussbudget have a budget of fussing that he has to spend? No, fortunately, that's not it at all. A hint as to the proper direction here can be found in a couple of synonyms that arose around the same time as *fussbudget* (we're talking early 1900s here): *fussbox* and *fusspot*. The image we get with these terms is that the person has a collection of worries that he keeps in a box or pot to pull out at will. Luckily, there's an older sense (dating from the fifteenth century) of the word *budget* that means, "pouch or wallet." (This makes etymological sense since the word *budget* comes to us from the French term *bougette*, the diminutive form of *bouge*, "leather bag.") So the fussbudget has a metaphorical bag of worries that he dips into when the occasion warrants (or even when it doesn't).

gadget

The word *gadget* is an all-purpose placeholder for a small device or mechanism, but it's also a word to use when you don't know or have temporarily forgotten the proper name for something. It probably comes to us from the French word *gâchette*, a kind of catchall term used for various bits of machinery over the years. It's the diminutive form of the word *gâche*, "a staple or hook." Humans must be awfully forgetful creatures because we've coined many different nonsense words to use as placeholders for the names of things we've temporarily mislaid, such as *dingus, thingy, thingamabob, thingamajig, whatchamacallit, whatsit,* and *whoosit.* For nameless gadgets or trinkets, there are also *doodad, doohickey, gizmo,* and *widget.* There's some speculation that *widget* is a shortened form of *waffle-gadget,* a device used on ships in the Royal Navy.

Oojah Whatsit?

The *OED* lists yet another placeholder phrase to be used when the name of something stumps you: *oojah capivvy.* The *OED* suggests it comes from the Persian phrase *ujjat kafi fihi,* which means something like "there's no more to be said about it." This seems quite silly, but the *OED* isn't known for its sense of humor or a tendency to yank its readers' chains, so there you go. Amazingly, the *OED* only describes the phrase as "rare" (not, say, "archaic" or even "obsolete") and even includes a citation from 1992! (The *OED* also lists tons of variants, of which I'll only torture you with a few: *hooja-kapippy, oojah-capiff, oojah-cum-pivvy,* and *uja-ka-piv.*)

gadzooks

> "Upon my word I don't see how it's to be done," rejoined Nicholas.
>
> "Why, isn't it obvious?" reasoned Mr. Lenville. "Gadzooks, who can help seeing the way to do it?—you astonish me!"

Wouldn't you just *love* to live in a time when you could use, as Charles Dickens does in the above citation from his 1838 novel *Nicholas Nickleby*, an off-the-scale fun oath such as *Gadzooks* and not be thought an eccentric weirdo for doing so? I know I would, but that's because I love words that are a bit old-fashioned and anachronistic, but not so ANTEDILUVIAN that they're obsolete (antediluvian is a good example). Using such words is called *gadzookery*, a fun term that comes from the oath *Gadzooks*, the modern equivalent of which would be something dishwater-dull such as "Oh my gosh!" The word *Gadzooks* is probably a euphemistic variation on the phrase *God's hooks*, which refers to the nails or spikes that held Jesus Christ to the cross. Changing *God* into *Gad* to make an oath more acceptable in polite society was very common, particularly in the seventeenth century (when our hero *Gadzooks* was at its zenith in popularity). The *OED* lists a bunch of these, including the following: *Gadsbobs, Gadsbodikins, Gadsbud, Gadsbudlikins, Gadslid, Gadsnouns, Gadsokers, Gadsookers, Gadsprecious, Gadswookers, Gadswoons,* and *Gadzookers*.

galaxy

The terms *Milky Way* and *galaxy* would seem to be light-years apart (so to speak), but they're actually surprisingly close, linguistically. The phrase *Milky Way* is very old and comes to us directly from the Latin phrase *lactea via* ("milky way"). Other Latin writers used the phrase *lacteus circulus*, "milky circle," so you get the idea that humans have long regarded the thick strip of stars that dominates the night sky as having a definite milklike quality. Which brings us smartly to *galaxy*, a word that was originally synonymous with Milky Way, a fact attested to by the origin of the word, which is the Greek term *gala*, "milk." See also LETTUCE.

gargoyle

I love Gothic architecture, so my fascination with gargoyles (which are most closely associated with Gothic structures) isn't surprising. What does surprise me is the origin of the word: the Old French *gargouille*, meaning "throat." I guess that's because I always figured gargoyles were either purely ornamental or served to ward off evil. (That's why they're always grotesque figures facing outward: the idea is to scare off any demon or devilish imp who may happen along.) I forgot they originally also had the more mundane chore of draining rainwater away from a wall. It seems reasonable, then, to speculate that the draining water made a gurgling sound, much like liquid being gargled in a throat. And, in fact, the words *gargoyle* and *gargle* share the same root.

geezer

Older folks will sometimes say that they feel like they're wearing a mask or disguise when they look at themselves in the mirror (so different does their current visage look compared to the bloom of youth). Little do they know just how appropriate this is, at least linguistically, because the origin of the word *geezer*, "a senior citizen, particularly one who's eccentric or irritable," is the word *guise*, "a disguise or mask." Around the fifteenth century, the noun *guise* became a verb that meant "to attire fantastically; to go about in masquerade dress." People who would do this kind of thing became known as *guisers*, and by the nineteenth century the pronunciation of the word had changed to *geezer*. At first the word *geezer* referred to anyone who was odd or a bit of a character (an apt description of someone who would "go about in masquerade dress"), but early in the twentieth century people started applying the word to elderly men. (Although in Britain they still use *geezer* as a slang term meaning "chap; fellow.") See also FOGEY.

gerrymander

To *gerrymander* means "to adjust voting districts to favor one party over another." As weird as it may sound, it was the combination of the last name of Elbridge *Gerry*, a former governor of Massachusetts, and *salamander* (a small lizardlike amphibian) that gave us the word gerry-mander. This strange beast was formed when Governor Gerry reshaped his state's voting districts to favor his party. One such district looked suspiciously like a salamander and was drawn as such in an editorial cartoon by Gilbert Stuart. His editor immediately dubbed the creature a *Gerry-mander*, and the name stuck. (Some trivia: Stuart was the same man who painted the portrait of George Washington that appears on the U.S. $1 bill.)

get down to brass tacks

When it's time to *get down to brass tacks*, it means it's time to concern yourself with the fundamentals or the essentials of a situation. What tacks are we talking about here? The most common explanation is that they were a series of brass tacks stuck to a table precisely 1 yard apart in a nineteenth-century general store or any place that sold fabric. Examining a bolt of fabric was one thing, but if you were serious about buying, you'd bring the fabric down to the brass tacks for measuring the amount you needed. Another possibility is that nineteenth-century furniture makers would often use brass tacks or brass nails to stick fabric to the underside of a chair, sofa, or other piece of furniture. If you wanted to see whether the furniture was well made, you'd get down to the brass tacks underneath the piece. This theory is helped a bit by the fact that sometimes the phrase *get down to brass nails* has been used instead of *get down to brass tacks*. A third theory—that *brass tacks* is rhyming slang for *facts*—isn't likely since *get down to brass tacks* originated in America, and we don't do rhyming slang on this side of the pond. (See RASPBERRY for a sidebar that explains what rhyming slang is all about.)

get off scot free

See SCOT FREE.

get the sack

If a person loses his job, we say that the poor fellow *got the sack* or, more succinctly, that he was *sacked*. There is no actual sack involved here, of course, but there used to be. Back in medieval times, workmen and artisans carried around their tools in a sack (this being a few hundred years before the first toolbox was invented). When a worker started a new job, he would take out his tools and give the employer his sack for safekeeping. When the job was complete, the worker would get his sack back, load up his tools, and then move on to the next gig. However, if things didn't work out on the job and the employer wanted to fire the worker, he would hand him his sack and tell him to leave immediately. He literally "got the sack," and we still use the phrase to this day, although in the figurative sense.

You're Fired!

There are some wonderfully fanciful ideas about where the verb *fire*, "to dismiss from employment" comes from. My favorite is the tall tale that a worker who committed an egregious offense (such as stealing) wouldn't GET THE SACK for his tools, but would have the tools themselves confiscated and burned so that the miscreant couldn't work anywhere else. A clue to the actual origins of the verb is the fact that it was originally a verb phrase—*to fire out*—which tells us that it comes from the firing of a gun.

G

go postal

Postal workers are the archetypal angry employees. That reputation began on or about August 20, 1986, when a disgruntled postal worker opened fire on his coworkers, killing 13 of them. Over the next seven years, there were nine more such incidents involving postal workers, and a total of 34 people were killed. These gruesome statistics are the source not only of postal workers' violent reputation, but also of a phrase that today is used with dark humor: *go postal*, "to become extremely angry, possibly to the point of violence."

goatee

See TRAGUS.

gobbledygook

Gobbledygook refers to any impenetrably pretentious verbiage, particularly if it's someone speaking or writing in a professional, political, or other official capacity. It's a fun and fanciful word based on *gobble*, "the noise made by a turkey." *Gobbledygook* was the invention of a United States congressman with the great name Maury Maverick. In the May 11, 1944, edition of *The New York Times Magazine*, he said that he got his "baptism under 'gobbledygook' ... its definition: talk or writing which is long, pompous, vague, involved, usually with Latinized words. It is also talk or writing which is merely long." He said that he was inspired by the turkey, "always gobbledy gobbling and strutting with ludicrous pomposity." If you're wondering about the name Maverick and whether that's something I ought to be investigating in this book, you're absolutely right: see MAVERICK.

goody two-shoes

A *do-gooder* is a humanitarian who sincerely tries to do good deeds but who suffers from naïve and unrealistic expectations. While practicing his do-goodism, the person may also be called a *goody-goody* or, more intriguingly (and perhaps a bit more insultingly), a *Goody Two-Shoes*, although both terms have the sense of someone who is overly virtuous in a sickly sweet kind of way. "Goody Two-Shoes" is the name of the main character in a children's story called *The History of Goody Two-Shoes*, which was published in 1765. She lived most of her life with only one shoe, but when she received a second shoe, she went around yelling "Two shoes! Two shoes!" until nobody could stand the sight of her.

googol

This book is about the origins of words, but sometimes a word simply has no historical background. Linguists say that such words are produced *ex nihilo*, which means they are created out of thin air (literally, "from nothing"). The *OED* contains several thousand words that are classified as "of obscure origin," "origin obscure," "origin unknown," "of doubtful origin," or "uncertain origin" (the *OED*'s etymological descriptions aren't very consistent). This list includes obscure words such as *bazoo*, *gongoozler*, and *pilliwinks*, but it also contains many surprisingly common words, including the following: *aye, beach, bet, boy, capsize, caucus, charade, condom, cub, dog, dud, garbage, gravy, hog, hug, job, lad, moniker, muffin, niche, oat, plot, puke, pun, queer, sleet, slush, slut, smidgen, sneak, stooge,* and *wife.* Modern words with unknown origins include *jazz* (1909), *bozo* (1920), *hijack* (1923), *gig* (1926), *gimmick* (1926), *jive* (1928), *pizzazz* (1937), *raunchy* (1939), *gismo* (1943), *scam* (1963), *dork* (1964), *zit* (1966), *hoagie* (1967), *reggae* (1968), *humongous* (1970), and *mosh* (1987). Another relatively modern word created out of thin air is the mathematical term *googol*, which represents the number 1 followed by 100 zeroes. It was coined by nine-year-old Milton Sirotta in 1938, who made it up when his uncle, the mathematician Edward Kasner, asked him to think of a word for a very large number.

From Googol to Google

The name of the popular Internet search engine Google was supposed to be Googol. In 1997, the search engine had the temporary name BackRub, and the founders—Larry Page and Sergey Brin—quite rightly decided a new name was needed. Since the search engine was handling immense amounts of data, Larry Page suggested the name Googol (he's a math geek). He asked someone nearby to see if the domain named googol.com was taken. Unfortunately, that person typed "google.com," instead. That name was available, Page and Brin decided they liked that version of the name, and they then registered what is now almost certainly the most famous Internet name in the world.

govern

I'd like to take this opportunity to clear up a linguistic mystery that has been confounding people for a very long time. First, we need to take a look at the history of the word *govern*. The source is the Greek word *kubernan*, "a person who steers a ship." This became *gubernare* in Latin, then *governeur* in French, and then it passed into English as *governor* (noun) and *govern* (verb). No surprises there. However, *gubernare* also became the old English word *gubernator*, "ruler; governor," which led to the adjective *gubernatorial*, "of or relating to a ruler or governor." So *that* is why you hear things related to governors (especially the governors of U.S. states) described a "gubernatorial."

grok

This word means "to understand in a deep and exhaustive manner." It originated in Robert Heinlein's classic science-fiction novel *Stranger in a Strange Land*, where it was used as a Martian word that meant "to drink" (in its literal sense) and "to be one with" (in its metaphoric sense).

grubstake

This term refers to the initial money provided to a start-up company, usually by a venture capitalist or an angel investor (a wealthy individual). Grubstake goes back to about the mid-1800s when it was used to mean a supply of food (otherwise known as *grub*) and other equipment that a wealthy investor would give to gold prospectors in exchange for a share of whatever gold was found.

gubernatorial

See GOVERN.

hair of the dog

The expression *hair of the dog* is a shortened form of the original phrase: *hair of the dog that bit you* (or me or him or her or whomever). It means, as all non-TEETOTALERS know, "a hangover cure consisting of an alcoholic drink the same as or similar to the alcoholic drink that caused the hangover." There's a slight possibility that there might be a hair in that morning-after drink, but if so it would only be there accidentally and is not part of the "cure." So why a "hair" and why a "dog"? The phrase *hair of the dog* goes way back to ancient times when, in the spirit of "like cures like," people believed that the proper treatment of a dog bite, particularly if the cur in question was rabid, was to somehow get some of that dog's hair, bind it together, and then apply this puppy poultice directly to the wound. Since a hangover can feel as painful as a dog bite, and since a drink in the morning can make one feel better (however temporarily), taking that drink was like applying dog hair to a bite, and by the mid-sixteenth century, the expression *hair of the dog that bit you* was a firmly established proverb.

Halloween

This scary holiday, which falls on October 31 each year, was originally *Hallow-e'en* or *Hallowe'en*, a contraction of *All-Hallow-Even*, the night before All Hallows Day—now All Saints Day—which is November 1. Of much newer vintage is the term *Falloween*, an extended celebration or observance of Halloween, often beginning several weeks before the day. This word unites the words *fall* and *Halloween* to recognize the lengths to which many people now go to celebrate the latter. If you see houses bedecked with pumpkins and skulls and cobwebs in early October, then you know those people are fully immersed in the Falloween thing. A similar idea is embodied in the phrase *Christmas creep*, the gradual trend to begin displaying Christmas-related merchandise and advertising earlier each year.

hanged, drawn, and quartered

See DRAWN AND QUARTERED.

hangnail

You and I know that a *hangnail* is a bit of partially detached skin around a fingernail. So there's hardly anything weird about the origins of this term, right? It's a rogue bit of epidermis that appears to "hang" off the "nail." Easy-peasy, as the people on British television shows say. Hah, you wish! You don't get off that easy, my friend, so settle in. To understand where *hangnail* came from, you have to use a completely different extremity: the foot. Back in the days of Old English, the word *angnæl* referred to a corn on the foot. *Angnæl* combines *ang*, "compressed, painful" and *næl*, "nail," with the latter referring not to a toenail or fingernail, but to the iron spikes that you drive into wood with a hammer (which then smashes a fingernail when you miss your target). The journey from foot to finger involves a metaphor and a couple of mistakes. The metaphoric part of the trip is that people began to see the hard substance growing on the ends of their fingers and toes as being something nail-like. Some wags actually called them *man-nails* (to differentiate them from, say, doornails), but eventually we began to use the terms *fingernail* and *toenail*. The first of the mistakes was that some folks took the French word *angonailles*, "ulcers; sores," saw the *-nailles* part, and assumed the word referred to any painful swelling or sore near the toenail or fingernail. The second mistake was actually a two-for-one deal: that in the word *angnæl*, the *ang* part sounded like "hang," and the *næl* part referred to a "nail" such as a fingernail. The rest is easy: "I say, Rosemond, look at this wee bit of partially detached skin around my fingernail. That must be what they call a *hangnail*."

happy as a clam

Whenever I give a couple a wedding present, I always sign the card "May you both be clam-happy and horse-healthy." My adjective "clam-happy" comes, of course, from the famous colloquialism *happy as a clam*, "well pleased, contented." We all know and use that phrase, but have you ever stopped to wonder just what the heck your average clam, being a mere shellfish and all, has to be happy about? Not getting dug up and turned into clam chowder would be a good start, but it hardly seems like the full story. To get that story, we must turn to the *OED*, which quotes one Jonathan Slick in his 1844 collection of letters, *High Life in New York*:

> They seemed as happy as clams in high water.

Hmm. Similarly, check out this citation from John Hanson Beadle's 1873 book *The Undeveloped West*:

> A thousand or more negroes thronged the streets "happy as clams at high tide."

I think you see what's going on here. You have your trusty clam shovel at your side, but there's nothing you can do until it's low tide. It follows that no one can go clamming during high tide (or "high water," which is the same thing), so that's when clams are safest and therefore, one presumes, happiest. The full phrase *happy as a clam at high tide* would have been quite familiar to most Americans in the nineteenth century, so using the shortened form *happy as a clam* would have been fine because other people would mentally fill in the rest of the phrase. Over time, however, we kept using the shorter phrase, but the longer version was forgotten. Happy?

hat trick

If you score three goals in a hockey or soccer game, if you ride three consecutive winners in horse racing, or if you accomplish just about any feat three times (particularly three times in a row), then people will applaud your *hat trick*. (In hockey, the fans will go so far as to throw their hats onto the ice in a kind of millinery mania.) The *trick* part comes from a now rarely used sense of the word—"a feat of dexterity or skill"—but what's up with the *hat* part? For that bit of inexplicableness, you can thank the otherwise inexplicable game of cricket, where in the late nineteenth century any skillful bowler who knocked down three wickets on three consecutive throws would earn a prize: a new hat (or perhaps a bit of money collected from the appreciative spectators by passing around a hat).

haywire

When something or someone goes *haywire*, it means that the thing or person is functioning or behaving erratically or unpredictably. I always used to think this word came from the fact that the wire used to bind bales of hay would shoot off erratically when someone cut it. Not so! The *OED* tells me the origin is the phrase *haywire outfit*, a poorly equipped and maintained logging operation. The "haywire" part came from the constant use of pieces of haywire to effect makeshift repairs to logging equipment. The phrase first appeared about 1905, and by the 1920s the word *haywire* had come to refer to anything that malfunctioned or was confusing or unpredictable, including people.

heebie-jeebies

The *heebie-jeebies* are feelings of nervousness and anxiousness. You can thank the cartoonist Bill DeBeck for the invention of this barrel full of linguistic fun. He used it in the 1920s in his strip "Barney Google," which was also the source of gems such as *hotsy-totsy*, "wonderful; pretentiously fashionable," and *horsefeathers*, "nonsense; rubbish."

highfalutin

Highfalutin describes something that is pompous or pretentious. Highfalutin (or, if you prefer, *highfaluting*, but that just doesn't sound right to my ear) has been around since the middle of the nineteenth century, but nobody knows how it got started. The SCUTTLEBUTT is that it comes from the image of a person pompously playing high notes on a flute, or "high-fluting."

Hoity-Toity

An equally fun adjective to toss out is *hoity-toity*. I mentioned earlier in the book that onomatopoeia is one of the ways that new words are formed. Another is *reduplication,* a word-forging process that creates a new word by doubling all or part of an existing word. ("Reduplication" sounds like a redundancy, I know, and that's borne out by the word's history: it comes from the Latin word *reduplicare: re-,* "again," plus *duplicare-,* "duplicate.") It's the origin of such classics as *goody-goody, fiddle-faddle, wishy-washy,* and RIFF-RAFF. In the special case called rhyming reduplication, two words that rhyme are combined, as in *bow-wow, harum-scarum,* HODGEPODGE, *super-duper, teeny-weeny,* and, of course, *hoity-toity* (from the obsolete verb *hoit,* "to romp").

H

hippocampus

The *hippocampus* is the bit of brain tissue that stores memories and regulates emotions. This may come as a bit of a shock, but the word *hippocampus* implies that you have a sea horse in your head! Let me explain. The word comes from the Greek word *hippokampus,* which combines *hippos,* "horse," and *kampos,* "sea monster." It was the name of the creature ridden by the god Poseidon, and it was later applied to the marine animal known as a sea horse. In turn, the hippocampus brain structure got its name from its resemblance to the sea horse.

hobnob

If you *hobnob* with a person or group that is wealthy or powerful, it means that you hang out or mingle with them, usually with the implication that you may be fraternizing a rung or two above your normal perch on the social ladder. In the nineteenth century, however, to hobnob with someone simply meant you were on close or even intimate terms with that person. This sense of *hobnob* came from the phrase *hab-nab,* a shorter version of *habbe nabbe,* which meant, variously, "get or lose," "succeed or fail," or "give or take." This, too, was a short form, this time of phrases such as *habbe we, nabbe we* and *habbe he, nabbe he,* which translate as "have we, have we not" and "have he, have he not." Such phrases eventually came to be used with the social custom of alternating the responsibility for buying a round of drinks for one's companion. If I buy this round, you buy the next one. So first I have the pleasure of treating you, and then I don't have it. We are, in short, *hab-nabbing*. This is a convivial way to spend time with someone, so that's how *hab-nab*—and then *hobnob*—came to mean "on close terms." The word *hobnob* probably got its more modern connotations by association with the word *nob*, which is a slang term for a wealthy person.

hobo

A *hobo* is a homeless person who travels around looking for work. (The "looking for work" part is important, say the hoboes, because it's what differentiates them from those no-good *tramps* who travel to avoid work, and the even more worthless *bums* who neither travel nor work.) It's likely that the word *hobo* comes from the greeting "Ho, bo!" where *ho* is an exclamation to attract attention (something like *ahoy* or, these days, *yo*) and *bo* (also *Bo* or even *Beau*) is a generic form of address (something like *buddy* or *brother*). *Hobo* may also come from the phrase "Ho boy!" uttered by railway workers either as a greeting to their peers or, more to the point here, as a challenge to railway interlopers (such as homeless people traveling around looking for work).

hodgepodge

A *hodgepodge* is a mixture of all kinds of things, particularly if the result is a clumsy, confused mess. (The *OED* not-quite-helpfully defines *hodgepodge* as "a medley, FARRAGO, gallimaufry.") This nice bit of rhyming reduplication (see the sidebar near HIGHFALUTIN) comes to us via our friends in France, who used the word *hochepot* to refer to a stew made from a variety of ingredients. This word combines the verb *hocher*, "to shake together," and *pot*, "pot." *Hochepot* entered English in the fourteenth century and went through a number of forms, including *hogpoch*, *hogepotche*, *hotch-potch*, and *hodge-pot*, until finally settling on *hodgepodge*.

hoi polloi

This phrase (it's pronounced *HOY puh·LOY*) refers to the masses or the common people and has a hint of looking down upon the crowd. This phrase is a bit of a head-scratcher for some people because the original Greek phrase translates as "the many." Therefore, if you say "the hoi polloi," you're really saying "the the many." Hmmm. However, check out how off-kilter things sound when you drop the "the":

> At the state fair, Deirdre kept her caviar pancakes under the counter because she didn't want hoi polloi eating them.

For this reason (as well as the fact that we're not speaking Greek here), a great many professional writers and language authorities accept "the hoi polloi."

Hoi, Not High

Some people mistakenly use hoi polloi to mean "the elite," which is the opposite of its real meaning. It may be that hoi sounds like "high" or because it's reminiscent of hoity-toity.

honeymoon

Some folks would have you believe that the word *honeymoon* refers to some ancient custom that required the bride and groom to spend the first month (or, really, a full lunar cycle, or "moon") drinking mead, an alcoholic drink made with honey. The very idea that your average newly minted man and wife could spend 27 days drunk as skunks should be enough to put the lie to this old chestnut. Unfortunately, however, the real story is quite a bit more cynical. The deal is that at the beginning of a marriage, the bride and groom's love for each other is as sweet as honey and burns as bright as the full moon. However, just as the full moon's brightness eventually wanes, so too will the couple's love for each other. Boo!

hooker

Etymology is generally an obscure business that plies its trade among dusty books and dusty languages. However, tales about the origins of certain words and phrases are fairly famous and often used as cocktail party fodder. One of these famous fables concerns the origin of the word *hooker*, "a prostitute." It seems there was a certain American Civil War general by the name of Joseph Hooker who was infamous in his time for having "camp-followers" (a euphemism of the day for prostitutes) and his headquarters was called "a combination of bar-room and brothel." Seems pretty definitive, but hold your horses. This took place during the Civil War, which lasted from 1861 to 1865. However, the *OED* includes the following citation from an 1845 issue of *Tarheel Talk:*

> If he comes by way of Norfolk he will find any number of pretty Hookers in the Brick row not far from French's hotel.

So although General Hooker was certainly instrumental in popularizing the term *hooker,* he's obviously not the source. For that we must turn to an early version of the verb *hook,* which meant "to snatch with a hook; to seize by stealth," and people who would do this were called *hookers.* The idea that prostitutes "seize" men by the stealth of their feminine wiles was prominent in those days, so this was seen as a kind of hooking. In fact, there's a famous lithograph published around 1850 that shows a couple of ladies-of-the-night (to use yet another euphemism) standing on a New York street corner in bonnets and hoopskirts, no less, propositioning gentlemen in top hats and tails. The picture is titled "Hooking a Victim." So in the same way that earlier thieves who hooked watches and other items became known as hookers, so too did prostitutes who hooked men become known as hookers.

horns of a dilemma

See BETWEEN THE DEVIL AND THE DEEP BLUE SEA.

hullabaloo

This word refers to a great noise or commotion; a hubbub. This is a fun word to use in conversation, and it's perfect if you need an unusual synonym for *noise* or *commotion*. It's just obscure enough that it doesn't get overused, but it's not so obscure that most people won't recognize it and chuckle to themselves. Hullabaloo began its life as the word *halloo,* meaning to urge or incite with shouts. Then, using rhyming reduplication (see the sidebar near HIGHFALUTIN), the *balloo* part was added to form *halloo-balloo,* which eventually morphed into *hullabaloo.*

humble pie

See EAT HUMBLE PIE.

hussy

If you know a woman who manages the affairs of her household, you'd be unlikely to call her a *hussy*, since that term refers to an immoral or mischievous woman (most often magnified by the adjective *brazen*). However, a few hundred years ago, you could call such a woman a hussy and not have to duck away from what would now be an inevitable slap in the face. That's because the word *hussy* was originally a shortened form of the word *housewife*, and the two were synonyms for a few hundred years. Both come from the old word *huswif*, literally "house woman." Over time, crabby people started using the short form *hussy* as an insult for women they thought were beneath them or who exhibited wanton behavior, and after a while this negative sense stuck.

hypochondriac

The word *hypochondriac* (referring to a person who complains of having the symptoms of a disease, but those symptoms are not physically present) is an amalgam of the Greek words *hypo*, "under," and *chondros*, "rib cartilage." Say what? The story is that the ancient Greeks thought organs (such as the upper abdomen, the spleen, and the liver) that reside under the ribs—that is, in an area they called the "hypochondria"—were the source of black bile and hence the cause of melancholy. And since imagining you have a disease is a kind of melancholy, people with this neurotic affliction became known as hypochondriacs. See also PHLEGMATIC.

iconoclast

An *iconoclast* is a person who attacks traditional or popular ideas or established institutions. The word literally means "image-breaker," and it originally referred to a person who smashed religious images (*icons*). The first iconoclasts weren't antireligious, as you might expect. Rather, they were extremely devout, and they considered the viewing of religious imagery to be idolatry (the worship of idols).

idiot

A private person is one who keeps to himself, and I suppose if that fellow was an idiot, to boot, then his solitary lifestyle would be no concern of yours. It would also be rather appropriate, linguistically speaking. That's because the word *idiot* harkens back to the Greek word *idiotes*, "a private person." This also had the sense of someone who held no political office or other public position, so the word *idiot* became associated with the common man. In Greek times, the common man was almost always an uneducated man, too, so *idiot* eventually came to refer to someone who was ignorant or without learning. The extremely ignorant were seen to be actually mentally or intellectually deficient, and that's where our current sense of the word *idiot* has stayed for the past few hundred years.

imp

We use the word *imp* to refer to either a mischievous child or a little devil (or both, depending on the child). Could you call a garden gnome an imp? I guess it depends on the gnome's expression (a demonlike leer would help), but probably not. No matter, the question gives me a chance to segue into the origins of the word *imp*, which are related to gardening, believe or not. We take our lexical time machine back to the Latin term *putare*, "to prune," and then to its opposite, *imputare*, "to graft." Grafting something onto a plant results in a young shoot, and that's the meaning the shortened form *imp* had when it entered English way back in the ninth century. By the early fifteenth century the English metaphor machine had taken over and folks were using *imp* to refer to any child (since a child is a kind of human "young shoot"), but also particularly to the scion of a noble house. Now at the risk of sounding uncharitable, it should be said that scions of noble houses aren't always the most pleasant tykes on the block. This may explain why by the sixteenth century *imp* had taken on its "mischievous child" sense. You might even call such a brat a "child of the devil" or a "devilkin," so in other contexts people took up just the "devil" part and that gave *imp* its "demon" sense.

Growing More Words

The Latin term *putare* has been a prolific source of English words. One of its other senses is "to consider; to think." From this branch have grown the English words *putative* ("commonly thought; reputed"), *reputation*, *compute*, and *dispute*.

in cahoots

See CAHOOTS.

infantry

If you're thinking that the "infant" part of *infantry* couldn't possibly have anything to do with children, think again! The story is that, although we generally think of an infant as a newborn baby, in the Middle Ages the word was used for any young person (equivalent to what we would call a "minor" today). In Italy, a youngster was also expected to perform military duties, and in that capacity, he was called an *infante*. As a group, they were called the *infanteria*. From there, it was only a short march to the English word *infantry*.

it's a dog's life

See DOG'S BREAKFAST.

jaywalker

If you cross the street against the light or without the benefit of a cross-walk, the driver of the car that had to slam on its brakes to avoid mow-ing you down may scream "Stupid jaywalker!" at you. You, as a riposte, would be well within your rights to yell back "Redundant screamer!" Okay, well, it's not exactly a zinger, but it does have the virtue of being linguistically apropos. That's because the word *jaywalker* combines the old insult *jay*, "a stupid or silly person," with *walker*. Some legal fussbud-gets believed that anyone who would risk their life to cross the street illegally was acting stupidly, so that "walker" is a "jay"—a *jaywalker*. Why *jay* for a stupid person? No one's quite sure, but it probably has something to do with the traditional belief that birds are dumb because they have such tiny brains (hence the insult *birdbrain*).

jejune

The word *jejune* means "insipid, dull," but it began its linguistic career as part of the human anatomy, namely part of the small intestine. Now it's true that the intestines aren't particularly interesting to those of us who aren't internists or gastro-intestinal specialists, but that's not how the modern meaning of the term came about. The origin is the Latin word *jejunus*, "fasting," which became *jejunum*, "a section of the small intestine." (The lexical leap here was that this particular section of the intestine was rumored to be always empty at death. Yes, language can be *very* weird.) The word inserted itself into the English language in the seventeenth century, and it kept the original Latin meaning of "fasting," but it also meant "hungry; without food." However, it didn't take long before the metaphor machines began doing their work, and *jejune* began being used for things or people that were considered to be insubstantial or unsatisfying in some way. From there, it wasn't much of a jump to the "insipid; dull" sense that dominates today. While we're still here, I should point out that Latin also had the word *disjejunus*, which meant literally "to break one's fast." In French, that became *déjeuner*, "to breakfast," which eventually turned into the English verb *dine* (and the noun *dinner*).

A Naïve Coinage

Some people use *jejune* to mean "childish, naïve," and that sense probably came about by mistake since *jejune* looks a lot like the Latin term *juvenis* and the French term *jeune*, both of which mean "young."

jovial

If you come across someone whom you'd describe as *jovial*, "jolly, convivial, full of mirth," it's unlikely you'd also describe that person as "godlike." (I'm not sure what circles you run in, so I don't want to be *too* presumptuous here.) However, you'd be well within your linguistic rights to describe that person as such, because a god does indeed lurk behind the word *jovial*. That god is none other than Jupiter himself, the Big Kahuna of the Roman pantheon. The name *Jupiter* comes from *Jovis-pater*, a term that combines *Jovis*, "Jove," and *pater*, "father." It was because of this that folks would often refer to Jupiter as just Jove, and the Latin word *jovialis* meant "Jove-like," and that adjective was later shortened to *jovial*. That's how it entered the English language, although with the meaning "majestic." However, another of Jove's characteristics was that he was a jolly, convivial sort, so over time the word *jovial* also took on those same qualities.

More Planetary Coinages

The jovial-Jupiter connection isn't an obvious one, but other planet-themed words are more accessible. For example, the word *mercurial*, "lively, unpredictable," comes from *Mercury*; the word *saturnine*, "melancholy, morose," comes from *Saturn*; the word *martial*, "warlike," comes from *Mars*; and the word *plutonic*, "dark, gloomy," comes from *Pluto*. We don't call anyone "Venusian," although there was an old sense of the word *venereal* that meant "relating to sexual pleasure," and that word came directly from *Venus* (and, of course, now refers to a disease). There are no common words based on Neptune or Uranus.

judge

The word *judge* comes from the Latin word *judice*, which combines *jus*, "law," and *-dicus*, "speaker." So a judge is one who literally "speaks the law." (The word *verdict*, "the decision of a jury in a trial," has a related past. It combines the Latin *ver*, "true," with *dit*, "speech." So someone rendering a verdict literally "speaks the truth.") The same Latin root also produced *judicial*, which describes anything related to the courts, judges, or the administration of justice. Another form of the Latin *jus* was *juris*, "law," from which we get words such as *jurist*, *juridical* (which describes anything related to the administration of justice; the *-dical* suffix goes back to the Latin *dicere*, "to say"), *jurisdiction* (the *-diction* suffix means "declaration"), and *jurisprudence* (the *-prudence* part comes from the Latin *prudentia*, "knowledge").

juggernaut

You may know that *juggernaut* refers to "a force that's relentlessly destructive or unstoppably crushing." My use of the word "crushing" here was slyly deliberate because there's a story of literal crushing behind the word *juggernaut*. In 1321, a Franciscan missionary named Friar Odoric published a first-hand account of a Hindu festival in honor of Jagannath, one of the titles of Krishna, the eighth incarnation of Vishnu. (The name *Jagannath* means "lord of the world.") According to the good Friar, during this festival in Orissa, India, an idol of Jagannath would be mounted on an enormous vehicle that would then be paraded through the streets. Devotees of Jagannath would sometimes throw themselves under the giant wheels of the vehicle, where they would be crushed to death. It's a horrific story, to be sure, and it's one that was likely exaggerated for effect (a not uncommon occurrence when Westerners return with tales of "pagan" religious practices). However, everyone loves a good yarn, and this tale took England by storm, which helped the anglicized version of Jagannath—*juggernaut*—find a permanent place in the language. It originally referred to any institution or practice that caused blind devotion, but by the nineteenth century it had taken on its current meaning of an unstoppable force. (By the way, in Britain they use *juggernaut* to refer to a large, heavy truck or *lorry* as a Brit would be more likely to say.)

July

See SEPTEMBER.

jump the gun

If you *jump the gun*, then shame on you for doing something before you're supposed to. This phrase comes to us via the noble sport of track and field, where since at least 1942 the phrase *jump the gun* has referred to a false start in a race, and the "gun" in question is the starter's pistol. Okay, but why "jump"? First there's the image of some twitchy sprinter leaping out of the blocks ahead of his competitors. However, there's a sense of the verb *jump* that's been around for over 300 years and refers to making a kind of premature mental leap. For example, we might say that someone "jumped to a conclusion." So the verb *jump* has a lengthy pedigree of prematurity, you might say.

jump the shark

If a television show *jumps the shark*, it means that the show has included an over-the-top scene or plot twist that's indicative either of an irreversible decline in the show's quality or of a desperate bid to stem the show's declining ratings. The phrase refers to an episode of the *Happy Days* TV show in which the previously cool character Arthur "Fonzie" Fonzarelli water-skis (while still wearing his trademark leather jacket) up a ramp and over a tank containing a shark.

Jump the Couch

The verb phrase *jump the couch* means "to exhibit frenzied or aberrant behavior that makes it appear as though one is completely out of control or even insane." This just-so phrase was inspired both by JUMP THE SHARK and by actor Tom Cruise's infamous and eyebrow-raising couch-jumping antics on the May 23, 2005, *Oprah Winfrey* show.

June

See SEPTEMBER.

junta

A *junta* is a group of military types who take over a country after a coup. It's a group that you probably wouldn't want to join, and it's unlikely they'll ask you anyway. However, it used to be that with juntas you could do nothing *but* join. That's because the word *junta* comes to us via the Latin term *juncta*, a form of the verb *jungere*, "to join." It's the source of our word *join*, as you might expect, but it also became *junta* in Spanish and Portuguese, where it referred to an administrative council or committee. That sense entered English as *junta* in the early seventeenth century, and a hundred years or so later the sense changed to the post-coup cabal that we use today.

kangaroo court

You don't get more Australian than a kangaroo, so surely the phrase *kangaroo court*, "an official or illegal tribunal or legal proceeding," must have originated in Australia. Ah, if only etymology were so logical and convenient. Alas, there isn't a shred of evidence that links *kangaroo court* directly with the Aussies. On the other hand, the first recorded use of *kangaroo court* comes from an American publication in 1853, the time of the California gold rush, and we know that lots of Australians were 49ERS (from the year 1849, the start of the main gold rush, although gold was first discovered there in 1848). So it's possible these Down Under gold-diggers could have brought the phrase with them. However, a more plausible explanation comes from some of the illegal activities of the day. In particular, if you took over someone else's mining claim without permission, you were said to be a *claim jumper*, a phrase that dates as far back as 1839. (This comes from an old sense of the verb *jump* that meant "to rob or cheat.") California in those days was still a work in progress, so the courts set up to prosecute claim jumpers weren't exactly models of the judiciary process. Combine this with the fact that kangaroos are, of course, world-class jumpers, and it's not hard to imagine some wag calling these loose legal proceedings against the claim jumpers a *kangaroo court*.

Getting the Jump on Neonatal Care

Premature babies, isolated in a separate ward or under an oxygen tent, suffer because they lack human contact. In the 1980s, doctors in Colombia began taking the opposite approach and allowing mothers to tuck their premature newborns under their clothing and hold them twenty-four hours a day. This arrangement looked just like a baby kangaroo tucked inside its mother's pouch, and so was born the phrase *kangaroo care:* "neonatal care in which a premature baby is held on the chest of the caregiver with skin-to-skin contact." Best of all, it worked: not only did more *kangarooed* (yup, it's a new verb) babies survive, but they thrived, with many leaving the hospital days or even weeks earlier than normal.

keep up with the Joneses

If you try to *keep up with the Joneses*, it means that you extend yourself financially to appear as though you're in the same socioeconomic strata as your neighbors. This sounds like a term from economics, but it actually comes from a comic strip named *Keeping Up with the Joneses*, published by Arthur R. Momand from 1913 to 1941. Momand got the idea for the strip after living for several years in the upscale community of Cedarhurst, New York. Momand explained that he and his family ...

> had been living beyond our means in our endeavor to keep up with the well-to-do class which lived around us in Cedarhurst. I also noticed most of our friends were doing the same: the $10,000 chap was trying to keep up with the $20,000-a-year man. I decided it would make good comic-strip material.

The title of the strip was going to be *Keeping Up with the Smiths*, but in the end Momand "finally decided on *Keeping Up with the Joneses* as being more euphonious." Good call!

Sounds Good!

The adjective *euphonious* means "pleasant-sounding." It comes to use from the Greek term *euphōnos,* a euphonious combination of the prefix *eu-,* "good" and *phon,* "sound."

kibosh

A *kibosh* (pronounced *KYE·bosh*) is a thing that stops or restrains some-thing else. However, it's always used as part of the phrase *put the kibosh on* something. The world's linguists have occasional skirmishes over the origin of this word, but the winning theory seems to be that it comes from the Gaelic phrase *cie bas* (pronounced the same as kibosh), which means "cap of death." In ancient Ireland, a judge would slip on this cap before he sentenced a person to death, which is about as stopped or restrained as you can get.

kit and caboodle

If you've got your whole *kit and caboodle* with you, then you've got everything you need, the complete collection, the whole lot. What's the deal with this curious phrase? The *kit* part is no big whoop because the word has long referred to the collection of equipment required by a soldier, the collection of tools used by a workman, or the collection of personal effects that a traveler requires for a trip. The word *kit* might come from the Middle Dutch term *kitte*, "a wooden vessel made of hooped staves," presumably because one might carry one's kit in such an object, although that seems a bit dodgy to me. *Caboodle* is more prob-lematic, but it's certainly a variation on *boodle*, which comes from the Dutch word *boedel*, "possessions, estate." So the phrase was originally *kit and boodle*, but I guess that wasn't enough fun to say, so people added the "ca" sound to give the alliterative version *kit and caboodle* that we use today. See also LOCK, STOCK, AND BARREL.

K

lackadaisical

Near the end of Shakespeare's *Romeo and Juliet*, Juliet's nurse and Juliet's mother, Lady Capulet, tell Juliet's father the bad news:

> NURSE   She's dead, deceased, she's dead. Alack the day!
>
> LADY CAPULET   Alack the day. She's dead, she's dead, she's dead!

Nothing lackadaisical ("without energy or enthusiasm") about those lamentations! However, the clue we seek for the origins of the oddball word *lackadaisical* lies in those two lines: the phrase *alack the day*. The archaic word *alack* was long used as an exclamation of regret or dissatisfaction, and it combines the interjection *A*, meaning "Ah!" or "Oh!" with the word *lack*, which in this sense means "shame, reproach, or fault." So when something bad happened, people would exclaim *Alack the day!*, meaning "shame to the day" or "woe to the day." *Alack the day* later became a single word, *alackaday*, and then (as English speakers have a habit of doing), the *a* disappeared and we ended up with *lackaday*. Folks having fun with the language extended this term to *lackadaisy*, and anyone who was given to uttering this term was described as *lackadaisical*. People without energy or enthusiasm would often complain about how hard their lives were, part of which included frequent "lackadaisy" reproofs, so the adjective eventually stuck to them.

laconic

The word *laconic* described a person who uses few words. It goes back all the way to an ancient Greek people called the Laconians. One day, a fellow named Philip of Macedon threatened to invade Sparta, the Laconian capital city. He sent them a note: "If I enter Laconia, I will level Sparta to the ground." The Laconians returned a single-word reply: "If." Now *that's* laconic!

lame duck

If a political incumbent loses an election, he becomes a *lame duck*, the holder of a political office between the election date and the date when the successor is inaugurated. The implication is that, although he still holds office, he's "lame" because he can no longer wield the power of that office. So why is a lame duck a duck and not some other animal? No one really knows for sure. The most plausible explanation I've seen is that a duck that's lame would not fly as well as the healthy ducks, so it would soon fall behind, which is sort of what happens to a defeated incumbent. Others believe it's a play on the phrase *dead duck*, "a doomed person." In this case, the loser isn't officially "dead" until his term ends, so between the election and then he's merely "lame."

last-ditch

If you describe some effort or strategy as *last-ditch*, you mean that it's your final chance to avert defeat or disaster. Not that in such a dire situation you'd have much time for such things, but it might occur to you to wonder just what ditch you're talking about, and why it's the last one. The ditch in question is probably more accurately (and helpfully) described as a trench, particularly a defensive trench dug during a war. Armies generally dig a series of trenches as they advance. If things go awry, however, the army might have to retreat to a previous trench (where they would then *retrench*, one supposes). If things went *really* badly, the army might find itself retreating all the way back to its first trench. There's no place else to go, so this represents the army's final chance to avoid defeat, so they're in their "last ditch." The latter phrase eventually came to refer to giving one's all in war, as evidenced in a 1798 declaration by the citizens of Westmoreland, Virginia, that "In

L

War We ... know but one additional Obligation, To die in the Last Ditch or uphold our Nation." The more general sense of the phrase as a last chance to avoid disaster didn't enter the language until about the mid-twentieth century, when Marshall McLuhan, in his 1951 book the *Mechanical Bride*, wrote of "A last-ditch stand of denuded minds."

laughingstock

If a person is a *laughingstock*, it means the poor dear is the object of ridicule, and "object" is the operative term here. The word *stock* has long been used to refer to things: a block of wood (this comes from the earliest sense of the word, "tree trunk," which goes back to the ninth century), the stock in a store, livestock, and so on. So to describe someone as "stock" means that you see that person as a mere object, incapable of feeling. People who do stupid deeds fall into this category, and we've long called them by names that indicate how ridicule-worthy they are: *jesting-stock*, *mocking-stock*, *sporting-stock*, and *talking-stock*. The one that's stuck is *laughing-stock*, which was first recorded in 1533 and is now such a comfy citizen of the language that we routinely make it a single word: *laughingstock*.

lettuce

Milk is a fine accompaniment to many foods, particularly cookies and peanut butter and jelly sandwiches, but I bet there aren't many people who think milk goes well with lettuce. Yuck! Milk and lettuce may not have much of an epicureal connection, but they have a genuine etymological one. That's because the word *lettuce* comes from the Latin *lactuca*, which in turn is derived from the prefix *lact-*, "milk." The connection here is that some types of lettuce contain a white, milklike juice. The Latin word entered English as *letuse* (no one's quite sure how we got from *lactuca* to *letuse*, but there you go), and the spelling became *lettuce* by about the mid-seventeenth century. See also GALAXY.

Lilliputian

See BROBDINGNAGIAN.

lock, stock, and barrel

Your workaday firearm has three basic pieces: the *lock*, which is the firing mechanism; the *barrel*, which is the tube down which the bullets travel after being fired; and the *stock*, which is the wooden piece to which the lock and barrel are attached. That's the entire gun: lock, stock, and barrel. Soldiers probably as far back as the American Revolution were using the phrase *lock, stock, and barrel* to refer to the entirety of their gun assemblies, but by the mid-nineteenth century civilians had appropriated the phrase to refer to anything in its entirety. Interestingly, the variant phrase *stock, lock, and barrel* appeared in written form as early as 1817, while the more familiar *lock, stock, and barrel* didn't show up until at least 1842. See also KIT AND CABOODLE.

lollapalooza

A *lollapalooza* is an outstanding person or thing or something that's an exceptional example of its kind. In his book *The American Language*, the great writer H. L. Mencken claims that this word (which is also spelled *lollapaloosa* and *lallapalooza*, among others) originated with the French phrase *allez-fusil*, "forward the muskets!" After the French landed in Ireland in 1798, the phrase passed into the local language and eventually became *allay-foozee*, "a sturdy fellow," and it somehow morphed into *lollapalooza* from there. This word has been taken over in recent years by a tour of alternative music bands called *Lollapalooza* that runs each summer. So (speaking of alternatives) here are some other words you can use instead: *corker, doozy, humdinger,* and *lulu*.

L

mad as a hatter

> "Then you should say what you mean," the March Hare went on.
>
> "I do," Alice hastily replied; "at least—at least I mean what I say—that's the same thing, you know."
>
> "Not the same thing a bit!" said the Hatter. "You might just as well say that 'I see what I eat' is the same thing as 'I eat what I see'!"

In this passage from Lewis Carroll's *Alice in Wonderland*, the Hatter's sensible rhetoric belies his underlying madness, as we soon find out. You might think this memorable character was the source of *mad as a hatter*, but that phrase had been around before Carroll wrote his book. (In fact, it's likely that he was making a play on the phrase—that is, needing a character who the reader would recognize as mad, he choose a hatter.) First, you need to know that a *hatter* is a person who makes hats. (It has also been used to refer to a person who sells hats.) In the eighteenth and nineteenth centuries, felt hats were quite fashionable, and hatters would work long hours turning beaver pelts and rabbit skins into felt top hats and other fancy headgear. Unfortunately, part of the process of preparing the fur was to brush on a mercury solution to stiffen the hairs. The hatter sweatshops of the day were poorly ventilated, of course, so the women making the hats inhaled mercury vapors constantly. The resulting buildup of mercury in their systems damaged their brains, resulting in symptoms as mild as depression and anxiety, and as acute as outright madness. These symptoms were called *mad hatter syndrome*, resulting in the phrase *mad as a hatter* becoming part of the language.

maelstrom

When you think of grinding things (pepper, flour, your teeth), you usually think that whatever's doing the grinding is something hard (blades, stones, your teeth). But could it be something soft? Could it be, in fact, water? That seems a stretch, but that's the imagery behind the word *maelstrom*, "a powerful whirlpool." It began its linguistic life as the early Dutch word *maelstrom*, which was a blend of *malen*, "to grind," and *strom*, "stream." (The Dutch got the word *malen* from the Latin *molere*, "to grind," which also produced the word *mill* in English, as in *pepper mill, flour mill*, and the verb *mill*, "to grind in a mill.") The Dutch first used *Maelstrom* as the name of the system of eddies and whirlpools that form twice daily off the northwest coast of Norway. This is one of the most powerful tidal systems in the world, and apparently the Dutch thought it was so dangerous that it could grind unwary ships to bits.

magazine

You know that the word *magazine* is a synonym for a periodical, and you may also know that military types and gun-owners also use the word *magazine* to refer to the chamber or clip used to feed cartridges to a rifle or machine gun. These are wildly different senses, so what's the story behind them? The story is the Arabic verb *khazana*, "to store," from which came the noun *makhzan*, "storehouse." In the fourteenth century, this word entered Middle French as *magasin*, and by the late sixteenth century it had found its way into English as *magason*, then *magosine*, and finally *magazine*. Throughout all these lexical shenanigans, the "storehouse" sense was preserved. By the turn of the seventeenth century, the military started using *magazine* in the more specific sense of "a storehouse for ammunition, arms, and other military provisions." By the mid-eighteenth century, the meaning had specialized even further to "a chamber for bullets in a wind-gun," and then, a hundred years later, to the current sense of the rifle chamber or machine-gun clip. That's one side of the *magazine* story. The other side is more metaphorical, because people took the idea of a storehouse and applied it to encyclopedia-like books that were "storehouses" of ideas, facts, and information. So in 1639, a fellow named Richard Ward published a book titled *Animadversions of Warre; or, a Militarie Magazine of the*

M

Truest Rules, and Ablest Instructions, for the Managing of Warre. In 1669, one Samuel Sturmy, apparently a more succinct fellow than Mr. Ward, published a book called *The Mariners Magazine.* You can also think of periodicals as "storehouses" of articles and other literary tidbits, so it didn't take too long before they, too, became known as magazines. The first use of this sense of the word that we know of came in 1731 with the publication of a new periodical named *The Gentleman's Magazine; or, Monthly Intelligencer,* the introduction to which included the following bit of helpful background:

> This Consideration has induced several Gentlemen to promote a Monthly Collection to treasure up, as in a Magazine, the most remarkable Pieces on the Subjects abovemention'd.

If the use of the verb *treasure up* in this citation has you NONPLUSSED, your confusion is understandable. For help, see my entry for THESAURUS, later in the book. (Yes, I said *thesaurus.* You'll see.)

manure

If you're a *Seinfeld* fan, you may think you already know the origins of the word *manure.* In one episode, George tries to impress a date by inexplicably parsing the word *manure:* "Horse manure's not that bad. I don't even mind the word 'manure.' You know, it's 'newer,' which is good, and a 'ma' in front of it. Ma-newer. When you consider the other choices, 'manure' is actually pretty refreshing." Now, I'm not saying that you *shouldn't* use TV sitcoms for etymological research, but in this case you'd be wise to look elsewhere. Where? Right here: The word *manure* comes to us from the Latin phrase *manu operari,* "to perform manual labor," which later gave rise to *manurare,* "to till or cultivate," and this became the verb *manure.* Back in those days, "manuring" involved much manual labor, including tilling the soil and adding fertilizer. That fertilizer was, naturally, animal dung of some description, so eventually the verb *manure* became the noun *manure.*

March

See SEPTEMBER.

maverick

Earlier in the book I told you the story of how one Maury Maverick coined the useful word GOBBLEDYGOOK. What about that irresistible last name? Yes, it *was* the source of the word *maverick*, meaning "a nonconformist; an independent thinker." However, it wasn't Maury Maverick who inspired the term, but rather his grandfather, the south Texas lawyer Samuel A. Maverick. It seems that at some point the elder Maverick was owed the significant sum of $1,200. The client couldn't pay, but he was able to clear the debt by giving Maverick 400 head of cattle. Maverick was a lawyer, not a cattle rancher, so I guess it's not all that unusual that he didn't seem to know what he was doing with his newfound herd. For one thing, he never branded the animals. In the tradition of the day, if an unbranded cow wanders off and is found by a neighboring rancher, that fellow can claim the animal as his own (and, being a proper cattle rancher, he would then brand the animal). Maverick eventually sold off what few cattle he had left, but his more enduring legacy is a linguistic one: the word *maverick* came to refer to any unbranded animal separated from its herd. It's not too much of a stretch to say that a nonconformist or independent person is one who refuses to be "branded," and by 1886 people were doing just that and labeling such people *mavericks*.

May

See SEPTEMBER.

McMansion

A *McMansion* is a large, opulent house, especially a new house that has a size and style that doesn't fit in with the surrounding houses. This word has only been a part of the lexicon since about 1990, but it has already undergone a fairly significant change in meaning. In fact, the word's current meaning seems to be almost the opposite of its original sense. *McMansion* originally referred to something similar to "cookie-cutter house"; that is, a house that has a bland style that's identical to all the nearby houses. This fits nicely with the formation of the word, which combined *McDonald's* (the fast-food) and *mansion*. After all, what could be more bland and "cookie cutter" than the fare served by McDonald's?

melting pot

In 1908, the playwright Israel Zangwill released a new production called *The Melting-Pot:*

> America is God's Crucible, the great Melting-Pot where all the races of Europe are melting and re-forming! Here you stand, good folk, think I, when I see them at Ellis Island, here you stand in your fifty groups, with your fifty languages and histories, and your fifty blood hatreds and rivalries. But you won't be long like that, brothers, for these are the fires of God you've come to—these are the fires of God. A fig for your feuds and vendettas! Germans and Frenchmen, Irishmen and Englishmen, Jews and Russians—into the Crucible with you all! God is making the American.

The play was a success and the *melting pot* metaphor—that the various races and cultures that populated the United States were "melted" down into a single national culture and identity—became a permanent part of the lexicon.

From Melting Pot to Salad Bowl

For the melting pot to function, immigrants have to give up their old cultures in favor of the American Way. That is, each immigrant becomes just another ingredient in what some people call the *American stew.* But there's plenty of evidence to show that many immigrants are hanging on to their cultural identity while still mixing with the larger culture. To some, this is reminiscent of the way that salad ingredients remain identifiable when mixed together. Therefore, they say, America isn't so much a melting pot as it is a *salad bowl,* an increasingly popular metaphor that first entered the language around 1975.

metrosexual

This infamous term refers to an urban male with a strong aesthetic sense who spends a great deal of time and money on his appearance and lifestyle. A metrosexual is a clotheshorse wrapped around a dandy fused with a narcissist. Like soccer star David Beckham, who has been known to paint his fingernails, the metrosexual is not afraid to embrace his feminine side. Why *metrosexual?* The *metro-* (city) prefix indicates this man's purely urban lifestyle, while the *-sexual* suffix comes from *homosexual*, meaning that this man, although he is usually straight, embodies the heightened aesthetic sense often associated with certain types of gay men. His opposite is the *retrosexual*, a man with an unde-veloped aesthetic sense who spends as little time and money as possible on his appearance and lifestyle.

Midas

See CROESUS.

mint

See MONEY.

mondegreen

Oronyms are two phrases that sound the same but have different mean-ings. For example, *I scream* and *ice cream*, and *some mothers* and *some others*. An oronym that comes from mishearing the lyrics of a song is most often called a *mondegreen*. The name comes from a misheard lyric in an old Scottish folk song called *The Earl of Moray*. The line "Oh, they have slain the Earl o' Moray and laid him on the green" was heard as "Oh, they have slain the Earl o' Moray and Lady Mondegreen." Perhaps the most famous mondegreen occurs in the Jimi Hendrix song "Purple Haze"; people regularly mishear "'Scuse me while I kiss the sky" as "'Scuse me while I kiss this guy."

money

Roman mythology tells us that the goddess Juno (wife of head honcho god Jupiter) was responsible for warning people of dangers, and in this capacity the Romans called her Juno Moneta. (In Latin, *moneta* means "to warn.") The Romans built a temple in her honor and a while later added a mint alongside the temple. So Juno also became the goddess of finance, and the coins created in the mint became known as *moneta*. That word eventually turned into the French word *monneai*, from which our word *money* came to life. So money has at its root a warning, which would explain why so many people through the ages have warned their fellow beings about the inherent dangers of money (it's the root of all evil, and so on). The Latin word *moneta* also became our word *mint*, "to produce money out of metal." This has given us the idiom *in mint*

M

condition, "as good as new." Also, minting produces coins, so *coin* is also a synonym for mint, and this has given us the idiom *to coin a phrase*, "to invent a word or phrase to express a new idea." Such a word is often called a *coinage*.

mortgage

A *mortgage* is a pledge of property as security for the repayment of a loan. This is a strange word on two accounts. First, its pronunciation (*MOR·gij*) seems a bit off, and second, the history of the word tells us that it means, literally, "dead pledge": *mort* is French for "dead" (and is pronounced *MOR*), and *gage* is an old word that means "pledge." The explanation for this is that if a person defaults on a mortgage, he ends up losing the property. It becomes, in effect, dead to him. So a mortgage is a do-or-die proposition.

muckraker

If a journalist is fond of sensationalist stories that focus on exposing misconduct and corruption in prominent individuals or institutions, we call him or her a *muckraker*. Muckraking came into the language in 1684 in a book titled *Pilgrim's Progress*, by John Bunyan. In it, he speaks of a man "that could look no way but downwards, with a Muckrake in his hand." It's a parable about people who can't see or do great things because they are so concerned with "raking the muck" of profits or other worldly concerns. The muckraking journalist ignores the good or great works of individuals and concentrates instead on their scandals and misdeeds.

The Buckraker

These days, a *buckraker* is a journalist who uses his or her connections and knowledge to earn a significant amount of money outside of his or her regular job. Witness the following citation from *The New Republic*:

"The same history might mark February 1985 as the start of the next era. That was when Patrick J. Buchanan went to work at the White House and his financial disclosure statement revealed, to widespread astonishment and envy, that he had made $400,000 as a journalist in 1984. This included $60,000 for his syndicated column, $25,000 for his weekly appearance on "The McLaughlin Group," $94,000 for Cable News Network's "Crossfire," $81,000 for a radio show, and more than $135,000 for 37 speeches. Welcome to the era of the buckraker."

mucky-muck

A *mucky-muck*—or, if you prefer, a *muck-a-muck* or a *muckety-muck*—is a person in a position of authority, particularly one who wields his or her authority in a self-important or overbearing manner. All the variations on this term come from the longer phrase *high-muck-a-muck*, which in turn is the English version of the Chinook phrase *hiyu muckamuck*, which combines *hiyu*, "plenty," and *muckamuck*, "food." So a *hiyu muckamuck* was a person with lots of food, which meant, at least back in the mid-nineteenth century, when this phrase entered the language, that the person had a certain amount of power or authority.

mumbo jumbo

If you come across some jargon or other writing that appears to be nothing but stuff and nonsense, you may want to call it a bunch of *mumbo jumbo*, unless you feel uncomfortable invoking the name of an African god as you do so. Yes, the seemingly secular phrase *mumbo jumbo* used to be *Mama Dyumbo*, a spirit once said to protect villages among certain African tribes in Senegal. Of course, this wasn't a real god, just a tribesman in a mask who would be called upon when a husband wanted to punish one of his wives for arguing or talking too much. At first the husband would threaten his wife that he'd call upon Mama Dyumbo if she wouldn't behave herself. If she persisted, Mama Dyumbo—dressed in a tufted mask (his name means "ancestor with a pompom")—would seize her and frighten her with hideous noises and sometimes even physical punishment (such as whipping). Eighteenth-century travelers who witnessed these nasty ceremonies anglicized the name Mama Dyumbo as Mumbo Jumbo, which is how this phrase entered the English language. Either because of the meaningless noises made by Mama Dyumbo, or perhaps because of the incoherent speech of the poor women frightened out of their wits by this "god," *mumbo jumbo* soon came to refer to any speech or writing that was meaningless or nonsensical.

muscle

Muscular people are usually big and strong, but you'd never know it from the history of the word *muscle*. It actually goes back to the Latin word *musculus*, which means "little mouse." Huh?! Word historians speculate that the ancients thought a big, rippling muscle looked something like a mouse. Makes sense, I guess, but it's kind of creepy.

namby-pamby

> Like the linnet green, in May,
> Flitting to each bloomy spray;
> Weari'd then, and glad of rest,
> Like the linlet in the nest.

I certainly don't consider myself a poetry connoisseur by any means, but these lines don't strike me as the height of the art. They were penned in 1725 by Ambrose Philips, a poet surprisingly much admired in his day, but largely forgotten now. Forgotten, that is, except in one sense: he's the inspiration behind the phrase *namby-pamby*, "weak, effeminate." This is one of those rare occurrences in English where we know exactly who coined a term and when. The story begins with the great poet Alexander Pope, who despised not only Philips's poetry, but his politics as well. The two had an ongoing feud, and Pope's friend Henry Carey took up the cause. In 1726, he published a poem titled *Namby Pamby: or, A Panegyric on the New Versification*:

> All ye Poets of the Age!
> All ye Witlings of the Stage!
> Learn your Jingles to reform!
> Crop your Numbers and Conform:
> Let your little Verses flow
> Gently, Sweetly, Row by Row:
> Let the Verse the Subject fit;
> Little Subject, Little Wit.
> Namby Pamby is your Guide;
> Albion's Joy, Hibernia's Pride.

...

As an Actor does his Part,
So the Nurses get by Heart
Namby Pamby's Little Rhimes,
Little Jingle, Little Chimes.

Ouch! Carey's purposefully childish pet name *Namby Pamby* struck a
chord, particularly with Pope, who used the name in his famous poem
The Dunciad, and the phrase *namby-pamby* found a permanent place in
the language. At first it referred to any sentimental or childish literary
work, but within a few years put-down artists were using the word to
denounce anything they saw as week or effeminate.

nausea

If you come down with a bout of *nausea,* "a feeling of sickness, usually
accompanied by an urge to vomit," it's safe to say that you're not feeling
exactly shipshape. That's true physically, but it's also true etymologically. That's because the word's origins are from ancient Greek, where
their word for seasickness was *nausia*. This term combines *naus,* "ship,"
and the suffix *-ia,* "sickness," so it's literal meaning is "ship sickness."
The word *nausea* meant "seasickness" in English, too, for a few hundred
years, but by the mid-seventeenth century it had acquired the more
general sense that we use today.

nemesis

A *nemesis* is an unbeatable opponent or a person who inflicts vengeance
or retribution. This word is another refugee from Greek mythology.
Nemesis was the goddess of retribution, which means "the dispens-
ing of something justly deserved." This usually implies a well-earned
punishment, but it can occasionally mean a reward as well. In any case,
there was no hiding from Nemesis once she decided to track you down,
so that's why her name has also come to stand for an unbeatable foe.

nerd

The word *nerd*—which one major dictionary defines, almost positively,
as "an enthusiast whose interest is regarded as too technical or scientific
and who seems obsessively wrapped up in it"—is older than you might

think. More than a few people believe the word *nerd* comes from the following lines in *If I Ran the Zoo*, by Dr. Seuss (1950):

> And then just to show them, I'll sail to Ka-Troo
> And Bring Back an It-Kutch, a Preep and a Proo,
> A Nerkle, a Nerd, and a Seersucker, too!

The illustration shows the Nerd to be an unpleasant-looking creature, and it was only a few years later that *nerd* came to mean "an uninteresting person; a dud; a square." It was in the computer-literate 1990s that nerd became fully associated with the technically savvy, and the word is now used as a compliment in technical circles.

newbie

The word *newbie* is Internet slang for a new or inexperienced user, especially one who is ignorant of Internet etiquette (usually called *netiquette*) and other online proprieties. Newbie is a variation of *new boy*, which the *OED* defines as a "schoolboy during his first term at a school, esp. one at a preparatory school or English public school."

nice

The word *nice* has several different meanings, including "subtle; fine" (as in "a nice comparison"), "well-executed" (as in "nice work!"), and "pleasant; agreeable" (as in "she's a nice person"). It's also popular with ironists and the sarcasm crowd ("Nice going, Sherlock!"). These current meanings seem quite fixed, but the word *nice* has had a number of jobs over its linguistic career. It began with the Latin word *nescious*, which combines the prefix *ne-*, "no," and the word *scire*, "know." (The word *scire* also gave us the word *science*.) So *nescious* means, literally, "no knowledge," but it's best translated as "ignorant." So the original meaning of the word *nice* was "foolish or silly"! Between that and the current dominant sense of "pleasant; agreeable," *nice* has meant, variously, "wanton," "extravagant," "elegant," "scrupulous," "fussy," "cowardly," "slothful," "fragile," "pampered," "rare," "shy," "trivial," and "dexterous." What a ride! The *OED* calls the path of the word *nice* through English "unparalleled in Latin or in the Romance languages."

Working the Semantic Shift

When a word changes meaning over time, linguists call the process a *semantic shift,* and it isn't even remotely rare. For example, people originally used *silly* to mean "deserving of pity," and a *hearse* has over the years referred to a candlestick, a framework for holding tapers, a coffin, and a corpse. In some cases, the meaning of a word broadens. For example, *bird* originally meant "a small fowl" and now it means "any winged creature." Similarly, *dog* went from "a hunting breed" to "any canine." The opposite process—*semantic narrowing*—also goes on under our noses. *Meat* used to mean "any type of food" and now it means "flesh of an animal." *Disease* once referred to "any unfavorable state" and it now means "an illness."

nickname

An awfully long time ago, an informal or humorous name used in place of a person's given name was said to be that person's *ekename.* The old word *eke* here means "extra" or "additional," and it survives today in phrases such as "to eke out a living." Error or mishearing is a common source of new English words, and *ekename* gives us a good example of this strange-but-true process at work. Whenever someone would say the phrase "an ekename," there was always a good chance that some listener (who had never heard the word before) would think the person was actually saying "a nekename." In this case, that mistake happened often enough that *ekename* turned into *nekename,* which then turned into our word *nickname.* A similar process turned the word *napron,* "a small cloth" to *apron* (because "a napron" sounds just like "an apron").

Drop That Syllable!

The process of creating a new word by lopping off the initial letter or syllable of an existing word (as in the origins of *nickname* and *apron*) is called *aphaeresis* (which means "to take away"). This not-as-uncommon-as-you-might-think process was behind words such as *mend* (a shortening of *amend*), *spy* (from *espy*), *cute* (from *acute*), and *squire* (from *esquire*).

niggardly

This adjective refers to spending or giving only the smallest possible amount, and even that is doled out grudgingly. The word *niggardly* comes to us from the Middle English word *nigon*, "miser." It is not in any way related to a certain disgusting "n-word." This knowledge didn't help a fellow named David Howard, who was driven from his job in the Washington, D.C., mayor's office after he used the word and some people thought he was making a racial slur. You have two choices here: you can use this word and educate those who misread it, or you can avoid it knowing that some people will always remain ignorant and will give you grief over it.

NIMBY

You use this acronym for a person who hopes or seeks to keep some dangerous or unpleasant feature out of his or her neighborhood. It's based on the phrase "not in my back yard." Similar monikers are *GOOMBY* (from "get out of my back yard") and *NUMBY* ("not under my back yard"). Other I'm-against-it acronyms are NOTE ("not over there, either"), BANANA ("build absolutely nothing anywhere near anything"), and NOPE ("not on planet Earth"). This last name is, one hopes, the last word on these anti-development acronyms. After all, there isn't anywhere else for them to go. What's next, ZOOM (zilch on our Moon) or HOOSS (hands off our solar system)?

nincompoop

A *nincompoop* is a person who is stupid or silly. The great lexicographer Samuel Johnson once speculated that this word came from the Latin phrase *non compos mentis*, "of unsound mind," which comes up often in the medical and legal professions. Doctors and lawyers often shorten this phrase to *non compos*, so it doesn't seem unreasonable for nonprofessionals to have shaped this into nincompoop. Another theory is that it came from a combination of the French word *nicodême*, "a simpleton" (which in turn comes from the name Nicodemus, which appears in the Bible), and *poop*, "a clown." The *OED* pooh-poohs such suggestions and calls nincompoop "a fanciful formation." The *OED* also mentions some other rather hilarious forms of the word, including *nincompoopish*, *nincompoopery*, *nincompoophood*, and *nincompoopiana*.

nonillion

See BILLION.

nonplussed

A person who is *nonplussed* is bewildered and is at a loss as to what to think, do, or say. Many people think this word actually means the opposite, that the nonplussed individual remains unfazed and composed. This even happens with big-time writers and publications. For example, check out the following citation from the February 20, 2000, edition of *The New York Times:*

> The owner happens to be a computer security expert [who] knows about the attacks because his computer has a fire wall, which keeps intruders out and tells him when they have come by. Yet he was nonplussed by the number of attacks on that single day last week. "I think it's fairly typical," he said.

I think the reason for this confusion is that the *non-* ("not") prefix makes it sound as though nothing happened ("the guy didn't get plussed"). It doesn't help that the *-plussed* part comes from the Latin root *plus*, which means "more." So the Latin phrase *non plus* means, "no more." One way to remember it is to think of some poor, bewildered soul throwing up his hands and saying "No more! No more!"

not worth a tinker's damn

See TINKER'S DAM.

November

See SEPTEMBER.

October

See SEPTEMBER.

off the cuff

If you give your after-dinner speech to the Ladies Auxiliary *off the cuff*, it means that you speak without notes or rehearsal or preparation of any kind; you speak, in a word, extemporaneously. (The word *extemporaneously*, by the by, comes from the adverb *extempore*, "without preparation," which in turn came to us from the Latin phrase *ex tempore*, "out of the time; out of the moment.") The image behind the phrase *off the cuff* is that even though you don't have a written speech in front of you, you're speaking as though you have notes jotted down on the cuff of your shirt. That is, you seem to be reading "off the cuff." Some language authorities take this to mean that at some point people literally wrote their speech notes on the cuffs of their shirt. Unfortunately, no one has any direct evidence for this. However, it's true that once upon a time you could get shirts with detachable cuffs, and so you could just throw out any cuff that you ruined by writing on it. (Depending on the writing implement you used and the size of your shirt-cuff budget, you could also detach the cuffs and wash them separately.) It's also true that detachable cuffs were around in the 1930s when the phrase *off the cuff* first appeared, so the literal meaning of the phrase has at least a chance of being true.

More Cuff Guff

A phrase that was common in the 1930s and 1940s (and first appeared in 1927) but is now rare today is *on the cuff*, "on credit." Again this is related to writing on shirt cuffs. This time, we supposedly have bartenders jotting down customer debts on their shirt cuffs during times when they were too busy to use their more formal accounts book.

old fogey

See FOGEY.

old geezer

See GEEZER.

on tenterhooks

See TENTERHOOKS.

on the wagon

> JERRY: Oh, wait a second, I believe we have a heckler ladies and gentlemen. Hey Dick, I don't know what your problem is. It's not my fault you're back on the wagon.
>
> DICK: It's *off* the wagon.
>
> JERRY: In the old days how do you think they got the alcohol from town to town?
>
> DICK: I don't know.
>
> JERRY: On the wagon. Don't you think they broke into a couple of those bottles along the way?

In this bit of banter from the old *Seinfeld* show, Jerry is confused about the meaning of the phrase *on the wagon*, and compounds the error by giving a false derivation of the phrase. If you can't trust a comedy show to give correct etymologies, who can you trust? To be fair, lots of people get tripped up on the meaning of *on the wagon*, so let's set the record straight once and for all: if you're *on the wagon*, it means you're abstaining from alcohol. It helps to remember that the "wagon"

involved here is actually a water-wagon, and that the phrase was originally *on the water-wagon*. In the early 1900s, it was still common in
American towns and cities to have a horse-drawn water-wagon drive
around and hose down the unpaved streets to keep the dust to a minimum in the summer months. Someone who was no longer drinking
alcohol would probably drink mostly water, instead, so speaking metaphorically that person was "on" the water-wagon. Within a few years
folks dropped the "water" part, and we've used *on the wagon* ever since
(although the *on the water-wagon* version grimly held on until well into
the 1930s).

one-night stand

This euphemism for a casual sexual encounter that lasts just one night
seems strange at first blush, particularly since one expects that in most
cases there's very little standing involved. The mystery resolves itself
when you realize that in the original use of the phrase, the word *stand*
referred not to the assumption of an upright position, but to a stop
on a tour, particularly that of a theater company. To keep costs down
and maximize gate receipts, promoters would often book just a single
performance in small towns, and these became known as "one-night
stands." Sexual trysts have the element of performance about them, too,
so love-'em-and-leave-'em types started using *one-night stand* to describe
their brief encounters.

ornery

At first you might think that there's nothing ordinary about the word
ornery, "cantankerous, contrary." However, I assure you the word is
quite ordinary, quite literally. That's because *ornery* began its linguistic
path as a colloquial pronunciation of *ordinary*. You see this quite clearly
in a citation from Farmer Brown's journal for 1816, later published as
part of the *Maryland Historical Magazine*:

> The Land is old, completely worn out, the farming extremely
> ornary in general.

Eventually the word *ornery* came to refer to anyone who was common
or inferior. By the late nineteenth century, the word had shifted over
the people who were mean and cantankerous, and the term has sat
there ever since.

ounce

You know, I'm sure, that an *ounce* is one-sixteenth of a pound (or about 28 grams if your brain and the metric system are on speaking terms). Do you also know that an *ounce* is a member of the cat family? We also call it a snow leopard these days, but it used to refer to a lynx (also some other members of the feline family, such as the puma and the cheetah), and that's where the two senses of the word *ounce* are related. No, I'm not talking here about a *really* small cat. Instead, the word *lynx* goes back to the Greek word *lunx*, which became *lynx* in Latin as well as in English. In French, however, the word turned into *lonce*, and that's when things got interesting. Somebody out to prove the old adage that a little knowledge is a dangerous thing assumed that *lonce* was actually meant to be *l'once*, short for *la once*. The *once* error then entered a side door in the English language and became *ounce*, even though the "weight" sense of that word had already been around for a couple of hundred years. *That* sense came to us from the Latin term *uncial*, meaning "a twelfth part" (the original definition of *ounce* was "one-twelfth of a pound").

over a barrel

When you have someone helpless and at your mercy (for example, holding the last doughnut at arm's length to thwart your shorter-armed spouse, but our household shenanigans are, I'm sure, of little interest here), why do we say that we have that person *over a barrel?* You might think some kind of gun metaphor was at work, but that doesn't quite ring true because then you'd have the hapless person "in front of a barrel." It turns out that the phrase comes from the old (and now, thankfully, little-used) practice of clearing water from the lungs of someone who has nearly drowned by physically placing that person over a barrel. Such a person would obviously be quite helpless in that position, so although the rescue technique is obsolete, the phrase it's based on has found a useful place in the language.

oxymoron

An *oxymoron* is a phrase that combines two words that have contradictory meanings. For example, the phrases "pretty ugly" and "deafening silence" are oxymorons. Happily, the word *oxymoron* is itself an oxymoron! It comes from the Greek *oxumoros*, "pointedly foolish." However, the roots of the word are *oxus*, "sharp," and *moros*, "dull."

O

pants

If you have nothing but lions festooned on your pajama pants, that's apropos given the origins of the word *pants*. Our story begins in the Italian city of Venice, where the patron saint has been San Pantaleone for many hundreds of years. Pantaleone is a common Italian surname, and translates literally as "all lion" (from *pan-*, "all," and *leone*, "lion"). Over the years, in Italian commedia dell'arte, a character named Pantaleone was developed, and he was typically a slightly buffoonish old man who wore a red costume consisting of Turkish slippers, a tight jacket, and (crucially for our purposes here) trousers instead of stockings. The character's name became Pantaloon in French, and after a while his trousers became known as *pantaloons*. Our modern word *pants* was born when waggish types began shortening *pantaloons*, a linguistic turn of events mocked by the great American jurist Oliver Wendell Holmes in his 1846 book *A Rhymed Lesson:*

> The thing named "pants" in certain documents,
> A word not made for gentlemen, but "gents."

For another word that comes to us via commedia dell'arte, see ZANY. If you've got a minute, see also DANDELION.

paparazzi

Paparazzi are freelance photographers who aggressively pursue celebrities to take candid pictures to sell to newspapers and magazines. The singular form is *paparazzo*, and that word became associated with annoying celebrity photographers thanks to Federico Fellini's film

La Dolce Vita (*The Good Life*), which included a street photographer named Signor Paparazzo. Appropriately, *paparazzo* means "buzzing insect" in dialect Italian.

parting shot

When you give someone a *parting shot*—a cutting or hostile comment made while leaving—is it a "pointed remark" or an "arrow that hits close to home"? Both would be apropos considering the history behind the phrase *parting shot*. That history begins with the Parthians, an ancient race who lived in the region that we now call Iran. Parthian soldiers were expert horsemen and archers, and combined the two skills to deadly effect. Their signature move was to ride away from the enemy as though retreating. When the enemy followed in hot pursuit, the Parthians would turn on their mounts and fire arrows at the charging enemy, with usually devastating results. In the mid-nineteenth century, writers began using the phrase *Parthian shot* to refer to any cutting remark or hostile act made at the point of departure so that the other person had no chance to respond. *Parthian* sounds like *parting*, and a Parthian shot occurs at the moment of parting, so it's no surprise that people eventually started substituting *parting* for *Parthian*, and by the late nineteenth century the phrase *parting shot* had taken hold. Surprisingly, however, the phrase *Parthian shot* didn't wither away as you might expect given its now obscure origin and the more obvious meaning of *parting shot*. You still see *Parthian shot* fairly often in newspapers and novels, such as the July 21, 2007, article in *The Spectator* about the old screwball comedies where "women and men gave as good they got, artists at one-upmanship and masters of the Parthian shot."

pea

I mentioned earlier (see BUTTONHOLE), that new words are often created through mistakes. The most common of these errors is something called *back-formation* or *false analogy*. This means that someone sees an existing word, falsely places it in a particular grammatical category, and then proceeds to modify the word based on that false assumption. For example, the noun *pease* originally meant what we know of today as the pea. However, the word *pease* was both singular and plural (something like PANTS or *scissors*). But sometime around 1600 someone thought *pease* was plural, so they started using the word *pea* as the singular.

Got Yer Back-Formations

The *OED* lists over 700 such back-formations, including *agoraphobe* from agoraphobia, *exurb* from exurban, *sleaze* from sleazy, *burgle* from burglar, *enthuse* from enthusiasm, *televise* from television, *couth* from uncouth, *ept* from inept, and *gruntled* from disgruntled. Other examples are *surveil*, *baby-sit*, *diagnose*, *donate*, and *reminisce*.

peace out

The slang expression *peace out* is hipster talk for "goodbye; see you later." It's all the rage as I write this in late 2007, but the phrase has actually been around for a bit. The earliest known use is from the 1988 Beastie Boys song "3-Minute Rule" ("So peace out ya'll I'm PCP so I'm out"; yeah, I don't know what that means either). However, the use of just *peace* as a kind of valediction dates to at least the mid-1960s, although back then "peace" (like "aloha") was used for both farewells and greetings. I can't help but wonder if this use of the word *peace* is unconsciously derived from the old expression *peace be with you*, which first surfaced in the language in the fourteenth century.

pecuniary

This term means "of or relating to money," and it's strange, at least etymologically. To understand why, let's travel back in time to the Roman era and the Latin word *pecus*, "cattle." In those days, cattle were a form of currency, so the related word *peculum* came to mean "a person's property." From there came *peculiaris*, meaning "distinctive," which eventually became our *peculiar*, "strange or odd." As you've probably guessed, the currency value of cattle inspired the Romans to come up with a cattle-related word for money, *pecunia*, which eventually became our *pecuniary*. There's also the *pecuniary gland*, a whimsical monetary "gland" said, somewhat uncharitably, to be a part of the mental anatomy of lawyers, doctors, and other professionals who bill for their time. See also PICAYUNE and VACCINE.

pen

The increasing ubiquity of computer keyboards and the decreasing
popularity of pastimes such as letter writing have led to the decline of
printing and writing in longhand. These days, most people's penman-
ship is embarrassingly bad (I count myself among the worst offenders),
and that's because we use pens so seldom. So go ahead: pick up the
nearest pen and weigh it in your hand. How does it feel? If you said
"light as a feather," then I thank you for contributing to the progress
of this minihistory. That's because the word *pen* comes to us from the
Latin *penna*, "feather." As you know from watching movies that take
place in days of yore, the standard writing instrument used by scribes
was a feather with its quill sharpened and split to form a nib for dipping
in an inkwell. For a while the word *penne* referred to any writing tool,
but by the time the word was shortened to *pen*, it referred only to the
quill and then to our modern-day pens. By the by, you might think that
the similar word *pencil* must surely be a variation on the "pen" theme,
but no, sorry, thanks for playing. *Pencil* actually comes to us from the
Latin word *penicillus*, which means "paintbrush." This word entered
English as *pincellis* and then *pinsel* (or *pensel*), where it referred to any
implement for drawing or writing, and the word *pencil* as we know it
didn't show up until the late sixth century.

pencil

See PEN.

penicillin

Unless you've already read my entry for the word PEN, you might be
surprised to learn that the antibiotic penicillin is distantly related to a
paintbrush. It's true! To get from here to there, let's go straight to the
horse's mouth, so to speak, and hear from Sir Alexander Fleming himself, the discoverer of penicillin. Writing in a 1929 issue of the *British
Journal of Experimental Pathology*, Fleming coins the word *penicillin* right
before our very eyes:

> In the rest of this article allusion will constantly be made to experi-
> ments with filtrates of a broth culture of this mould, so for con-
> venience and to avoid the repetition of the rather cumbersome

phrase 'Mould broth filtrate,' the name 'penicillin' will be used. This will denote the filtrate of a broth culture of the particular penicillium with which we are concerned.

The "penicillium" that he's talking about here is a type of fungus that causes foods to go mouldy, although some versions are used to make delectable cheeses such as Brie and Roquefort. The word *penicillium* comes from the Latin *pēnicillus,* "paintbrush," because under a microscope some versions of the penicillium fungus appear as a long "stalk" with frayed ends, making them look like a bit like little brushes.

pescetarian

A *pescetarian* is a person who supplements a vegetarian diet with fish. The alternative spelling *piscetarian* for this vegetarian-with-an-exception is seen only rarely in the written record which is a shame since it makes more sense etymologically as a blend of *pisces* (Latin for "fish") and *vegetarian.* The prefix *pesce-* probably comes from the Italian word *pesce,* "fish," and is used from time to time to create new fish-related words. For example, I've seen *pescevino,* a wine that goes with fish, and *pesce-phobe,* a person who dislikes eating or is scared to eat fish.

philodendron

In your average garden, the flowers probably aren't too crazy about any nearby trees, because they compete with the trees for water and sunshine, and those rude trees are always thrusting their roots where they don't belong. The exception to this anti-tree attitude would seem to be the members of the philodendron family of plants. Why? Because the word *philodendron* comes to us via the Greek *philodendros,* which combines the prefix *philo-,* "loving," and *dendros,* "tree." Of course, philodendrons aren't actually "in love" with trees (at least, as far as I know), but they do enjoy *climbing* trees, which I guess is the next best thing.

phishing

This techno-term refers to creating a replica of an existing web page to fool a user into submitting personal, financial, or password data. It comes from the fact that Internet scammers are using increasingly sophisticated lures as they "fish" for users' financial information and password data. The most common ploy is to copy the web page code from a major site—such as eBay or America Online—and use that code to set up a replica page that appears to be part of the company's site. (This is why phishing is also called *spoofing*.) A fake e-mail is sent out with a link to this page, which solicits the user's credit card data or password. When the form is submitted, it sends the data to the scammer while leaving the user on the company's site so he or she doesn't suspect a thing. Hackers have an endearing tendency to change the letter *f* to *ph*, and *phishing* is but one example. The f-to-ph transformation is not new among hackers, either. It first appeared in the late 1960s among telephone system hackers, who called themselves *phone phreaks*.

phlegmatic

This word (it's pronounced *fleg·MAT·ik*), describes someone who isn't easily excited or provoked into action. It has come down to us through the ages from medieval physiology and its theory of the four "humors" (body fluids): phlegm, blood, yellow bile, and black bile. The relative concentrations of these humors were thought to determine a person's behavior. For example, a tad too much phlegm (pronounced *flem*) caused sluggishness and calmness, so that's where we get phlegmatic. A predominance of blood was said to make a person courageous and hopeful. The old French word for blood was *sanguin*, which gives us *sanguine*, "confident; optimistic." Yellow bile was also called choler, and it caused a person to be bad-tempered, from which we get *choleric*, "easily angered." Finally, excess black bile caused low spirits, and it gives us our word *melancholy*, "sadness or depression" (from the French word *melancolie*, "black bile"). See also HYPOCHONDRIAC.

picayune

You use the adjective *picayune* to describe something as trivial, trifling, or unimportant, and you can take that to the bank. Actually, you used to be able to take a picayune to the bank, literally. In the nineteenth century and for much of the twentieth, a *picayune* was a Spanish half-real coin which was much used in the southern United States, particularly in Louisiana. This term came from the French *picaillon*, "a small coin." The ultimate source here was the Latin *picaioun*, "a small copper coin," which came from a Latin term we've seen already: *pecunia* (see

PECUNIARY). Back in more modern times, the word *picayune* also came to refer to any small amount of money, and soon trivial things were said to be *not worth a picayune*. From there, the adjectival form of the word came to refer to anything trivial or unimportant. Note that this money-to-adjective trajectory is very similar to what happened with terms such as *two-bit* (see TWO BITS) and *twopenny*, which also refer to things that aren't worth very much.

picnic

If you eat nothing at your next picnic, that would be etymologically appropriate (but socially a bit weird). Let me explain: Our word *picnic* comes from the late-seventeenth-century French term *pique-nique*, which referred to a fashionable social event to which each invited guest brought along a dish. The phrase combines the word *pique*, "pick," and *nique*, "nothing," although it's probably better translated as "nothing much" or "a trifle." The term entered the English language in the middle of the eighteenth century as both *pique-nique* and *pic-nic*, and at first it also referred to a fashionable bring-your-own-grub social event. However, people must have started having these affairs outdoors frequently, because in 1826 we have the great British statesman Benjamin Disraeli (Earl of Beaconsfield at the time, but later the Prime Minister) writing that "Nature had intended the spot for pic-nics." From that point on the word *picnic* referred exclusively to an informal meal eaten out of doors, particularly as part of an excursion to a park or the countryside.

pie in the sky

> You will eat, bye and bye,
> In that glorious land above the sky;
> Work and pray, live on hay,
> You'll get pie in the sky when you die.

These lyrics are from a song called "The Preacher and the Slave," written by Joe Hill in 1911 and meant to be a parody of the old standard "In the Sweet Bye and Bye." The song became quite popular, particularly the opening stanza above, with people especially picking up on the evocative and tasty "pie in the sky" image, and that phrase soon entered the language on its own. At first the phrase *pie in the sky* referred somewhat cynically to a reward one might receive in heaven (what one wag of the day called "bourgeois heaven") for one's Earthly virtue or suffering. By the 1940s, however, the phrase had come to refer to any unrealistic prospect of future happiness, and then to anything good or pleasant but unlikely to see the light of day.

pigeonhole

If you *pigeonhole* something, it means that you label it or categorize it without putting much thought into the effort. Any label or category that people use in such a mindless way is also called a *pigeonhole*. What do pigeons have to do with any of this? Back in the sixteenth century, people noticed that pigeons liked to nest in little holes, and that they'd rarely stray too far from those holes. So folks who were into raising domestic pigeons had an idea: why not create a series of small, open compartments either on an outside wall or in a separate dovecote so that pigeons could use them for nesting? It was a jolly good idea, and the compartments soon became known, not even remotely surprisingly, as *pigeon-holes*. A hundred years or so later, someone came up with the idea of outfitting a desk with a series of small, open compartments that desk jockeys could use to sort mail, store papers, display knickknacks, and so on. Of course, these compartments looked just like pigeon-holes, and that's what people started calling them around the end of the seventeenth century. You can just imagine the detail freaks of the day loving these pigeon-holes because they enabled a person to always put the mail here, the accounts book there, and so on. This rigidity found its way into the meaning of the word *pigeonhole*, which by the middle of the nineteenth century had come to refer figuratively to the fixed categories of thought in many people's minds. Not long after that, the verb *pigeonhole* took on the more general sense of rigidly or mindlessly assigning something to a particular category.

pioneer

The early North American pioneers may have carried guns to keep bears and wolves at bay, but most of them probably weren't soldiers. However, they used to be exclusively soldiers, foot soldiers in particular. Our word *pioneer* comes from the Old French term *pionier*, "foot soldier," a word derived from *pion* (or *peon*), "pawn," which in turn comes from the Latin *pedon,* "foot soldier." In the sixteenth century, *pioneers* were infantry soldiers who would go ahead of an army or regiment to prepare the way by repairing roads and bridges, digging trenches, and clearing the terrain. This idea of someone leading the way to prepare or open up the territory ahead applied to civilians, too, and by the early seventeenth century, such people were being referred to a *pionners,* then *pioniers,* and finally *pioneers.*

placebo

A *placebo* is an inert substance that causes beneficial effects because the person taking the substance expects those effects. Placebos were originally intended for HYPOCHONDRIACS who insisted that the doctor prescribe *something* for their perceived pains. This is reflected in the history of the term, because the Latin word *placebo* means, "I will please." You might be wondering if the opposite is also true. That is, is there an inert substance that causes *harmful* effects because the person taking the substance expects those effects? Yes, there is, and doctors call such a substance a *nocebo.*

plumcot

See PLUOT.

pluot

This term (you pronounce it *PLOO·awt*) refers to a fruit created by cross-pollinating a plum and an apricot in such a way that the resulting hybrid has dominant plum characteristics. An initial cross between a plum and an apricot is called a *plumcot* (or *plum-cot*), and the resulting hybrid is 50 percent plum and 50 percent apricot. Cross the plumcot with yet another plum and the result is the pluot: 75 percent plum, 25 percent apricot. Mad fruit scientists also cross plumcots with apricots to create the *aprium,* which is 75 percent apricot and 25 percent plum.

Wacky Tomaccy

All of these fruit blends are called *interspecific hybrids,* a general term that refers to crosses between different but related types of fruit. On the vegetable front, some notable new blends are *broccoflower,* a cross between broccoli and cauliflower, and *tomacco,* a hybrid created by grafting a tomato plant onto the roots of a tobacco plant. (Yuck!, I hear you say. Amen. However, this one's more of a joke than anything else, because the idea came from an episode of *The Simpsons.* You won't find tomaccos in your neighborhood grocery store anytime soon.)

podcasting

Podcasting is a new technology that enables people to publish audio content that other people can subscribe to and have transferred to a music program or digital audio player. This was originally done with Apple's iPod player, so *podcasting* is a shortened form of the phrase *iPod broad-casting.*

poetaster

> Beside all this, he serv'd his master
> In quality of poetaster;
> And rhimes appropriate could make
> To ev'ry month i' th almanack
> What terms begin and end could tell,
> With their returns, in doggerel;
>
> —Samuel Butler, *Hudibras,* 1664

A *poetaster* (it's pronounced *POH·uh·tas·tur*) is a bad or inferior poet. It brings together the word *poet* and the suffix *-aster,* which has been used through the ages with nouns and adjectives to express, as the *OED* delicately puts it, "incomplete resemblance." *Poetaster* is the only word using this suffix that's still in regular use, but other examples from days gone by are *astrologaster, grammaticaster, historiaster, mathematicaster, medicaster, musicaster, philosophaster, philologaster, politicaster, scientaster,* and *theologaster.*

point-blank

If you tell someone *point-blank* what you're thinking, it means you've been direct and to-the-point, perhaps even blunt. If you shoot at something *point-blank*, it means you've taken the shot from very close range. These seem like wildly different meanings, but they're very closely related. To see why, think of firing an arrow or gun over a long distance. At first the bullet or arrow will travel in a straight line, but thanks to gravity the projectile will eventually follow a trajectory that curves down toward the ground. If you want to fire a shot where the bullet or arrow doesn't curve, then you need to get close enough to your target so that the bullet or arrow is still flying in its initial straight line when it reaches the target. In archery, being that close means that you can aim directly as the bull's-eye. This area used to be known in Middle French as *de pointe en blanc*, "white point," since the bull's-eye is white, and this phrase entered English as *point blank*. So *point-blank range* referred to being very close to the target, close enough to aim directly, which gave us the "direct; blunt" sense of *point-blank*.

political correctness

As I'm sure you know, *political correctness* is the conformity to liberal or progressive opinion on matters of gender, race, ethnicity, disabilities, or sexual preference, especially via the deliberate use of language or actions that avoid giving offense. However, if you take a step back from this infamous phrase, you see that it's a strange linguistic mix: Why *political?* Why *correctness?* To understand the origins of this phrase, you need to know something of the history of political correctness, which I view metaphorically as the history of contrasting tools. In the late 1960s and through the 1970s and 1980s, political correctness was used as a kind of goad, a stimulus to improve people and society. For feminists and their gender politics and for Black Power radicals and their race politics (to name just two groups who adopted PC codes of conduct), political correctness was used to prod people into behaving non-offensively. This is the positive side of political correctness, and its basis was most likely the writings of Chairman Mao Zedong, particularly a piece titled "Where Do Correct Ideas Come From?" which appeared in his 1963 *Little Red Book*. The phrase "correct ideas" was often translated into English as "correct thinking," and most scholars believe this was the source of the "correct" part of political correctness. But political correctness has also been used as a metaphorical sword, cutting down to size those who appear to be mindlessly conforming to liberal orthodoxy. This has certainly been the case since at least the mid-1980s when conservatives began using the charge of "political correctness" to slice up left-wing opponents and their positions. Today, *politically correct* is used as a grievous insult that implies the person is a humorless, self-righteous slave to the liberal party line. Interestingly, this negative side of political correctness first appeared in the 1930s and 1940s (although at the time it was just referred to as "correctness"). Back then it was used by leftists to criticize the old guard on the left who adhered too slavishly to Marxist doctrine.

politician

The word *politician* is based on the adjective *politic*, which in turn comes to English via a Greek word meaning "citizen." That sounds like a noble pedigree, but the earliest incarnation of *politician* is a negative sense that means "a shrewd schemer; a crafty plotter or intriguer." This meaning was active in the late sixteenth century and still exists today in the phrase *office politician*, someone who engages in office politics (a phrase that, somewhat surprisingly, has been in the language since at least 1917). The sense of the word *politician* that refers to a person who makes politics his or her profession doesn't appear until about 40 years after the original negative sense.

poll

See TADPOLE.

poodle

As you know, when someone mentions that "It's raining cats and dogs," you're obligated to reply, "Don't step in any poodles!" You might think you're using a clever (but oh so old) pun, but linguistically you're being quite serious. That's because the word *poodle* comes our way via the German word *Pudel*, which in turn is a shortened form of *Pudelhund*. This word combines *puddeln*, "to splash about in water," with *hund*, "hound; dog," a combination that reflects the German Pudelhund's use as a waterfowl retriever. Not even remotely surprisingly, the verb *puddeln* migrated to English to become the noun *puddle*, so you see that *poodle* and *puddle* are peas in an etymological pod.

It's Raining Cats and Dogs

What's up with the curious expression *It's raining cats and dogs?* One suggestion is that back in the days when houses were topped with thatch, such roofs were cozy spots for animals such as cats and dogs to curl up for a snooze. (Cats I can see, but dogs? Not so much.) When the rain would start, these animals would bail out of their hidey-holes, and it would look like it was raining cats and dogs. Another possibility is that because the roads in those days were so poorly constructed, at least a few cats and dogs would drown in a heavy downpour. People would later see these poor animals and it would look as if they had come down with the rain.

pork barrel

> I had the old bear salted: ... her fat filled half a pork-barrel.
> —George Cartwright, *A Journal of Transactions and Events, During a Residence of Nearly Sixteen Years on the Coast of Labrador*, 1792

Pork barrel refers to government legislation or projects that provide jobs and other benefits to a politician's district. This is now more commonly abbreviated to just *pork*. Originally, a pork barrel was exactly that: a barrel in which pork or pork fat was kept. How full the barrel was became a symbol of a person's wealth, so eventually pork barrel came to mean simply "wealth" or "a supply of money." The cynical politician who wanted to remain on good terms with his constituents would pass legislation enriching his district or, figuratively, filling their pork barrels.

portmanteau

This word comes to us from the French word *portemanteau*, meaning "coat carrier." The mundane meaning of portmanteau—a large leather suitcase—isn't what interests me here. Instead, I prefer the second meaning: a word formed by merging parts of two different words. This usage of portmanteau comes from the great British writer Lewis

Carroll. In his book, *Through the Looking Glass*, Alice is puzzling over the meaning of some of the words in the poem Jabberwocky, and asks Humpty Dumpty for help. Here's what he has to say about the word *slithy:*

> Well, "*slithy*" means "lithe and slimy." ... You see it's like a portmanteau—there are two meanings packed up into one word.

Other portmanteau words are *chortle* (a blend of *chuckle* and *snort*; this is another Jabberwockian word), *brunch* (*breakfast* and *lunch*), telex (*teleprinter* and *exchange*), and *contrail* (*condensation* and *trail*).

posthaste

To tell someone that you want something *posthaste* means that you want that thing as quickly as possible. It's a slightly antiquated (and somehow nicer) synonym for ASAP. You might think the "post" part here means "after," as though you're asking the person to perform that task at whatever speed comes after "haste." Nope. The "post" we're talking about here is actually an older sense of the word from the sixteenth century. In England back then, the king would have a series of messengers stationed along certain roads, and each person's job was to take a message from the king as fast as possible by horse to the next stage. This relay was called a *post*, and it meant that the king's messages were always delivered speedily. Later, the use of posts was broadened to include messages from people besides the king (mostly dukes and earls and other noble types). To get this speedy delivery, the sender would write the phrase *haste, post, haste* on the envelope or package. Eventually the word *post* came to mean "express; with speed or haste." So if you wanted something quickly, you'd say you wanted it "with haste," but if you wanted it *really* fast, then you'd say you wanted it "with post-haste." By the early seventeenth century, the word *posthaste* had come to mean "as quickly as possible."

pothole

The linguist Allen Walker Read once said that "jubilance is an explanation for a lot of the things that happen in language." That lovely sentiment seems to underlie our current use of the word *pothole*, "a depression or hole in the surface of a road." That sense dates to about

1889, but long before that geologists and geographers used *pothole* to mean "a deep, bowl-shaped hole formed by erosion or some other natural process." Some jubilant language jokester must have seen a particularly wide and deep hole in a road and dubbed it a "pothole." His irony lives on.

precocious

If you described a child you know as *precocious* to some wandering band of etymologically savvy cannibals that just happened to be passing by, they'd understand you to mean that the child has been cooked ahead of time! This curious misunderstanding resolves itself when you realize that the adjective *precocious*, "relating to someone who shows outstanding development or talent, particularly at a young age," comes from the Latin term *praecoquere*, which smushes together the prefix *prae-*, "before," and the verb *coquere*, "to cook." The original sense here was to cook something ahead of time (think: parboiling). However, in the sense that a plant ripening is somewhat akin to a meal cooking, the term eventually came to refer to any plant that ripens or flowers early, and the word became *praecox*. That word and meaning entered English as *precoce*. From there, it didn't take too much of a metaphorical bent to apply the idea to early blooming children, and so *precoce* became *precocious*. (Eagle-eyed readers may be wondering where they've seen the term *praecox* before. Ah, you're most likely thinking of the phrase *dementia praecox*, literally "premature loss of mind," the now archaic term for schizophrenia. Good eye!)

preposterous

If someone "put the cart before the horse" or "hanged a man first and then tried him afterwards," would you say that person was being preposterous? Perhaps, since *preposterous* means "utterly absurd; outrageous." However, you could definitely call that person preposterous if you're going by the literal meaning of the word. That's because it comes to us from the Latin term *praeposterus*, a combination of *prae-*, "before," and *posterus*, "later, next," that referred to something put in the wrong or unnatural order, particularly two things that are inverted (like the proverbial cart and horse). The word *preposterous* eventually came to mean anything that was contrary to nature or common sense, and it then morphed into the current sense of something absurd or outrageous.

More Oxymora

With a literal meaning of "before-next," *preposterous* is a kind of one-word OXYMORON. Other examples of one-word oxymora are *sophomore* (literally, "wise-fool"), *pianoforte* ("soft-loud"), *ballpoint, bittersweet, fire-water,* and *wholesome.*

procrustean

This adjective describes anything that produces conformity by ruthless or arbitrary means. It comes from the Greek word *prokroustes,* stretcher. In Greek mythology, Procrustes was a giant said to be the son of Poseidon. He lived beside the road and would offer hospitality to passing travelers. His "hospitality," however, consisted of fastening each person to a bed and "adjusting" the unfortunate soul so they fit: he'd stretch short people and lop off chunks of tall people. Nice fellow! (He received his comeuppance in the end, though: the hero Theseus gave him a taste of his own medicine.) These days, the term "procrustean" is used to describe anything that requires a grim or arbitrary conformity.

proof is in the pudding

Do a search for the phrase *the proof is in the pudding* in a media database such as Lexis-Nexis, and you'll get back more results than you can count. Journalists and your average Joe and Josephine use this phrase to mean something like "you won't know until you try" or even "I'll believe it when I see it." That's fine, I guess, but what a curious phrase! How can there be "proof" in a "pudding," of all things? The mystery resolves itself quite nicely when we learn the original phrase on which this shortened (and rather mangled) version is based: *the proof of the pudding is in the eating.* Here, the word *proof* is being used in the older sense of "test," so this phrase's literal meaning is that you won't know if a pudding is any good until you taste it. More generally, the phrase means that you can't know if something works the way it's supposed to until you try it. This phrase first appeared in written form in 1605 (although it's probably much older), and it remained intact until about 1970 when people started shortening it to *the proof of the pudding,* meaning that which puts something to the test. A vestigial memory of the remainder of the phrase must have still been floating around in the Zeitgeist, so the "is in the" part of *is in the eating* got swapped with the "of the" part of *the proof of the pudding,* and the result was the nonsensical *the proof is in the pudding,* which has been around since at least 1979.

protean

This useful word described a person who has talents or tendencies that can assume a variety of forms. The term comes to us from the name of the Greek god Proteus, who could change his shape and form at will. If you captured Proteus, he would attempt to escape by changing into various forms such as a lion or dragon. If you held on until he returned to his normal shape, he would tell you a prophecy.

purple state

This new term (it's only been hanging around in the language since about 2002) refers to an American state in which the Democratic Party and the Republican Party have roughly equal support. Why purple? On U.S. election night maps in recent times, Republican states are always shown in red and Democratic states are always shown in blue, so pundits of both political stripes now routinely talk about *red states* and *blue states* (both terms entered the language in 2001). Of course, there are a few states that give both parties roughly equal electoral support—these are the so-called *swing states.* That makes them an equal blend of blue and red, hence they're *purple states.* (Of course, the electoral battles fought in these keys states are so fierce—they're not also called *battle-ground states* for nothing—that "purple" may refer to the color of the figurative bruises the combatants have picked along the road to the ballot box.)

q.t.

If you've got a secret to tell someone and you want that person to keep it under his hat, you could ask the person to "keep this under your hat." Or you could say something like "this is strictly on the q.t." You might think *q.t.* stands for "quite tight-lipped" or something even sillier. Nope. Sometimes what's weird about a word's origins is that they're not all that weird at all. This is a case in point, because *q.t.* is nothing more (or less) than an abbreviation of the word *quiet*.

quadrillion

See BILLION.

queen

The next time a woman goes to her gynecologist, she'd be well within her rights to call her (assuming the gynecologist's a she) "Your Highness." I'll explain. In the ancient proto-language Indo-European, the word *gwen* meant "woman." That word jumped straight into Old English as *cwén*, which at first meant "woman," but by the late ninth century it had come to refer to a king's wife and then later the female ruler of a country. The spelling "queen" didn't show up until the seventeenth century (having gone through innumerable variations, such as *cwene*, *quene*, *quyene*, and *qwhene*). Meanwhile, the Indo-European *gwen* kept busy, including a move into Greek as the term *guné*, "woman." That word eventually became the English prefix *gyneco-*, "woman," which of course gives us *gynecology*, "the study and treatment of women's health, particularly reproductive health."

Oh, Those Crazy Indo-Europeans!

Approximately one third of the world's languages came from a single language that scholars now call *Indo-European*. One branch of this language eventually turned into Latin, which gave rise to the Romance languages (such as French, Italian, and Spanish). Other branches generated language families such as Slavic (Czech, Polish, Russian, and others), Indo-Iranian (Sanskrit, Persian, and others), Greek, and Celtic. Another branch led to the Germanic languages, including Dutch and German. It was in this latter family that English was raised. However, the German influence is so old (it dates back to the times when the Angles, Saxons, and Jutes invaded England in the fifth century) that the English words derived from it have long since been fully incorporated into the language.

quibble

Two stereotypical characteristics of lawyers lie behind the word *quibble,* "a petty or trivial objection." One is the tendency for lawyers to use high-blown language, and the other is to be obsessed with details, many of which you and I would call "petty trivialities," but which a lawyer would no doubt call "fine distinctions." *Quibble* is probably a diminutive form of *quib,* which came to us from the Latin *quibus.* This last term is a form of the pronoun *qui,* meaning "who; which," and was often used in legal texts for phrases such as "to whom" and "from whom." The frequency with which Latin lawyers used such terms meant that *quibus* became associated with petty details of all kinds. The English word *quib* referred to a kind of evasiveness where the person's argument depended on either a trivial circumstance, on some small difference between words, or on a subtle parsing of a word's meaning. (President Bill Clinton's famous defense "It depends upon what the meaning of the word 'is' is" fits the bill—no pun intended—nicely here.)

quiche

"Let them eat cake." Legend has it that those famous words were uttered by the French QUEEN Marie Antoinette. I'll deal with the legend in a sec. For now, I simply want to note that it's too bad the quote wasn't "Let them each quiche." That's because not only is quiche a distinctly

French dish, but its linguistic origin is the Alsatian German term *küche*, a diminutive form of the German *küchen*, "cake." Now to the legend: if you've always thought that Marie Antoinette spoke those disdainful words, think again. The first confirmed use is actually from the French philosopher Jean-Jacques Rousseau in his 1766 book *Confessions*, where he wrote that a "great princess" said of the peasants, "Qu'ils mangent de la brioche." This translates to "Let them eat brioche." A brioche, as you may know, is a sweet and savory French bread made from dough that's been enriched with butter and eggs. (The word *brioche* comes from the French verb *brier*, "to knead.") It's delicious and quite decadent, although not quite as decadent as cake. Anyway, this "great princess" must be Marie Antoinette, right? Nope. In 1766, Marie Antoinette was a mere 10 years old and still living in Austria. Rousseau didn't tell us the name of the princess, and at this point it's unlikely we'll ever know.

quintillion

See BILLION.

quiz

In Dublin, Ireland, way back in 1791, an apparently bored theater manager named Richard Daly made a bet with some cronies that he could think up a nonsense word and have it known throughout the city within 48 hours. A bold bet, indeed! So one night after a performance, Daly gathered his staff, gave them cards with the word *quiz* written on them, and told them to go forth and paint the word on walls through-out the city. When the 48 hours were up, the word was on everyone's lips and soon thereafter became a full-fledged member of the lexicon. Great story, right? Sure, but I'm afraid that it's almost certainly *not* the true origin of *quiz*. The problem, you see, is that the word already existed prior to 1791, although it had the now obsolete sense of "an odd or eccentric person." So what's the *real* story? No one knows for a fact, but most language mavens think it probably came from the Latin phrase *qui es?* (pronounced *KWEE·iz*), which means "who are you?"

radio

It's a fact long forgotten by most people, but the word *radio* is actually a shortened form of its original name, *radiotelegraph*, a term that first appeared in 1898. However, our story is much older than that, and to get the full scoop we need to go back to the Latin term *radius*, which originally referred to a staff or stake, but later came to refer to a spoke (as in the spokes of a wheel) and a ray. It's this last sense that's pertinent to us here, as it led to the Latin term *radiāre*, "emit rays," which eventually gave us the English terms *radiate*, "to emit energy in the form of rays," and *radiation*, "energy emitted in the form of rays." This led to scientists using the prefix *radio-* to describe something that emits energy as rays, hence terms such as *radio-conductor* and *radioactive*. It was also used, of course, to coin *radiotelegraph*, so-named because it uses electromagnetic waves to broadcast data, rather than the wires used in a regular telegraph. (Amazingly, people in Britain still use the term *wireless* for a radio.) The use of *radio* as a noun first appeared in the early 1900s.

rain check

If someone cancels a get-together or offers you something that you can't take right now but would be willing to take later, then you might respond by saying something like, "That's okay, I'll take a rain check." You say this, mind you, even on days when there's not a cloud in the sky. What in blue blazes are you talking about? These days we use the phrase *rain check* to refer to a kind of informal promise that a present offer will at least be considered in the future. A bit more formally, a merchant might offer you a rain check—an actual coupon or something similar—if it's out of stock of some sale item. Again, there's no rain in sight here. However, rain checks used to be *all* about rain. Back in the late 1800s, baseball teams started noticing that on days when rain was forecast, attendance would drop precipitously because people with even a minimum of common sense wouldn't want an outing at the ballpark ruined both by being rained on and by having the game delayed or canceled. So the baseball teams got smart: they promised that, if a game was rained out, they would give people coupons that would enable them to come to another game in the future. There was still the risk of getting soaked, but at least you could be assured that your money wasn't wasted on an incomplete game. The marketing ploy worked like a charm, and by 1884 the coupons had become popularly known as *rain checks*. By the 1930s, the phrase had taken on the more general sense that we use today.

raining cats and dogs

See POODLE.

rainmaker

This business term refers to an executive with an excellent record of bringing in new clients and generally increasing sales and profits. This word was originally used for the member of a tribal community who would use (or, really, would *claim* to use) magic to bring rainfall, which would help the crops grow and bring prosperity to the tribe.

ramshackle

R

A house that could be described as *ramshackle*, "run-down, rickety, falling apart," isn't likely to be one that you'd want to *ransack*, "plunder," so we'll just stick with a bit of etymological pillaging instead. As you've no doubt guessed, the words *ramshackle* and *ransack* are related, and not just because they sorta kinda look the same. The verb *ransack* comes from the Old Norse term *rannsaka*, built from *ran*, "house," and *saka*, "to seek." *Ransack* immigrated to English around the thirteenth century, and it originally meant "to search for something stolen or missing." By the turn of the fourteenth century the meaning had become "to search thoroughly, particularly a house," and then by the late fourteenth century the sense of "to search with the intent to rob; to plunder" had taken over. The variant *ransackle* appeared in the seventeenth century, and not long after we see the first appearance of the adjective *ransackled*, meaning "wrecked or destroyed by plundering." The idea of a house (or whatever) being wrecked stuck to *ransackled* and to its later variant *ramshackled*, and when the latter was shortened to *ramshackle* in the early nineteenth century, the "wrecked" sense had morphed into "rickety; run-down." While I'm rambling on about *ramshackle*, it's worth mentioning that the *OED* mentions another possible origin of the word: the verb *camshacle*, "to distort to twist," a Scandinavian term that's a blend of *cam*, "crooked," and *shacle*, "distort."

rap

> Sometimes used synonymously with street conversation, "rap" is really a special way of talking—repartee. Street repartee at its best is a lively way of "running it down," or of "jiving" (attempting to put someone on), trying "to blow another person's mind," forcing him "to lose his cool," to give in or give up something. For example, one needs to throw a lively rap when he is "putting the make on a broad." —John Horton, *Trans-Action*, 1967

"Putting the make on a broad"? Sheesh. Sexist sixties locutions aside, the "rap" part of rap music existed before the music itself. In fact, the *OED* lists a sense of the word *rap*, "talk, chat" with a citation from 1898! The more specialized sense of "lively banter, repartee," only came about in the 1960s, and by the 1970s the meaning had changed slightly to refer to any kind of impromptu talk. Poets in New York City took up rap, and the addition of complex and clever rhymes made the new style a big hit. DJs and other street artists added music and strong beats, and by about 1980 a new musical genre was born.

More Rapping

You may be wondering if the *rap* in rap music is in any way related to the *rap* in phrases such as *bum rap*, *beat the rap*, *pin the rap on someone*, and *rap sheet*. In a word, no. Not even in the form of rap music known as *gangsta*. The sense of *rap* that we're looking for here goes back to the eighteenth century, and it meant "adverse criticism; a rebuke." Early in the 1900s the meaning expanded to include "a criminal charge," and that sense is the source of the criminal cant phrases I mentioned earlier.

raspberry

No, not the delicious fruit but the slightly scandalous noise that erupts when you stick out your tongue between lightly closed lips and blow. You can do this to indicate to the person sitting across from you (who is, hopefully, at a suitable distance; there are spray issues here) that you don't appreciate what they've just said or done. (Or, of course, you can "blow a raspberry," as they say, just for the sheer fun of it; try it out on the nearest toddler.) This use of the word *raspberry* comes from the phrase "raspberry tart," which is rhyming slang for a four-letter "f" word that means "flatulence" (the derivation of which term is left as an exercise for the reader). A raspberry is also known as a *Bronx cheer,* a nicely ironic locution (since it's really the polar opposite of a cheer) that comes from the sounds that often emanate from fans of the New York Yankees baseball team, the home of which (Yankee Stadium) resides in the Bronx (a New York City borough).

Rhyming Slang

Rhyming slang—also called Cockney rhyming slang because it emerged from the Cockney population of London's East End—is a form of slang that replaces a word with a phrase where the last word rhymes with the original word. So, for example, *feet* becomes *plates of meat* and *face* becomes *boat race.* Rhyming slang is also an efficient producer of other slang terms. For example, you may find yourself telling the clueless person standing in front of you to "use your loaf." The slang term *loaf* comes from the phrase *loaf of bread,* which is rhyming slang for *head.*

R

rat race

The phrase *rat race* has long been used as a disparaging metaphor for the daily struggle to survive and get ahead in a competitive world. No one's too sure where the phrase came from, but the *OED* offers a tantalizing clue. It quotes a 1937 edition of the journal *American Speech* that defines a rat race as a "dance of low-grade nature." Inspired either by suppositions about what such a dance would entail, or possibly by images of rats running aimlessly through mazes or on exercise wheels, by the 1950s *rat race* had shifted to its current meaning and has since become a full-fledged and familiar member of the lexicon, albeit a negative one. Like the absurd intensity of a rat running on an exercise wheel, most folks see that there's an inherent folly in racing through life working ever-longer hours and rushing from one appointment to the next. And unfortunately, as comedian Lily Tomlin once observed, even if you win the rat race, you're still a rat. (One of my favorite new phrases is *rat-race membership fee*, the costs associated with buying clothes and other things that are needed for one's job.)

razzmatazz

Razzmatazz is a flashy, gaudy display designed to impress people and get them excited. Razzmatazz probably originated as a variation of *razzle-dazzle*, which means "an amazing or bewildering display." It's the "bewildering" component that gives razzle-dazzle an additional meaning of "an action designed to confuse," which is often used in sports ("the old razzle-dazzle play"). This also explains why *razzmatazz* is sometimes used to mean "double-talk; ambiguous or evasive language."

read the riot act

Our Sovereign Lord the King chargeth and commandeth all persons, being assembled, immediately to disperse themselves, and peaceably to depart to their habitations, or to their lawful business, upon the pains contained in the act made in the first year of King George, for preventing tumults and riotous assemblies. God Save the King.

This rather HIGHFALUTIN speech is the full text of what a justice of the peace, sheriff, or other official in a position of authority was supposed to recite "openly and with loud voice" if that person came across a group of rioters. The mind reels at the comic possibilities. The part of the speech that refers to "the act made in the first year of King George" was a piece of legislation enacted in Britain in 1714. The official title was the ponderous "An act for preventing tumults and riotous assemblies, and for the more speedy and effectual punishing the rioters." However, to all and sundry it became known more popularly as the Riot Act. The act required any on-hand official to read the text above, so the phrase *read the Riot Act* became synonymous with the idea of breaking up or dispersing a riot. By the early nineteenth century, the phrase *read the riot act* (although often still with the capital *R* and capital *A*) had taken on the more general sense of reprimanding someone for unruly behavior that we still use today. (By the way, the Riot Act is no longer in force; Britain repealed it in 1973.) If you're wondering about the word *riot* itself, it goes back to the Old French word *riote*, "debate; quarrel." Strangely, it didn't enter English with that meaning. Instead, in the early thirteenth century, the word *riote* meant "loose or wasteful living; debauchery." By the late fourteenth century, *riot* had come to mean "a noisy feast or wanton revel," and soon after that it took on its more common sense of "a violet disturbance of the peace."

recipe

See Rx.

red herring

If you happen to catch a herring one of these days, be sure to eat it right away or it will spoil in no time flat. The alternative is to heavily salt the fish and then smoke it over a fire for a day or two, in which case it will keep for months. Don't be alarmed, however, when you see the fish turn a deep red color. Yes, this is the origin of the phrase *red herring*, and these crimson fish were the staple of many a poor person's diet for a few hundred of years, beginning in the fifteenth century. Okaaaay, I hear you say, but what about the idea of a red herring being a misleading clue or something introduced to divert attention? Ah, that's where our story gets a wee bit murkier. We do know that red herrings gave off a powerful smell, and that in the late seventeenth century huntsmen would train their dogs by dragging a red herring for a few miles and loosing the hounds to follow the scent. Unfortunately, that's where the linguistic trail goes cold. In the late nineteenth century, *to draw a red herring across the path* was already in proverbial use, and it meant "to divert attention from the real question," and the thing doing the diverting was called a *red herring.* How we got from training hunting dogs to diverting attention is a bit of a mystery. Some folks believe there were early antihunting groups that would drag red herrings around to ruin a hunt in progress by distracting the dogs. Another theory is that escaped prisoners would pilfer a red herring or two and drag the fish behind them to confuse the pursuing bloodhounds. Either one

R

sounds at least plausible, but they could be just stories planted to throw an intrepid etymologist off the scent.

red-letter day

A *red-letter day* is a good day, indeed, referring as it does to "a very special, memorable, or fortunate day or occasion." But what letters are we talking about, and why do they insist on being red? To solve these conundrums, you'd need to go back to the calendars and almanacs published around the eighteenth century. In those august tomes, the names of the saint's days, church festivals, feast days, and other holidays were written in red ink or printed in red type. These were the original red-letter days, and the phrase eventually became associated with any special day.

red tape

The *OED* offers an invaluable historical record of the language, and to both amateur and professional etymologists, one of the joys of the *OED* is watching the progress of a word or phrase over the years. The phrase *red tape* provides an excellent example:

> 1696–1715—The Map … upon the Backside thereof sealed with his Excellency's Seal at Arms on a Red Cross with Red Tape.

> 1736—Let Wilmington, with grave, contracted brow, Red tape and wisdom at the Council show.

> 1814—Drawing from his pocket a budget of papers, and untying the red tape.

> 1837—My dear, you mistake John Barnsley … Dearly as he loves a bit of red tape, you never saw him try to inspire any other man with the love of business.

> 1839–1840—His brain was little better than red tape and parchment.

> 1869—All the morning at the custom-house, plagued with red tape.

So you see that *red tape* originally referred innocuously to the red-colored tape used to secure legal documents or other collections of official correspondence. Over the years, the phrase at first became more generalized ("he loves a bit of red tape") and then it becomes a negative thing ("plagued with red tape") as people began associating the tape itself with bureaucracy and its rigid adherence to unnecessary and over-complicated rules and regulations.

refurbish

When you refurbish something, you restore, renovate, or repair that thing so that it's cleaner, newer, or more functional than before. If all that work includes the cleaning and polishing of a sword or some armor, all the better because *refurbish* comes to us from the Old French verb *forbiss*, "to remove rust, to brighten by polishing, particularly armor, a sword, or other weapon."

remember

When you remember something, you're not repeating something done to a limb or to someone who belongs to a group (to cite just two senses of the word *member*). In fact, the word *remember* has nothing to do with the word *member* as we use it today. Instead, its origins lie in the Latin term *rememorārī*, which is a combination of the prefix *re-*, "again," and the word *memor*, "mindful." So the literal meaning was "to be mindful of something again." The Latin term *memor* is also the source of our words *commemorate* and *memorandum*.

restaurant

This word comes to us from the French verb *restaurer*, "to restore." In other words, a restaurant is a place where you go to eat and drink and thereby restore your energy and good spirits (if not your bank balance).

R

rhubarb

If you've ever had the distinctly frustrating task of removing a rhubarb plant from your garden (it's practically an all-day job, as I can attest from bitter—that's a pun, by the way—experience), then you won't be surprised to learn that the words *rhubarb* and *barbaric* are related. *Barbaric* comes from the Greek word *barbarous*, which means "foreign, rude," and is thought to be a mocking imitation of foreign (read: non-Greek) language. Those wacky Greeks knew of rhubarb, of course, and they called it *rha* or *rheum*. At one point you could only get this plant from foreign lands such as China and Tibet, so it was known as either *rhabarbarum* or *rheubarbarum*, literally "foreign rha" or "foreign rheum." From there, it was only an etymological hop, skip, and a jump to our modern word *rhubarb*.

rich as Croesus

See CROESUS.

riff-raff

Only a person who was among the dregs of society would plunder loot from the bodies of those who died in battle, so perhaps it's appropriate that this is the history of the phrase *riff-raff*, "disreputable people from the lowest classes of society." Our tale begins with the Middle French words *rifle*, "plunder," and *rafle*, "to snatch; to carry away." The combined phrase *rifle et rafle* referred to plundering the battlefield dead and making off with the loot. That phrase wandered into English as *rif and raf*, where the meaning was "everything" or "every single one" (probably a hint at the thoroughness of some post-battle plunderers). The meaning changed to "everyone" a while later, and then it came to refer to the common folk. Along the way the phrase itself morphed into *riff-raff* and, perhaps still carrying a whiff of those nasty battlefield thieves, the meaning sunk to its current lowest-of-the-low sense.

A Short History of Rifle

As you might have guessed by now, the French term *rifle*, from the verb *rifler*, "to plunder," is the source of the English verb *rifle*, "to ransack or search thoroughly."

rigmarole

If you're faced with an absurdly complex or confusing task, you might want to call that task a *rigmarole* (or, more rarely, a *rigamarole*). You're also at liberty to use this word for a long and overly elaborate explanation. Where did this strange lexical beast come from? One hint is that in the earliest uses (we're talking mid-eighteenth century here), the word was actually a phrase: *rig-my-role* or *rig-my-roll*. These phrase versions, particularly the latter spelling, hint that these are alterations of the earlier phrase *Ragman roll*. This refers to a scroll used in a medieval gambling game. This scroll was a piece of parchment on which was written a list of characters, each of whom had specific personality traits, and strings were attached to each character. A player would select a string at random and would then have to "play" that character for the evening. What fun! The first of these characters was named Rageman the Good, so the parchment became known as the *Rageman Roll*, which was later altered to *Ragman roll*. The game itself became known as *Ragman*, and later the word *ragman* came to mean "a long discourse," perhaps because of long-winded speeches given by the game's characters. That sense also attached itself to *rigmarole* when it entered the language. The "long discourse" sense also hatched a "long procedure" sense in the mid-twentieth century. I'll stop there to avoid this history from itself becoming a rigmarole.

riot

See READ THE RIOT ACT.

riot act

See READ THE RIOT ACT.

robot

> The best sort of worker is the cheapest worker. The one that has the least needs. What young Rossum invented was a worker with the least needs possible. He had to make him simpler. He threw out everything that wasn't of direct use in his work, that's to say, he threw out the man and put in the robot. Miss Glory, robots are not people. They are mechanically much better than we are, they have an amazing ability to understand things, but they don't have a soul. —Karel Čapek, *R. U. R.*, 1921

R

The quotation above is from a play titled *R. U. R.*, which is famous not only for its powerful take on human slavery and forced labor, but also for coining the word *robot* (the R. U. R. of the title comes from Rossum's Universal Robots, a company in the play that makes robots).

The word comes from the Czech term *robota*, "forced labor," and it entered English in 1923 when an English translation of the play was performed in London. Čapek's robots were artificial humans, but as mechanical automatons became more popular, the word *robot* came to refer exclusively to machines (with the word *android*, literally "man-like," taking over the "artificial human" niche of the automaton world).

rocket

The powerful thrust and roar of a rocket in flight stands in the sharpest possible contrast with a person using a spinning wheel to create yarn from flax or wool. But the two activities are very closely related behind-the-linguistic-scenes, as it were. That's because the word *rocket* is derived from the word *rock*, another name for the *distaff*, a wooden board attached to a spinning wheel and used to hold the fibers to be spun. This kind of rock has a roughly cylindrical shape, and is wide at the bottom and skinny at the top. It looks, in other words, like (to use the *OED*'s prolix definition) "an apparatus consisting of a cylindrical case of paper or metal containing an inflammable composition, by the ignition of which it may be projected to a height or distance." This described an early (seventeenth century) type of rocket, and that word came to English via the Italian *rochetta*, a diminutive form of *rocca*, "rock; distaff." The first recorded use of the word *rocket* as we think of it today (that is, a cylindrical craft propelled by a powerful engine) came in 1919.

round-robin

Your average, well-fed robin does have a bit of a rotund shape, but that's not the source of the phrase *round-robin*, "a tournament where each person or team plays the other in turn." Instead, you need to go back to the eighteenth century when people with a grievance or gripe of some kind would write it up and then sign their names in a circle so that no one's name stood out as the initiator of the complaint or as the ringleader. (It's said that in not-so-merry old England, if the King received a written petition or protest, he'd pick the first few names on the list of signers and behead them!) Sailors of the day would often resort to this technique and it's thought the phrase started with them. Where did they get it? No one's absolutely certain, but the most plausible explanation I've seen is that it comes from the French phrase *rouban rond*, "round ribbon." This was a circular ribbon on which protesters signed their names, with the circularity preventing any one name from standing out. In the late nineteenth century, this everyone's-the-same idea was applied to tournaments where teams or players took turns competing against each other, and such tournaments were called *round-robin*s.

rule of thumb

The phrase *rule of thumb* refers to a procedure, method, or guideline that's based on experience or practice that produces an acceptable result. Why "thumb"? It has to do with the humble thumb's place as a quintessentially human physical characteristic. One dictionary defines *man*, in part, as "a member of the genus Homo, family Hominidae, order Primates, class Mammalia, characterized by erect posture and an opposable thumb." In other words, that cannily positioned, two-jointed stranger in the house of fingers that soothes toddlers and enables us to hitchhike and rate movies is a symbol for humanity. So it's no wonder we trot it out linguistically at a moment's notice. A person has a *green thumb*; something *sticks out like a sore thumb*; you *thumb your nose at someone*; you can have someone *under your thumb*; you can give something the *thumbs-up* (or *thumbs-down*). It's also convenient that on a male with average-sized hands, the distance between the tip of the thumb and the first knuckle is about one inch. That rough-and-ready measure was used by many an old-time carpenter, and it's also the source of the phrase *rule of thumb*. For even more on the thumb (if you can stand it), see THIMBLE.

R

All Thumbs

The thumb is the digital age digit-of-choice. This newfound popularity is a result of a newfangled use for the thumb's opposability: operating the teensy keypads and buttons that are standard equipment on modern cell phones and PDAs. In fact, the word *thumb* has morphed into a new verb that means "to enter data into a cell phone or other device using one's thumb or thumbs." So now hipsters talk about *thumb culture*, "people who are skilled at using their thumbs to manipulate objects." The thumb-proficient are called the *thumb generation* and a device that can be operated using the thumbs is described as *thumbable*. Finally, a computer game that's all hand-eye coordination with little strategy or thought required is called *thumb candy*.

Rx

Why do we use the short form Rx to refer to a prescription? The short answer is that it's an alteration of ℞, the classic symbol associated with prescriptions. That symbol is a capital R with a small stroke through it, and it's short for the Latin word *recipe*, which means (in this case) "take." In medieval times, the ℞ symbol would appear at the beginning of the prescription, so it was an instruction to the patient to take the following medicines in the specified dosages at the specified intervals. Some folks saw that a medical prescription, with its medicines and instructions for taking them, was similar to food preparation, with its ingredients and instructions for cooking them. So early in the eighteenth century, a specific cooking procedure became known as a recipe.

sabotage

If a vote was held on the most unlikely starting point for a word's ety-mology, *sabotage*—"damage inflicted in secret to impair an enemy's ability to fight"—would be a "shoe"-in for the top 10. That's because it comes from the French verb *saboter*, "to walk noisily in wooden shoes"! (See what I mean?) Opinions vary on how this verb was transformed, but the most reasonable path is that it eventually came to mean "clum-siness" and then "to work badly" and then "to destroy machines delib-erately."

sack

See GET THE SACK.

sad sack

During World War II, a U.S. Army sergeant by the name of George Baker created a comic strip character named Sad Sack, who made his debut in the June 1942 issue of *Yank, the Army Weekly*. Sad Sack was a bumbling private with a big, bulbous nose, a perpetually forlorn expres-sion, and a penchant for getting himself into all kinds of trouble. *The Sad Sack* comic ran right through the war, was a syndicated newspaper strip until 1960, and appeared in comic book form regularly until 1982. However, the comic was very popular almost right away, and the term *sad sack* came into more general use astonishingly quickly. For example, the December 28, 1943, edition of the *Baltimore Sun* quoted one GI as follows: "A forlorn look, a G.I. haircut, an oversized fatigue uniform and all the paraphernalia that goes with them branded me as a typical 'sad sack'." Just a few years later, in 1951, Marshall McLuhan wrote of a "Model mother saddled with a sad sack and a dope." (This comes from his book *The Mechanical Bride*, which also features the phrase LAST-DITCH, which I talked about earlier.) The sense of the word *sad sack* as an inept, ineffectual, pathetic person has been with us ever since.

salary

When you receive your salary, do you salt it away? If not, then according to the history of the word *salary*, perhaps you need to rethink your financial strategy. Back in the days before bar fridges and coolers, keeping food fresh was nearly impossible, but keeping it somewhat edible was doable as long as you had access to salt, which can act as a preservative. That's what Roman soldiers used to do when they were off conquering the barbarian hordes. In fact, salt was so important to the average Roman grunt that they were all given money to purchase salt for use as a preservative. A kind of salt per diem, if you will. That bit of cash was called the *salarium*, a term derived from the adjective *salarius*, "relating to salt," both of which come from the root word *sal*, "salt." After a while, *salarium* came to refer not just to the salt stipend, but to all the wages given to the soldiers. This meaning stayed in place while the word entered English a few hundred years later as *salary*.

sandwich

> A minister of state passed four and twenty hours at a public gaming-table, so absorpt in play that, during the whole time, he had no subsistence but a bit of beef, between two slices of toasted bread, which he eat without ever quitting the game. This new dish grew highly in vogue, during my residence in London: it was called by the name of the minister who invented it. —Pierre Jean Grosley, *Tour to London*, 1765

The "minister" mentioned in the above citation was a Brit named John Montagu, a politician and statesman, but most famously for our purposes, he was also the fourth Earl of Sandwich. And, yes, the "new dish" consisting of "a bit of beef, between two slices of toasted bread" was called a *sandwich*. Actually, for the first few years of its existence, it was spelled with a capital "S" in honor of its inventor. Consider, for example, the following excerpt from the famous historian Edward Gibbon's journal from November 24, 1762 (a mere few months after the Earl of Sandwich's late-night nosh began the new trend):

> Twenty or thirty ... of the first men in the kingdom ... supping at little tables covered with a napkin, in the middle of a coffee room, upon a bit of cold meat or a Sandwich.

Within a few years the sandwich branched out to include other fillings, various types of bread (toasted or untoasted), and nongambling venues, and lunches were never the same again.

sandwich generation

This relatively new phrase refers to adults who must care for both their children and their aging parents, particularly when the parents move in with them. The idea behind the metaphor is that the adults are "SANDWICHED" between the slice of kids on the one side and the slice of parents on the other. A similar idea lies behind the phrase *club-sandwich generation*, adults who provide care for their parents, children, and grandchildren. The American Association of Retired Persons estimates that 11 percent of grandparents who are over 50 are helping to raise their grandchildren. Since many of those grandparents also have children and elderly parents to care for, their metaphorical sandwich has an extra layer of bread, making it a club sandwich.

sarcasm

> Blows are sarcasms turned stupid: wit is a form of force that leaves the limbs at rest. —George Eliot, *Felix Holt, The Radical*, 1866

If you've ever referred to a bit of sarcasm as a "biting" or "cutting" remark, you may not have any idea just how appropriately you wielded either adjective. That's because *sarcasm*, "a mocking, derisive remark that means the opposite of what it seems to say," comes from the Latin word *sarcasmus* and before that the Greek *sarkazein*, both of which mean "to tear flesh." When the word entered English in the sixteenth century, it was most often used as the name *Sarcasmus*, a personification of those who use sharp, bitter, ironical remarks. As a noun straight up, *sarcasm* first appeared in 1619.

satellite

> A projectile, animated with an initial speed twenty times superior to the actual speed, being ten thousand yards to the second, can never fall! This movement, combined with terrestrial attraction, destines it to revolve perpetually round our globe. ... Two hundred thousand dollars is not too much to have paid for the pleasure of having endowed the planetary world with a new star, and the earth with a second satellite. —Jules Verne, *The Begum's Millions*, 1880

In the above citation, the great French novelist Jules Verne uses for the first time ever the word *satellite* to refer to a man-made object orbiting Earth. Note that he speaks of a "second satellite," the first being the Moon, because since at least the mid-seventeenth century we've used the word *satellite* to refer to any smaller astronomical object that orbits a larger one. Before that, however, a satellite wasn't a heavenly body, but an Earthly one. That is, it used to refer to a person who was an attendant for someone important, having come to us from the Latin term *satellit-em*, "attendant; guard." It seems the notion of a moon orbiting a larger planet was just too reminiscent of a person "running around" a larger personage to resist, and the word *satellite* has been raised to new heights ever since.

Of Moons and Months

Just in case you're curious (although, since you're reading this book, curiosity would seem to be a natural state of mind for you), the word *moon* goes back to Old English times and it's based on the word *month*, since a complete cycle of the various phases of the moon constitutes a *lunar month*. In turn, the word *month* comes from the Latin *mens*, "measure," which also gave us words such as *immense* and *dimension*.

satire

> I wear my Pen as others do their Sword.
> To each affronting sot I meet, the word
> Is Satisfaction: straight to thrusts I go,
> And pointed satire runs him through and through.
>
> —John Oldham, *Upon a Printer*, 1681

Do you, like the English poet John Oldham quoted above, get satisfaction out of satire? If so, that's appropriate both literarily and linguistically. The word *satire*, "the use of ironic, sarcastic, or derisory wit to criticize faults," came to English via the Latin *satira*, a later variation on *satura*, "a poem that uses ridicule to denounce follies or vices." Before that, *satura* referred to a piece of writing that discussed a variety of subjects, which came from another sense of *satura*: "medley." This second sense came from the phrases *per saturam*, "collectively" and *lanx satura*, "a dish containing many different ingredients," which combines *lanx* "dish," and *satur*, "full." The word *satur* also produced *satis*, "enough," which was the source of our word *satisfaction* (not to mention *sate* and *saturate*).

sawbuck

The word *sawbuck* as slang for a ten-dollar bill may be on its way out of the language. A search of the Lexis-Nexis media database (an impressive collection of thousands of newspapers, magazines, journals, newsletters, press releases, and blogs) turned up less than 200 citations from the previous year. It's not in the language graveyard yet, however, so let's take a look at the origins of this curious term. The word *sawbuck* migrated to English from the Dutch term *zaagbok*, which referred to a rack or trestle used to hold wood for sawing (what we usually now call a SAWHORSE). The original sawbuck had two supports on each end, and those supports crossed each other to create an X-shape. In the mid-nineteenth century, U.S. bills used Roman numerals: I for the dollar bill, V for the five-dollar bill, and X for the ten-dollar bill. That "X" reminded people of the X-shapes holding up a sawbuck, and the name transferred over to the bill and was first used in that sense about 1850.

sawhorse

See EASEL.

scallywag

If you come across a person who's a disreputable good-for-nothing and you want to insult that person, albeit mildly and with a trace of humor, then by all means call that person a *scallywag* (or, if you prefer, a *scalawag*). You'd be unlikely to also call that person a "skinny cow," but that's exactly what you would have been doing if you'd hurled the epithet "scallywag" at someone in mid-nineteenth century America. For, indeed, the word *scallywag* (actually *scalawag* back then) probably was first used to describe scrawny or undersized cattle. I'm hedging my etymological bets a bit here because the first recorded use of *scalawag* in the "scrawny cow" sense was 1854, but the first recorded use of *scalawag* in the "disreputable person" sense was 1848. Hmmm. No matter, people who've studied these things believe the cow came before the person here, so I'm willing to believe them and move on with my life. Specifically, I'll move on to the history of the word *scallywag*, notwithstanding the discouraging fact that the *OED* lists the word's etymology as "origin obscure." Fortunately for us, there's no shortage of fun and interesting theories. The most plausible of these is the suggestion that the word comes from Scotland's Shetland Islands, one of which is named *Scalloway*. You may be familiar with the Shetland pony, a miniature and oh-so-cute horse, but Scalloway is also home to dwarf cattle (probably not so cute), so it seems reasonable for people to have adapted the name *Scalloway* to any undersized or undernourished cattle stateside. Another Scottish theory is that *scallywag* comes from the Scots word *scurryvaig*, "vagabond," which may have come from the Latin phrase *scurra vagas*, "wandering fool" (perhaps because it reminded people of the phrase "scurrilous vagrant").

scapegoat

A *scapegoat* is a person who takes the blame for other people. Who then will take the blame for what appears to be the rather serious lexical error that brought this word into the English language? A good candidate is William Tindale, whose 1530 translation of the Bible included the following for Leviticus 16:8:

> And Aaron cast lottes ouer the
> gootes: one lotte for the Lorde, and another for a scape-goote.

The "scape-goote" (scapegoat) here was Tindale's translation of the Hebrew word *Azazel*, which he thought meant "escape goat," which he rendered poetically by lopping off the *e*. From this the legend grew that this "escape goat" was one to which the people's sins had been confessed, and it was therefore released into the wilderness so that it could take (symbolically, at least) the sins of the community with it. That idea gradually morphed into the current meaning, where we place actual blame on a person for some wrongdoing. Not so fast, however. It now appears that Azazel was actually a name from Hebrew mythology, and it represented a demon that ruled the wilderness. So, really, one goat was the "Lord's goat" (free of sin) and the other was "Azazel's goat" (loaded with sin). The goat didn't "escape" at all, but was probably sacrificed. Not that I'm suggesting this should be the new fate for all our modern-day scapegoats.

scofflaw

If there's one thing people hate, it's a gap in the language. For example, what do you call the adult with whom you regularly go out on dates? ("Girlfriend" and "boyfriend" are too juvenile, and "lover" is too intimate, too romance-novelish.) What should we call the first decade of the 2000s? (We have the sixties, seventies, eighties, nineties, and then ... what?) Why is there no genderless third-person singular pronoun? ("He" is traditional, but is now considered politically incorrect; "they" is grammatically controversial.) Despite the language's half a million words, these kinds of gaps are legion, and contests to fill these gaps are a thriving cottage industry. One of the earliest such contests was launched by a TEETOTALER named Delcevare King, who in 1923 was alarmed at the number of people who were flouting the U.S. Constitution's Eighteenth Amendment, which prohibited the manufacture and sale of liquor. Mr. King decided that what the world needed was a word to name these "lawless drinkers," these "scoffers." He offered a $200 prize (a princely sum in those days) for the best word. By the contest deadline, more than 25,000 people had responded with suggestions ranging from *boozlaac* to *hooch-sniper* to (my personal favorite) *law-loose-liquor-lover*. The winning entry, submitted independently by Kate Butler of Dorchester, Massachusetts, and Henry Dale of Andover, Massachusetts, was *scofflaw*, a word that found a permanent place in the language, although today it refers to anyone who ignores or disregards the law.

Skycap!

A few years after *scofflaw* became part of the language thanks to a contest, a similar situation gave us another now-familiar word. In a 1940 contest, people were asked to come up with a name for the porters who worked at the Airlines Terminal in New York. According to an article in the December 24, 1940, edition of the *New York Herald Tribune*, 2,780 people vied for the $100 prize, which was won by Willie Wainwright of New Orleans, Louisiana. His suggested word was *skycaps*.

scot free

The Scottish have a reputation for being frugal, perhaps even a tad tight-fisted; the uncharitable would say penny-pinching. It's one of those stereotypes with a nut of truth buried inside somewhere. (I speak with some authority here: my parents and their ancestors are nothing but Scottish as far back as you care to go.) Even so, I report with some glee that the Scots are in no way connected to the adjectival phrase *scot free*, "exempt from injury or punishment," most often seen in phrases such as *get off scot free* and *go scot free*. We've been describing people as *scot free* since at least the thirteenth century, and the phrase has gone through several incarnations: *scotfre*, *skot fre*, *scott free*, and so on. The word that links them all is *scot*, which originally referred to a payment or contribution, particularly one used to pay for entertainment. It was also called a *tavern score* or an *ale-house reckoning*. In the late fourteenth century, the word *scot* also took on the sense of a local tax. In both meanings, if you were somehow exempt from paying, you were said to be *scot free*. By the mid-sixteenth century, the phrase *scot free* had become more general and referred to getting out of some situation without injury or punishment.

scrimmage

War metaphors abound in football: from *offense* and *defense* to *blitz* (based on the German term *blitzkrieg*) and *bomb*. You can also add *scrimmage* to that list. In football, a *scrimmage* refers to a single play (that is, the action that occurs between the time the ball is snapped and the time the play is whistled dead). *Scrimmage* is a variation on the word *scrimish*, which was itself a variation on the word *skirmish*, "a brief battle; a fight between two people." *Scrimmage* and *skirmish* were synonyms for a few hundred years, until around 1880 when the football usage first arose for *scrimmage*, and that sense has been the main one ever since. (The secondary sense of a practice game between a team's offensive and defensive players first appeared around 1916.)

The Blitz Is On!

The word *blitzkrieg* refers to a swift and surprising military offensive that uses combined air and ground forces to overwhelm the enemy. This is a German term that brings together *blitz*, "lightning," and *krieg*, "war."

scuttlebutt

This term refers to gossip or rumors. Scuttlebutt brings together the word *scuttle*, "a hole or hatch," and *butt*, "a large cask." In days of yore, this word first referred to a cask that contained a sailing ship's drinking water. That cask had a hole in the top to allow a thirsty sailor to insert a cup or dipper and extract some water, and that water cask became known as the *scuttlebutt*. Humans are, of course, natural gossips, so not surprisingly the *tars* and *salts* (both informal terms for sailors) would gather around this nautical version of a water cooler and exchange the latest rumors and news. Over time, this gossip took on the name of the cask.

second

The word *second* is a curious lexical beast: as a noun it means "one-sixtieth of a minute" (measured by time or the angle of a circle) and as an adjective it means "next after the first." How in the name of Pete did one word end up with two radically different meanings? Did a whole bunch of people at one time lose races by just one second? Nope. The real deal begins with the Latin word *secundus*, which started off with the "next after the first" sense attached to it. So far so good. Back in those ancient times, scientists wrestled with the problem of measuring angles within a circle. Some tall-forehead type came up with the idea of dividing the circle evenly, and for whatever reason chose 360 as the number, hence the 360-degree circle was born. Scientists are usually precise people, and they soon realized that 360 degrees was too coarse a measure. To get more accuracy, they divided up each degree into 60 parts (they called this "sexagesimal division") and they gave these new units the surprisingly unscientific name *pars minutae*, "little parts." Scientists are a tough lot to please, however, and they soon realized that even the *pars minutae* were too big. So they did the whole sexages-imal division thing yet again, this time dividing up each *pars minuta* into another 60 parts. The first division then became known as the *pars minutae primae*, "first little parts," and the next division became known as the *pars minutae secundae*, "next little parts." Eventually, these unwieldy names became shortened: a *pars minuta prima* became just a *minute*, and a *pars minuta secundus* became just a *second*.

S

seersucker

When you picture someone in a seersucker suit, you just might picture that person sipping tea in some English country garden. If your imagination tends to include specific details, go ahead and picture that person with milk and sugar in his tea. Why? Because milk and sugar are part of the etymology of the word *seersucker,* which refers to a lightweight linen or cotton fabric with alternating smooth and puckered pinstripes. The word came into English via the Hindi term *sirsakar,* which was itself a corruption of the Persian phrase *shīr o shakkar,* "milk and sugar," apparently a reference to the light-colored stripes that are characteristic of the fabric.

sepia

You've probably seen your share of sepia-colored pictures from the early days of photography. *Sepia* refers to the brownish tone that was a natural byproduct of early photographic processes (and which can be added artificially to modern-day digital photos with a mere mouse click or two). You might be more than a little surprised to learn that the word *sepia* developed from the Latin term *sēpia,* which means "cuttlefish," of all things. It turns out that in the nineteenth century, watercolor painters would use the inklike secretion of the cuttlefish to create a rich, brown pigment, which became known as *sepia.* The color of this pigment was similar to the brown color seen in early photographs, so that color took on the name *sepia.*

September

You know, of course, that September is the ninth month on the calendar. What you may not know, however, is that the word *September* comes from the Latin term *septem,* "seven." Hunh? The mystery deepens when you learn that *October* comes from the Latin *octo,* "eight"; *November* comes from *novem,* "nine"; and December comes from *decem,* "ten." The mystery is solved when you learn that the old Roman calendar consisted of only ten months, and those months began in what we now call March. Ah! Working back from September, the original Roman name for August was *Sextilis,* from *sextus,* "six," and the original name for July was *Quintilis,* from *quintus,* "five." (The Romans later renamed these months after Julius Caesar and Augustus Caesar.) So, care to take a guess at the original Roman name for June? If you said "Quartilis," from the Latin *quartus*, "four," well, no, I'm sorry but that's just wrong. It was *Junius*, duh. This comes from the name of the Roman goddess Juno, and the rest of the month names are also god- or goddess-based: *Maius* (May) from Maia; *Aprilis* (April) from Aphrodite (a Greek goddess; go figure); and *Martius* (March) from Mars.

High Noon—at 3 P.M.?

A similar shift occurred with the word *noon*, which comes from the Latin word *nōna*, "the ninth hour of the day" (from *nōnus*, "ninth"). Strangely, *nōna* referred not to nine o'clock in the morning, but to three o'clock in the afternoon! It seems that *nōna* also referred to the canonical office for the ninth hour, and the Christian church day begins at six o'clock in the morning. Thus the ninth hour of the day is actually three in the afternoon. How did we get from *nōna* to *noon*, a three-hour shift? I wish I could tell you. The *OED* speculates that it "probably resulted from anticipation of the ecclesiastical office or of a meal hour," but I have no idea what that means.

septillion

See BILLION.

serendipity

You use the word *serendipity* to refer to a fortunate or useful discovery made by accident, or to the faculty or gift for making such discoveries. The word was coined by the author Horace Walpole in the mid-eighteenth century. It comes from an old Persian fairy tale called *The Three Princes of Serendip*. The tale's heroes were always making accidental discoveries as they traveled, so Walpole coined *serendipity* in their honor. (Serendip, by the way, is the country we now know as Sri Lanka.)

sextillion

See BILLION.

shambles

> Alastair learned, too, that all schemes ended in a "shambles" which did not mean, as he feared, a slaughter, but a brief restoration of individual freedom of movement. —Evelyn Waugh, *Put Out More Flags*, 1942

The word *shambles*, "messy disorder; chaos," has had quite a number of careers in its long linguistic life, and the citation above shows but one of them. To get the full biography of this word, we need to go back to the Latin term *scamnum*, "bench," which entered Old English as *scamel* or *schamel*, which at first (this is way back in the ninth century) referred to a stool or footstool, but later (in the tenth century) became a table for displaying goods for sale. Things held steady until the fourteenth century when the word changed to *schamil* or *shamell* and the meaning specialized to "a table or stall for the sale of meat." In the sixteenth century, the plural form *shambles* made its first appearance, and the meaning changed yet again, this time to refer to "a place where meat is sold." (The plural probably came from the fact that there were multiple tables—shambles—at such a market.) It was also called a *flesh-shambles*. Since in those days a meat market would be located near the place where the animals were slaughtered, the word *shambles* also took on the "slaughterhouse" sense. This was a crucial turning point, because soon after that writers started using *shambles* figuratively to refer to any scene or place of carnage or wholesale slaughter:

> O Jerusalem, not the infidel Romans which shall invade thee, and make thy city ... a shambles of dead bodies. —Thomas Nashe, *Christ's Tears Over Jerusalem*, 1593

By the twentieth century, although the "slaughter" sense still hung in the air (see the Evelyn Waugh quotation at the top of this entry), the word *shambles* had softened somewhat and was used for any scene of mere disorder, mess, or chaos.

shampoo

> Had I not seen several China merchants shampooed before me, I should have been apprehensive of danger. —Charles Noble, *Voyage to East Indies*, 1762

This citation has the distinction of being the earliest known use of the word *shampoo* in English. It also has the distinction of being perhaps the most perplexing use of the word. After all, what "danger" could possibly lurk behind getting shampooed, beyond getting a bit of soap in one's eyes? Ah, but there's the rub—literally. You see, the verb *shampoo* was borrowed from the Hindi term *champo*, which is itself a variation on the Hindi verb *champna*, "to press." What this means is that when the anglicized version *shampoo* (sometimes spelled as *shampo*) entered the language, it referred to a vigorous, full-body massage complete with all manner of oils and unguents. It wasn't until about 1860 that the verb *shampoo* settled down into its modern sense of, as the *OED* fussily defines it, "to subject (the scalp) to washing and rubbing with some cleansing agent, as soap and water, shampoo powder, etc."

shindig

No one's 100 percent sure about the origin of the fun word *shindig*, "a noisy and festive party." However, we do know that at one time the word *shindig* referred to "a kick in the shins," a sense first recorded in 1859. However, we also have the following citation from Theodore T. Johnson's 1849 book *Sights in the Gold Region, and Scenes by the Way:*

> One of our party commenced a regular hoe-down, knocking his shins with heavy boots when opportunity offered.

A *hoe-down* is a noisy, lively dance that wouldn't be out of place at a festive party, and if there was a great deal of shin-kicking involved, then why not call that part a "shindig"? Another possibility (perhaps working in tandem with the "shin-kicking" theory) is that *shindig* is a variation on *shindy*, "a disturbance or commotion," and in the mid-nineteenth century it was common in certain circles to *kick up a shindy*.

shirty

If you come upon a petulant person who is acting unreasonably angry, feel free to describe that person as *shirty*. This comes from the phrase *keep your shirt on*, which means "don't get angry or upset." What does a shirt have to do with anger? One story has it that, in olden times, there lived ferocious Viking warriors called "berserkers." They were quick to anger and, in their fury, would rip off their chain-mail shirts and fight bare-chested. So the phrase means that by keeping your shirt on, you avoid a potential battle. (These Norse hotheads also gave us the word *berserk*, which means "destructively frenzied.") Another (and generally more accepted) story on the origin of *keep your shirt on* is that American men in the mid-1800s wore overly starched shirts that were too stiff to fight in. So taking off your shirt was seen as a prelude to fisticuffs.

shopping mall

Although online shopping has become a popular way to buy things, most folks still do their buying by heading for a physical location to exercise their credit cards. The location of choice is the *shopping mall*, a term that dates to 1963 but had its origins 400 years before in, of all things, a golflike pastime. The game was called *Pall Mall*, a name derived from the French word *pallemaille*, literally "ball-mallet." Pall Mall was played in a long alley that had an iron hoop suspended above the ground at the far end. The object was to use a mallet to drive a ball down the alley and then through the hoop in as few strokes as possible. The alleys used for the game were often tree-lined, and proved to be pleasant places to go for a stroll, especially after the game fell into disfavor. By the mid-seventeenth century, the word *mall* was being used to refer to the alley itself. In the late seventeenth century and throughout the eighteenth century *the Mall* referred to a tree-lined walk in St. James's Park in London, which used to be a Pall Mall alley. By the mid-eighteenth century, a *mall* was any tree-lined or sheltered walk used as a promenade. In the 1960s, developers appropriated the term for their new indoor shopping centers that were designed to encourage people to walk around and browse in the shop windows.

Silicon Valley

The region in Santa Clara County, California, known as Silicon Valley is famous as a center for high-tech firms, and that NICKNAME has been used since at least 1974. Why "Silicon"? That term comes from the fact that Santa Clara Valley was the original home of many microelectronics companies, particularly those that built integrated circuits using small wafers of silicon as the base. Silicon is an element people used to think was a metal, so its original name was *silicium*, a combination of the prefix *silic-*, "silica," and the suffix *-ium*, "metal." However, in 1802 the chemist Thomas Thomson discovered that silicium wasn't a metal at all, so he coined a new name in his book *A System of Chemistry:*

> The base of silica has been usually considered as a metal, and called silicium. But ... as it bears a close resemblance to boron and carbon, it is better to class it along with these bodies, and to give it the name of silicon.

A World of Silicon Valleys

There's probably not a Board of Trade in the country that hasn't tried to "brand" their town or city as "Silicon Something." Here are some examples: Silicon Alley (New York, New York), Silicon Desert (Phoenix, Arizona), Silicon Dominion (Fairfax, Virginia), Silicon Forest (Portland, Oregon), Silicon Hills (Austin, Texas), Silicon Mesa (North Albuquerque, New Mexico), Silicon Mountain (Colorado Springs, Colorado), Silicon Parkway (Garden State Parkway, New Jersey), and Silicorn Valley (Fairfield, Iowa). Outside of the United States, other Silly-Con monikers are Silicon Alps (Carinthia, Austria), Silicon Isle (Irish midlands), Silicon City (Bangalore, India), Silicon Fen (Cambridge, England), Silicon Glen (Glasgow-Edinburgh-Dundee, Scotland), Silicon Valley North (Ottawa, Canada), Silicon Valley of the East (Penang, Malaysia), Silicon Vineyard (Kelowna, British Columbia), and Silicon Wadi (Jerusalem, Israel).

skeptic

A *skeptic* is someone who doubts that something or other is true. (You can also call him a *doubting Thomas*, a phrase that comes from Christianity's Saint Thomas, who doubted the resurrection of Jesus and wanted proof.) The original Skeptics were members of a Greek school of philosophy who believed that real knowledge was impossible (except, one assumes, the knowledge that real knowledge is impossible). The Greek source of the term is the word *skeptesthai*, "to look about," from the Latin *skepticus*, "inquiring; reflective."

He Was from Missouri

Your friendly neighborhood skeptic might be inclined to say "I'm from Missouri" when he disbelieves something. This curious phrase means that he has to be shown something before he'll believe it. The deal here begins with the fact that the unofficial motto of Missouri is "The Show-Me State." This was made famous by a speech given in 1899 by Democratic Missouri Congressman Willard Duncan Vandiver: "I come from a state that raises corn and cotton and cockleburs and Democrats, and frothy eloquence neither convinces nor satisfies me. I am from Missouri. You have got to show me."

skinflint

A *skinflint* is an exceptionally parsimonious person, a miser who would go to almost any length to save a buck. He would even—gasp!—skin a flint! Okay, so that means nothing to the likes of you and I, but if we lived in the seventeenth and eighteenth centuries, we'd be shaking our heads at such a sorry image. First, there's a long-standing sense of the verb *to skin* that denotes excessive parsimony or cheapness: a miserly sort would "skin a cat" or, even more evocatively, would "skin a flea for his hide and tallow" (to borrow a wonderful quotation from the *OED*). So far so good. Now to the flint: this refers to a hard stone that, when struck forcefully by steel or some other metal, would produce a spark that would ignite some nearby kindling (or the fluid in a lighter). Obviously, such a hard stone would be impossible to "skin," but that wouldn't stop your average skinflint from trying.

sleuth

If you come across a *sleuth* ("detective") with a good nose for tracking down criminals, you might be tempted to describe him as a "human bloodhound." Please feel free to use this simile at will because there's more to it than mere similitude. The word *sleuth* originally referred to a track or trail, particularly the trail of a person or animal. (It came to English around 1200 from the Old Norse term *slod*, "track; trail.") In the 1400s, people started tracking animals and fugitives using a type of bloodhound called a *sleuth-hound*. The name of these dogs was eventually shortened to just *sleuth* in the 1800s, and the characteristics of these dogs caused the name to transfer to keen (I want to say "dogged") human trackers, and then to detectives.

slogan

> An Act was passed to abolish the words Crom-a-boo and Butler-a-boo, the Slogans of these two clans. —Goldwin Smith, *Irish History and Irish Character*, 1861

If the marketing fuss kicked up by the likes of Coke and Pepsi, McDonald's and Burger King, or Leno and Letterman seem like wars to you, that's very appropriate. Why? I'm glad you asked. It's because the word *slogan*, "a short, catchy marketing phrase" comes from the Gaelic *sluagh-ghairm*, "battle cry" (*sluagh* means "host; army" and *ghairm* means "cry; shout"). These fearsome cries were often used by Scottish Highlanders and native Irish clans, and they usually included a clan's name or home. For example, with the battle cries mentioned in the citation that opens this item, the clans involved are the Fitzgeralds for "Crom-a-boo" (Crom was the name of their ancestral castle) and the Butlers for "Butler-a-boo." The "a-boo" part doesn't sound very manly, until you understand that it comes from the Gaelic term *a buadh* (pronounced *ah-BOO-ah*), which means "to victory." The use of *slogan* to refer to a war-cry entered English in the early 1500s. By the early 1700s, the term had broadened so that it also referred to the distinctive phrase or cry of a person or group. The marketing version of the word first started appearing in the late 1800s.

slugabed

A *slugabed* is a person who prefers to stay in bed out of laziness. This is a word that probably needs no commentary (not that that will stop me). Slugabed seems to me to be the perfect description for someone too lazy, too slothful, too sluggardly to drag themselves out of bed. The word combines the noun *slug*, "a slow, lazy person; a sluggard" and the adverb *abed*, "in bed," and was coined by William Shakespeare. The Bard first used it in *Romeo and Juliet*. In Act V, Scene IV, the nurse comes to wake Juliet from her "unnatural sleep" and says:

> "Why Lamb, why Lady, fie you slugabed!"

At least Juliet had an excuse!

smell test

This idiom—usually seen in the longer phrase *X doesn't pass the smell test*—refers to a metaphoric test used to determine the legitimacy or authenticity of a situation. This fragrant phrase comes from the idea of smelling food in advance as a test to see if it has gone bad. Some similar tests are the *gasp test*—used to determine whether something is shocking or provocative—and the *giggle test* (or *laugh test*)—used to determine whether something is legitimate or serious.

smithereens

> Then you have a beautiful calm without a cloud, smooth sea, placid, crew and cargo in smithereens, Davy Jones' locker, moon looking down so peaceful. Not my fault, old cockalorum. —James Joyce, *Ulysses*, 1922

This passage from Joyce's famous novel imagines the aftermath of a shipwreck, where the result is the "crew and cargo in smithereens." The great and fun word *smithereens*, "small fragments," is more often seen in phrases such as *blow to smithereens* and *smash to smithereens*. The word has been in the language since the early nineteenth century, where it first appeared as *smiddereens*. That early spelling isn't surprising because the word came to English from the Irish term *smidirin*, which has the same meaning. The Irish often pronounce "th" as "dd" (for example, the lovely ale Smithwick's is pronounced *Smiddicks* by the Irish and would-be Irish), so some proper Englishman must have assumed the opposite: that the "dd" in *smiddereens* must really be a "th," making the "correct" pronunciation of the word *smithereens*.

smoke-easy

A *smoke-easy* is a place where cigarettes are smoked illegally; a private smoking club. It's an illogical-but-fun play on *speakeasy*, a place where alcohol is purchased and consumed illegally. *Speakeasy* dates to 1889, but it was popularized during Prohibition (1920 to 1933) when it was illegal to manufacture or sell alcohol in the United States. The word comes from the practice of speaking quietly in such places so as not to attract attention. That's why *smoke-easy* is illogical: smoking, as far as I know, is never that loud in the first place, and one presumes that people would still speak quietly in a smoke-easy so as not to draw unwelcome attention from the *lung huggers* (a synonym for anti-smoking activists that I once heard on the radio).

sneeze

> Constantyne sayth that fnesynge is a vyolent meuynge of ye brayne to putte out superfluytees of fumositees therof.
> Constantine says that sneezing is a violent moving of your brain to put out superfluities of fumes thereof.

The quotation (my rather stilted translation is underneath) comes from John de Trevisa's 1398 publication *On the Properties of Things.* Of particular note here is Trevisa's use of *fnesynge* for *sneezing.* What's up with *that?* It turns out that our word *sneeze* was originally spelled as *fnese,* which came from the verb *fnesan,* "to sneeze," which originated as the Old Norse term *fnysa,* "to snort." If you have ever seen pictures of old handwritten manuscripts, you may recall that the scribes wrote an "s" the same way as they wrote an "f", just without the little crossbar. Someone coming across the word *fnese* in a manuscript might miss the crossbar and, particularly since the letter combination "fn" at the front of a word is pretty much unheard of in English, would make the honest mistake of reading the word as *snese.* This occurred sometime around the end of the fifteenth century, and by the mid-sixteenth century the modern spelling of *sneeze* had taken root.

Another Fn-word

Besides *fnese,* the only other word that has appeared in English with an "fn" front-end is *fnast,* an obsolete (duh) word for "breath."

snowclone

> Toyota Canada Inc. managing director Stephen Beatty likes to say that while Eskimos have 100 words for "snow," auto manufacturers have 100 words for "beige." —*Edmonton Sun,* 2007

> If Eskimos have dozens of words for snow, Germans have as many for bureaucracy. —*The Economist,* 2003

Have you ever heard the story about how Eskimos have a huge number of words related to snow? It makes sense given the northern climes that Eskimos call home, but it turns out that it's just not true. They use, in fact, about the same number of snow-related words that we do. That Eskimo *factoid* (an inaccurate bit of information that gets accepted as true only because of constant repetition) is the source of many phrases that use the general format "If Eskimos have N words for snow, X have Y words for Z." This kind of thing has been called an *adaptable cliché frame*, but the linguist Glen Whitman used the Eskimo/snow variation to come up with a much snappier term: *snowclone*. I talk about the origins of a few snowclones elsewhere in the book, so check out *we don't need no stinking X!*; *welcome our new X overlords*; *X and Y and Z, oh my!*; *X is the new Y*. Here are a few others to watch out for:

> *Don't X me because I'm Y.*—from a series of 1980s ads for Pantene shampoo, each of which opened with a model saying "Don't hate me because I'm beautiful."

> *I am X, hear me Y.*—from the 1972 Helen Reddy song *I Am Woman*, which includes the lyric "I am woman, hear me roar."

> *I'm an X, not a Y!* or *Dammit Z, I'm an X, not a Y!*—from a number of episodes of the 1960s TV series *Star Trek*, the canonical example being "Dammit Jim, I'm a doctor, not an engineer!"

> *I'm not an X, but I play one on Y.*—from a 1986 ad for Vicks Formula 44 cough syrup, in which the actor Peter Bergman, a star on the soap opera *The Young and the Restless*, said "I'm not a doctor, but I play one on TV."

> *If X is wrong, I don't want to be right.*—from the title of the soul song "[If Loving You Is Wrong] I Don't Want to Be Right."

> *In X, no one can hear you Y.*—from the tagline of the 1979 movie *Alien*: "In space, no one can hear you scream."

soccer

North Americans are often ridiculed by the British (and, indeed, by the rest of the English-speaking world) for using the word *soccer* instead of the word FOOTBALL. These criticisms have always seemed a bit daft to me, since both Americans and Canadians already have a sport named *football*, and the idea of having two completely different sports using the same name makes my head hurt. And besides, the word *soccer* was actually coined in—wait for it—Britain! Hah! The story is that the official name of what the Brits call "football" is actually Association Football, and they also often use the name Association all on its own (for example, a phrase such as "Association rules" refers to the rules of Association Football). English speakers shed syllables whenever possible, so inevitably the word *Association* became just *Assoc*. Then, using the same linguistic process that turned *rugby* into *rugger* (and also *football* into *footer*), *Assoc* became *socker* (or *socca*) and then *soccer*. All of this happened in Britain in the late 1800s, so if anyone from that side of the pond chastises you for using the word *soccer* instead of *football*, you've got something to toss right back at him.

Moms as a Political Force

With every U.S. election cycle, the pollsters and spinmeisters anoint a new demographic as the Key to Winning the Election, and these are often moms. For example, in 2004 it was the *security moms* (defined as "women with children who believe the most important issue of the day is national security"). In 1998 it was the *waitress moms* ("women who are married, have children, work in a low-income job, and have little formal education"). The first and most famous of these are the *soccer moms*, "white, suburban women who are married and have children."

software

The suffix *-ware* means "things of the same general type or made of the same material." It comes from the Old English word *waru*, "goods." Software, of course, isn't really soft, so how did "soft" and "ware" get together? The short version of the story is that the word *hardware*—the physical components of a computer system—already existed when programs were invented. Since these programs could be viewed as the non-physical components of the computer, somebody thought the opposite of hardware—*soft*ware—would be the appropriate name.

S

souse

A *souse*, as you know, is a drunkard, and describing such a person as "pickled" would be appropriate both bibulously and etymologically. (Let me interrupt your regular programming to let you know that *bibulous*, "relating to the consumption of alcoholic drinks," comes from the Latin verb *bibĕre*, "to drink," which is also the source of our words *beer, beverage, bib*, and *imbibe*. See also SYMPOSIUM. We now return you to your regularly scheduled program, already in progress.) That's because the word *souse* came to us via the Old French verb *sous*, "to pickle." The source of that term was the Old High German *sulza* (with the same meaning), which comes from the stem *sult-*, "salt," which makes sense since the most common liquid used to pickle something is brine, which is heavily salted water. *Souse* started out in English in the late 1300s and referred to any part of an animal that had been pickled. By the mid-eighteenth century, *souse* had come to refer to plunging, immersing, or drenching something in water. Early in the twentieth century, a *souse* was a heavy bout of drinking, and then a few years later folks started using *souse* to refer to the person doing the heavy drinking.

sousveillance

> You have zero privacy, anyway. Get over it. —Scott McNeally, 1999

Are we becoming what Queen's University professor David Lyon has called the "surveillance society"? Is there hope for privacy? Scott McNeally, the CEO of Sun Microsystems, might not think so, but an increasing number of people are fighting back by using a technique called *sousveillance*, a form of counter-surveillance where people take pictures of surveillance cameras or record people in positions of power or authority and post those recordings on the web. (It's also sometimes called *inverse surveillance*.) University of Toronto professor Steve Mann calls it "watchful vigilance from underneath," which is a clue to the origins of this new word. (Mann coined the term in 2001.) The "sous" in *sousveillance* is French for "under," which makes it the opposite of the "sur" in *surveillance*, which is French for "over." (In both terms, the "veillance" part comes from the French verb *veiller*, "to watch.") Think of it as the watched watching the watchers. (There's even a World Sousveillance Day, which occurs on December 24.)

More Surveillance

The need for more sousveillance is perhaps bolstered by the increasing prevalence of *dataveillance*, the ability to monitor a person's activities by studying the data trail created by actions such as credit-card purchases, cell-phone calls, and Internet use. The word *dataveillance* is an inelegant blend of *data* and *surveillance*. It has been around since the late 1980s, but its use has jumped significantly over the past few years thanks to the increasingly widespread concerns for individual privacy in the Internet age. The term was coined in 1988 by Roger A. Clarke, a professor of computer science at the Australian National University. A synonym that isn't as popular, but rolls off the tongue a little better, is *consumer espionage*, which was coined by former *Wall Street Journal* reporter Erik Larson in his 1992 book, *The Naked Consumer*.

spam

Spam originally meant "flooding a newsgroup with irrelevant or inappropriate messages." This original sense derived from the overuse of the word "spam" in a sketch performed by the comedy troupe Monty Python's Flying Circus. The sketch begins as follows:

MR. BUN: Morning.

WAITRESS: Morning.

MR. BUN: Well, what you got?

WAITRESS: Well, there's egg and bacon; egg, sausage and bacon; egg and spam; egg, bacon and spam; egg, bacon, sausage and spam; spam, bacon, sausage and spam; spam, egg, spam, spam, bacon and spam; spam, sausage, spam, spam, spam, bacon, spam, tomato and spam; spam, spam, spam, egg and spam; spam, spam, spam, spam, spam, spam, baked beans, spam, spam, spam and spam …

However, it didn't take long for the meaning of *spam* to change to the unsolicited commercial e-mail messages that are the bane of every Internet user's existence. Spam, in case you don't know, is a luncheon meat consisting of compressed pork shoulder with a bit of ham tossed in. Apparently, some people eat it.

S

speakeasy

See SMOKE-EASY.

speako

> The faster I speak, the better my tablet PC transcribes. It won't choke, even at bursts over 200 w.p.m. ... This machine is a master of speakos and MONDEGREENS. —Richard Power, *The New York Times*, 2007

A *speako* is an error in speaking, especially when dictating to a voice recognition system. It's a "spoken typo," if you will. The word *typo*, "an error in typing or printing," has been in the language since at least the early 1800s. It actually began its lexical life as a shortened form of the phrase *typographical error*. *Speako* is the natural oral equivalent for the mistakes that occur when you're having what I like to call a "bad tongue day."

speed

The word *speed* is very old, appearing in texts from as far back as about 725. However, back then *speed* didn't mean what it does today. Instead, it originally referred to success, good fortune, or advancement, as well as abundance or wealth. By the middle of the thirteenth century, *speed* had also come to refer to one's fate or lot in life, and people would often say to someone "God send you good speed" (or, for those they didn't like, "God send you evil speed"). This is the source of the benediction *God-speed*, which is short for *may God speed you*. That is, "God-speed" is a wish for success, not haste. I suppose people have always been in a hurry to be successful, because the word *speed* first starting showing up in the "quickness; rapidity" sense around 1000. I should note, too, that the same Indo-European root (see the sidebar near QUEEN for some background on Indo-European) that produced *speed* in English also led to the Latin term *speres*, "hopes," which ultimately gave us our words *prosper*, *prosperity*, and *despair* ("without hope").

spendthrift

A *spendthrift* is a person who spends lots of money, usually wastefully. The *spend* part makes sense, but what's up with the *thrift* part, since this word refers to *saving* money? Ah, you and I associate thrift with frugality and economy, but it wasn't always thus. The original meaning of *thrift* was "prosperity; success," and although this meaning has long been obsolete, it lives on in the word *thrive*. So a spendthrift, then, was a person who would give away (spend) his prosperity (thrift).

spin

All human endeavors have an element of art to them, where by "art" I mean a high level of skill. We have the "art of war," the "art of the deal," and even the "art of motorcycle maintenance, Zen and the." Political skill is most often seen in the art of *spin*, which means to convey information or cast another person's remarks or actions in a biased or slanted way so as to favorably influence public opinion. As a noun it refers to the information provided in such a fashion. This stalwart member of the political lexicon (it first appeared in 1977) probably came from phrases such as "putting a positive (or negative) spin" on something. In turn, this notion of influencing direction almost certainly made the leap from sports such as baseball and billiards where players impart spin on a ball to change its course.

More Spin Stuff

Spinning has become such an art form that it has generated its own vocabulary. For example, the adjective *spinnable* means "capable of or susceptible to being influenced by biased or slanted information." The word *Spinnish* means "the language used by spin doctors and other political operatives." Finally, there's *Zen spin*, "to spin a story by not doing any spinning at all."

spoils

The *spoils* are either the valuables or property seized by the winner of a conflict (in which case they're usually called the *spoils of war*), or the benefits and rewards that accrue to the winner of any kind of contest.

That's all well and good, but why in the name of Julius Caesar would anyone want "spoils"? Isn't that a bad thing? Not when you realize that instead of the "waste" sense of the word *spoil*, we're really talking here about the older sense of "theft," which came to English from the Old French term *espoillier*, "plunder," which in turn was based on the Latin term *spoliāre*. That word came from *spolium*, which at first referred to the hide stripped from a carcass, but later referred to armor stripped from a vanquished foe.

spyware

Spyware is a plague upon the earth that threatens to deprive a significant portion of the online world of its sanity, but what is it, exactly? As often happens with new concepts, the term *spyware* has become encrusted with multiple meanings as people attach similar ideas to a convenient and popular label. However, spyware is generally defined as any program that surreptitiously monitors a user's computer activities—particularly the typing of passwords, PINs, and credit-card numbers—or harvests sensitive data on the user's computer, and then sends that information to an individual or a company via the user's Internet connection. In other words, it's a program (hence the -*ware* suffix) used to "spy" on someone's computer activities. Linguistic proof of the cultural impact of spyware is the large number of synonyms that have popped up in the past few years. These include *sneakware, stealthware, snoopware, trackware, thiefware*, or, tellingly, *scumware*. A spyware program is also sometimes called an *E.T. application*, because it "phones home" to secretly send data to an online destination.

squirrel

Many people love to watch squirrels frolic on the ground and in the trees, and it must have been a squirrel fan who wrote the *OED*'s definition, which describes them as "slender, graceful, agile ... characterized by a long bushy tail, furry coat, and bright eyes." On the other hand, gardeners aren't big on squirrels since these members of the rodent family dig up bulbs and have the perverse habit of biting off the tops of tulips just as they're about to bloom! However, just about everybody admires a squirrel's tail, which may be how this animal got its name.

The original is the Greek term that combines *skia*, "shade," and *oura*, "tail" to give the name *skiouros*, "shady-tail." Apparently the ancient Greeks thought the squirrel used its large tail to protect itself from the sun, a supposition that may even be true.

stalking horse

A *stalking horse* is a political candidate put forward either to split the vote with an existing candidate or to conceal the candidacy of another person. This is a hunting term that refers to a horse behind which a sneaky hunter would hide while stalking his quarry.

starboard

The right-hand side of a ship is called the *starboard* side, but although early sailors would often steer by the stars, the word *starboard* has more to do with steering than stars. That's because the original word was the Old English *stéorbord*, which combines *stéor*, "steer," and *bord*, "board," and referred to a ship's rudder. Since the rudder was usually found on the right side of the ship, that side became known as the *stéorbord* as early as the ninth century, and the term eventually morphed into *starboard* by the seventeenth century.

On Your Left!

The left side of a boat is called the *port* side because when a ship is docked, it must sit with its left side to the pier since the rudder on the starboard side would be in the way. The opening on the left side of the ship used for loading and unloading cargo has long been known as the *port*, and that term eventually applied to the entire left side.

steal someone's thunder

In 1709, the playwright John Dennis opened a new production of a play called *Appius and Virginia*. The play itself is largely forgotten except for one technical detail: Dennis figured out that he could generate an effective simulation of the sound of thunder by having someone shake a large sheet of tin backstage. This innovation in sound effects notwith-standing, the play closed after just a few nights' run. It was replaced by a production of Shakespeare's *Macbeth* and, well, let me give the *Biographica Britannica* the honor of explaining what happened next:

> Some nights after, Mr. Dennis, being in the pit at the represen-tation of "Macbeth," heard his own thunder made use of; upon which he rose in a violent passion, and exclaimed, with an oath, that it was his thunder. "See," said he, "how the rascals use me! They will not let my play run, and yet they steal my thunder!"

The story was justly famous in its day and long after, and the wonderful phrase *steal my thunder* became part of the language. By the turn of the twentieth century, to *steal someone's thunder* meant "to prevent someone from receiving praise or acclaim for an idea or action by putting forth that idea or performing that action first."

He'll Be a Vile

For the record, I should also mention that John Dennis is famous for one other quotation: "A man who could make so vile a pun would not scruple to pick a pocket."

steampunk

This term refers to a relatively new literary genre, which applies sci-ence fiction or fantasy elements to historical settings and that features steam-powered, mechanical machines rather than electronic devices. Okay, fine, but where'd the weirdo name come from? First, you need to go back to another literary form called *cyberpunk*. This science fiction subgenre (although there are antecedents, William Gibson's 1982 novel *Neuromancer* is generally considered to be the first example) places com-puters, networks, and electronics (the *cyber-* part) inside a future that's anarchic and often dystopian (the *punk* part; from the anarchic, dysto-pian punk rock music of the 1970s). Move the setting to the past, espe-cially the Victorian Age, take out the electronics and replace them with mechanical devices, especially elaborate, steam-powered contraptions, and you have a new genre: steampunk. Steampunk often imagines what the past would have been like if the future hadn't happened so quickly. It imagines, in other words, what engineers and inventors might have come up with if they'd had another, say, 100 years to tinker with mechanical and steam-powered machines. (Some examples: a steam-powered flamethrower; a spaceship made of steel and wood.)

stem-winder

A *stem-winder* is a stirring political speech. This curious phrase comes from the stem-winding watch, the kind you wind by turning a small knob on the side. When these watches first came out in the latter half of the nineteenth century, they became instantly popular, and the adjective *stem-winding* was soon used to refer to anything that was first-rate, such as a particularly good speech.

Stepford

This adjective described a person who is unthinking, conformist, and uncritical. This comes from Ira Levin's 1972 book *The Stepford Wives*. (It was later made into a movie of the same title with a screenplay by William Goldman, as well as a remake starring Nicole Kidman.) The women of Stepford (a New York suburb) are creepily content with their lives as wives, mothers, and housekeepers. And no wonder: it turns out they're all automatons, programmed by their husbands to embrace "traditional" wifely duties and conform to their husbands' norms. Ever since, Stepford has been used to describe someone who goes through life robotically or compliantly. You sometimes see *Stepford* used as a standalone word, but it's most often seen right before a noun, particularly a type of person, such as *Stepford employee*, *Stepford children*, or *Stepford politician*.

story

You know full well that a *story* is a fictional or factual account of an event. It comes our way via the Greek word *historia*, "narrative; an account of events" (which, as you'll no doubt have guessed by now, was also the source of our word *history*). But what about the *other* meaning of *story*: "a floor in a building"? How the heck do we get from a narrative to a floor? The answer is that once upon a time there were floors that were actually narratives. Seriously. In particular, you often saw buildings, especially churches, where one floor would display a series of paintings or stained glass images that depicted some kind of narrative (such as a tale from the Bible). Architects of the day (this goes way back to at least the thirteenth century) called such a floor a *historia*. By the fifteenth century, this word had morphed to *story* and had generalized to mean "a floor or level of a building."

stringer

A *stringer* is a reporter who freelances or works part-time for the newspaper. He usually covers only a specific subject or geographical area and is most often paid by the column inch (which is an area of text or space that's one column wide and one inch high). This also gives the origin of the word: to get paid, the reporter would paste all his clippings together to form a string, and an editor would measure the string to find the total number of column inches.

stump

The word *stump* is a bit of political lingo that's used as the general term for the places where a candidate gives speeches. Why a *stump* of all things? Because in days of yore, candidates rarely had official podiums from which to regale their audiences. So, instead, they would often climb onto a nearby tree stump and hold forth from there.

A Stumper

Ever wondered why when a person is baffled by something, we described that person as *stumped*? This term, too, has tree roots, as it comes from the pioneer conundrum of trying to figure out a way to plow land that had been hastily cleared and so was still studded with difficult-to-remove tree stumps.

suburban

The word *suburban*, "of or relating to a residential district bordering a city," is a curious term. The "urban" part makes sense, because it comes straight from the word *urban*, "of or relating to a city." But what in the name of sidewalk-less streets is up with the *sub-* prefix? Snobby city types will tell you that it indicates the suburbs are "below" the city because there are fewer cultural institutions, fewer restaurants, and sidewalk-less streets. Nice try! The real story is that in this case the prefix *sub-* means "near," so the word *suburb* literally means "near a city." Interestingly, although both *suburban* and *suburb* feel like modern coinages, they have a Latin root in the word *suburbium*, a combination of *sub-*, "near," and *urbs*, "city."

suede

Do you have a pair of suede gloves? If so, did they come from Sweden? Probably not physically, but they certainly did etymologically. Back in the nineteenth century, the Swedes were known in fashionable circles for their soft, undressed kid-skin, a material they used to make gloves. These sought-after fashion accessories were fancy, but they didn't have a fancy name, being known simply as *gants de Suède*, "gloves of Sweden." Eventually the material was used for other clothing, and eventually the word migrated to English, first as *Suède*, then as *suède*, and finally as the accent-less *suede*, in the 1920s.

supercilious

> His mother eyed me in silence with a supercilious air. —Tobias Smollett, *The Expedition of Humphry Clinker*, 1771

To "eye" someone with a supercilious air is rather appropriate, as you'll soon see. The word *supercilious* means "haughtily contemptuous or arrogant," and has been a paid-up member of the English language since the sixteenth century. It came our way directly from the Latin term *superciliōsus*. Where things get weird is that this Latin word is derived from *supercilium*, which means, of all things, "eyebrow"! This term combines the prefix *super-*, "above," and the word *cilium*, "eyelash" (or "eyelid"). The thinking here is that a haughtily arrogant person would often show his feelings by raising an eyebrow to express superiority or by lowering his eyebrows as part of an overall look of stern contempt. This expressiveness eventually led to the adjective *supercilious*, meaning "to use one's eyebrows to express superiority or contempt," and later the word came to refer to just the feelings themselves.

surly

> In my stars I am above thee; but be not afraid of greatness: some
> are born great, some achieve greatness, and some have greatness
> thrust upon 'em. Thy Fates open their hands; let thy blood and
> spirit embrace them; and, to inure thyself to what thou art like
> to be, cast thy humble slough and appear fresh. Be opposite with
> a kinsman, surly with servants. —William Shakespeare, *Twelfth
> Night*, 1601

If you come across a man who's *surly*, "rude; bad-tempered," you probably wouldn't be inclined to call that person "sir," but back in the
fourteenth century you wouldn't have had a choice. That's because the
word *surly* is actually a variation on the now obsolete term *sirly*, which
had a literal meaning of "sir-like" (where *sir* refers to the title used
exclusively in those days by knights and baronets), but in actual use it
meant "lordly; haughty." In the sixteenth century the spelling changed
to *surly*, for some reason, and the meaning changed, too, from "lordly"
to "imperious" to "arrogant" and finally to the modern sense of "churl-
ishly ill-humored" (as the *OED* nicely puts it).

sweepstakes

A *sweepstakes* is a contest in which a prize is offered to the winning
name drawn from the contest entrants, or which offers monetary prizes
based on the amount of money the players have entered. Most modern
sweepstakes offer several prizes, but that wasn't always the case. It used
to be that the sweepstakes prize was given to a single winner, and that
explains the origin of the word, which combines *sweep* and *stakes*, the
latter referring to the sum of money involved in a game. The idea here
is to think of the winner "sweeping" all the money toward himself and
into his pocket or purse.

swill

You may be wondering if the noun *swill* ("unpalatable or inferior food")
and the verb *swill* ("to drink quickly, greedily, or in large amounts")
are related. Why yes, they are as a matter of fact. *Swill* was originally

the table scraps and other kitchen refuse that was fed to the hogs. That explains the noun sense of *swill*. The verb sense of *swill* comes from eating or drinking "quickly and greedily," which is what a hog would do.

symposium

To get to the origins of this word, let's begin with a seemingly misguided side trip to the word *imbibe*, which means "to drink, particularly an alcoholic beverage." The origin of this word is the Latin verb *biběre*, "to drink." (See SOUSE for a bit more on this Latin term.) An even earlier form of the Latin *biběre* eventually became our words *potable*, "fit to drink," and *poisonous*, "unfit or dangerous to drink (or eat, or whatever)." Completing the round trip, the old form of *biběre* also gave us *symposium*, "a conference for the discussion of a topic." How did *that* happen? It turns out that *symposium's* original Latin meaning was "drinking party"!

S

tabby

You might not think your cat is in any way connected with the city of Baghdad, and you're right, it's not. Unless, of course, you want to talk about *linguistic* connections (that's why we're here, after all), and on that score your cat just might have some Baghdad in its background. This is particularly true if she is a *tabby*, "a cat with a brownish or grey coat that's dark-striped or brindled." You see, long ago (as far back as the twelfth century) there was a section of Baghdad called Attābiy, which was named after Prince Attāb of the Omayyad dynasty. This area of Baghdad was famous for its striped silk taffeta, which was called *Attābiya*. That term migrated to France in the fourteenth century as *atabis* and then *tabis*. The word crossed over to England in the early seventeenth century, first as *taby* and later as *tabby*. The striping on these tabby silks reminded some people of the striping on certain cats, and in 1665 one writer referred to a cat as "tabby-coloured." By the end of the seventeenth century the phrase *tabby-cat* had become common, and the first recorded use of just *tabby* on its own came in 1774. For more "catymology," see TOMCAT.

tabloid

A *tabloid* is a smaller-format paper, usually about half the size of a broadsheet (that is, about 10 to 11 inches across and about 14 to 18 inches high). The *-oid* suffix in tabloid means "resembling or having the form of." Strangely, the *tabl-* prefix is short for *tablet*, one definition of which is "a small, flat pellet of medicine." It turns out that the original meaning of tabloid was a trademarked name for a pill-like medicinal substance invented and sold in the late 1800s! However, another meaning of *tablet* is "a small piece of material for writing," and that's probably where the newspaper form of tabloid came from.

tadpole

In the early days of a tadpole's life, this frog or toad larva looks pretty much like it's all head, with just a bit of a tail for getting around the pond. That observation is where the word *tadpole* comes from: the Middle English word *tadde*, "toad," plus *poll*, "head," so the literal meaning of the word is "toad-head" (which actually sounds like a pretty good insult). The old word *poll* came to English via the Middle Dutch term *pol*, "top," which later became *polle*, "the top of the head." We still see *poll* used in the "head" sense today (for example, in the phrase *poll tax*), but mostly we use the word to mean "a survey of public opinion," a sense that probably developed from the idea of counting people (a *head count*).

takes the cake

See CAKEWALK.

tantalize

This verb means "to torment someone by allowing that person to see something they strongly desire but can't have; to tease." *Tantalize* comes from the Greek myth of Tantalus, a mortal son of Zeus who was allowed to eat with the gods. When Tantalus took some of the gods' forbidden food and drink to earth, Zeus condemned him cruelly but appropriately: stricken with a constant thirst and hunger, Tantalus was placed neck-deep in water and with fruit hanging just overhead. But when he bent down to drink, the water drained away, only to return again when he straightened up. And when he reached for the fruit, the wind would always blow it just out of reach. A tantalizing fate indeed.

tawdry

If you hear something described as *tawdry*, you almost certainly think that thing is cheap, gaudy, and of poor quality. However, you'll no doubt be surprised to hear that for many hundreds of years the word *tawdry* was associated with items of the highest quality! The story behind this massive and surprising semantic shift begins way back in the seventh century when there lived a queen named Aethelthryth, also known, thankfully, as Etheldrida. She was a kind, pious woman who founded a monastery and devoted her entire life to helping the poor. Her only vanity was a love of scarves and necklaces of the highest quality, and when she later developed throat cancer, she saw this as divine retribution for her passion. After her death, her name was changed to Audrey, and she was eventually made a saint, with an annual Saint Audrey festival held in her honor. As a tribute to the old queen, festival merchants featured gorgeous scarves made of the finest lace, which eventually became known as *St. Audrey's lace*. By the middle of the sixteenth century, the last "t" in "Saint" had become stuck to "Audrey" (linguists call this common process *elision*) and the material had become known as *taudrey lace*, and then later *tawdry lace*. This material was still of the highest quality and much sought-after by those who could afford it, and it was famous throughout Britain. That fame led unscrupulous merchants to make cheaper and gaudier versions of the lace to sell to the masses. These eventually overran the market, and the knockoffs themselves became known as *tawdry lace*. This was eventually shortened to *tawdry*, first as a noun and then as an adjective, and by the late seventeenth century, the sense of cheapness and gaudiness associated with the fake lace had transferred to the word *tawdry* itself.

taxi

We don't normally associate taxis with taxes, but you're free to do so from a linguistic standpoint. Back in the 1890s, some enterprising German, tired no doubt of arbitrary fares charged when hiring a vehicle for transportation, invented the *taxameter*, a device that automatically computed the distance traveled and the fare owed. This word combined the Medieval Latin term *taxa*, "tax," with *-meter*, "measure." The French version was the *taximèter*, which blends *taxe*, "tariff" with *-meter*. Both terms were used in English for most of the 1890s and 1900s, but by 1907 the term *taxi-cab* and its shortened form *taxi* had entered the language for good.

technoburb

It used to be that the names sociologists and geographers used to label and describe populated areas were mostly related to their proximity to an urban center. A SUBURB is a community situated just outside the city, while an *exurb* or *edge city* is a community that lies just outside of the suburbs. Lately, however, the focus has shifted and areas now most often have labels that reflect their infrastructure, amenities, or population. For example, in recent years we've seen the rise of a new kind of exurb with decentralized, city-quality infrastructure, industries, and services: the *technoburb*. A technoburb is an example of an "accidental city," an exurb that, over time and without design, morphs into a true city, although with its amenities and services decentralized and spread throughout the community. Technoburbia forms part of what some call the "middle landscape," the area between where a large city's suburbs end and the rural regions begin. The word *technoburb* was coined by history professor Robert Fishman in his 1987 book *Bourgeois Utopias*. Why the *techno-* prefix for the citylike exurb? Because, as Fishman writes, "the real basis of the new city is the invisible web of advanced technology and telecommunications that has been substituted for the face-to-face contact and physical movement of older cities." This idea is reflected in some of the synonyms we're seeing for these emerging exurban cityscapes: *post-urban city, centerless city, urban village,* and *suburban downtown.*

teetotaler

> Teetotaler, n. One who abstains from strong drink, sometimes totally, sometimes tolerably totally. —Ambrose Bierce, *The Devil's Dictionary*, 1911

A *teetotaler* is a person who completely abstains from alcohol; it's a person who is ON THE WAGON. Lots of people think that the "tee" part of this word is a variation on "tea" because that what's an abstainer would (or should) drink instead of the hard stuff. Close, but no etymological cigar. The real story is that it's actually a form of reduplication (see the sidebar near HIGHFALUTIN). To see what I mean, first consider phrases such as "That guy's rich with a capital R" and "She's capital-B bossy." (Not to forget my personal favorite, "ugly with a capital ugh.") In each case, the adjective gets strengthened by emphasizing the first letter. That's sort of what happened with *teetotaler*. First consider this bit of Americana from 1832:

> It's a mercy, madam, that the cowardly varments had n't used you up, body-aciously. These Mingoes act mighty redick'lous with women and children. They aint the raal true grit, no how. Vile on them! They ought to be essentially, and particularly, and tee-totally obflisticated off of the face of the whole yearth.

The colorful language is from someone the author (Judge James Hall) calls a "Kentucky backwoodsman." Our concern here is the use of *tee-totally* as an adverb, where the addition of *tee* (the letter T spelled out) serves to strengthen the word *total*. This is a kind of reduplication. Around the same time (1833, in fact) a fellow named Richard "Dicky" Turner was said to have made a speech advocating total abstinence from alcohol, as opposed to just abstaining from hard liquor. In his speech, Mr. Turner used the word *tee-total* to describe such complete abstinence. The quickly became popular among other nondrinkers, and within a few years the noun *tee-totaller* (later *teetotaler*) had become a permanent part of the language. Interestingly, Richard Turner may be the only person in the world who coined a word and had this feat engraved upon his tombstone:

> Dicky Turner, now celebrated as being the author of the word Tee-total

tenterhooks

If you find yourself in a state of unbearable suspense, you might be inclined to describe yourself as being *on tenterhooks*. This figuratively painful-sounding state would have been a quite literally painful state a few hundred years ago when there still existed things called *tenterhooks*. These were small metal hooks (or sometimes bent nails) that ran along the bars of a device called a *tenter*, which was used for drying freshly woven wool. The wool was stretched between the frames of the ten-ter, and attached using the tenterhooks. The wool was then left out in a field for a while to dry. This was the last stage in the wool-making process, so it must have been hard for the weaver to wait for the wool to get ready so that it could be sold, and this state of suspense led to the modern meaning of the phrase *on tenterhooks*, even though both tenters and the hooks they used have long since faded into history.

that's not an X; *this* is an X

You use this SNOWCLONE when you want to contrast something you have with some other thing, particularly to point out how much more impressive yours is. The origin of this catchphrase is the 1986 movie *Crocodile Dundee*, where the title character (played by Paul Hogan) is threatened with a knife on the streets of New York. He gives the mugger's knife a disdainful look, says "that's not a knife," pulls out a massive bush knife, and says "*that's* a knife." Note that although the original phrase was "that's not a knife; *that's* a knife," most people use the snowclone with the second "that" replaced by "this": "that's not a knife; *this* is a knife."

thesaurus

You'd be unlikely ever to confuse a MAGAZINE and a thesaurus, but the two words are actually near-synonyms, at least etymologically. That's because, as I mentioned earlier, the origins of *magazine* lie in the Arabic term *makhzan*, "storehouse," and the origins of *thesaurus* lie in the Greek term *thesauros*, "storehouse." That Greek word also means "treasure" and that sense entered Old French as *tresor*, "treasure" (see TREASURE TROVE), and it infiltrated English back in the twelfth century as *tresor*, and was finally spelled as *treasure* in the early seventeenth century. The Greek term *thesauros* that started all this also made its way into Latin, where it became *thesaurus*, "treasury," and that term lurked in the Latin weeds for centuries while all this *treasure* business was going on. In the sixteenth century, some authors began using *thesaurus* to refer to a "treasury" or "storehouse" of knowledge, sort of like an encyclopedia or dictionary. The first such effort was the *Thesaurus Linguae Romanae et Britannicae* (that's the *Thesaurus of the Roman Tongue and the British* to you and I), published in 1565 by Thomas Cooper (and so more popularly known as *Cooper's Dictionary*). The big news came in 1852 with the publication of Peter Mark Roget's justly famous *Thesaurus of English Words and Phrases*. This may sound heretical, but Roget's thesaurus was *not* a collection of synonyms! Instead, he organized the book into various categories, and within each category he included a list of related words. People have an alarming tendency to see the world the way they want, and in this case they saw Roget's publication as a collection of synonyms, and by the turn of the twentieth century, the sense of *thesaurus* as "a book of synonyms" had become entrenched, established, ensconced, implanted, embedded, and rooted in the language.

thimble

You, dear reader, may use your thimble on your finger, but from an etymological point of view, the humble thimble is literally a "thumb instrument." Here's why: the word *thimble* comes from the Old English term *thýmel*, which was originally a sheath or covering for the thumb. It's a blend of the word *thúma*, "thumb," and the suffix *-el*, "instrument," which is an older version of the suffix *-le* used in words such as *handle* and *ladle*. By the early fifteenth century, the word *themel* had come to mean "a protective cap worn on a finger and used to push a needle through fabric." Later in the fifteenth century, some speakers felt there ought to be a *b* after the *m* (as in words such as *bumble*, *humble*, and *mumble*), and it's been all-thimble ever since.

Thimblerig

It would be a crying shame to pass by the word *thimble* without mentioning the terrific term *thimblerig*. This is an old game (the word first appeared in English in 1825) practiced by swindlers who'd place three thimbles on a table, ostensibly place a pea under one of them, and then shuffle the thimbles rapidly. The victim (also called the *mark*) would bet on which thimble held the pea, and would invariably lose since the pea was never placed under any of them! The game was also called, less creatively, *pea and thimbles*. Modern-day thumbleriggers run a similar con called the *shell game*, which replaces the thimbles with walnut shells, as well as a card-based con called *Three-Card Monte*.

thing

It's hard to find a word more bland and innocuous than *thing*, so you'd think there wouldn't be much of a history behind this workaday word. Think again! Way back in the oldest of Old English (we're talking the

600s here), the verbal phrase *thing gehégan* meant "to hold a meeting," and from that emerged just the word *thing*, "a meeting or assembly, particularly a court or council." Later, the meaning of *thing* broadened to "a matter brought before a court of law; a legal process," and later still to "a business, concern, or matter." This broadening just kept happening, and by about 1000, *thing* had come to refer to "an entity of any kind."

thug

Earlier in the book I told you the story of the *hashishiyun*, the murderous hash-eaters who gave us our word ASSASSIN. The word *thug*, "a ruffian or cutthroat," also comes to us from a notorious band of murderers: the Thag, a religious sect based in northern India who worshipped the goddess Kali. These ne'er-do-wells would rob wealthy travelers, strangle them, and then bury them. Nice bunch! In the seventeenth century they were known as *p'hansigars*, "stranglers," but by the early nineteenth century they were called Thags (or sometimes Thegs). This name comes from the Hindu word *thag*, "thief." The word bounced into English as *thug*, and our sense of a thug as a ruffian first entered the language around 1839, when the great writer Thomas Carlyle quoted some wag who referred to a gang as "Glasgow Thugs," and Carlyle called it a "witty nickname."

tidbit

Here's a *tidbit*, "a small piece of interesting news or gossip" about the word *tidbit*, "a bite-sized piece of tasty food." The food sense was the original, and it comes from the now-obsolete adjective *tyd*, which Samuel Johnson in his famous *Dictionary of the English Language* from 1755 defined as "tender; soft; nice." Combined with *bit*, "a small piece," you get a *tyd bit*, "a toothsome morsel" (as the *OED* mouth-wateringly defines it), a phrase that first showed up around 1640. The phrase turned into *tid-bit* by the turn of the eighteenth century, and then became *tidbit* a couple of hundred years later. For some reason, the Brits changed the *tid* part to *tit*, a word used to refer to any small animal, and also used in combinations such as *titmouse*, *titlark*, and *titling* (a kind of sparrow). So when you're in North America you hear *tidbit*, but when you're in Britain you hear *titbit*.

tinker's damn

The phrase *not worth a tinker's damn* (or a *tinker's curse*) means "useless or worthless." One explanation of this curious phrase is that the original tinkers (a *tinker* is a traveling craftsman who mends household utensils such as pots, pans, and kettles) apparently swore a lot, so a single curse didn't mean much. Others believe it's a corruption of *tinker's dam*, a wall (that is, a dam) made of dough or clay and placed around a spot where the tinker needed to pour solder. This dam would then be thrown away once the solder dried.

tissue

Tissue is a collection of similar cells and intercellular material that act together to form a structural component within the body. The four most common types are muscle, nerve, epidermal (the outer layer of skin), and connective (bone, cartilage, and other connecting and supporting structures). Tissue structures appear to be "woven" together, so it's not surprising that the word *tissue* goes back to the Latin *tistre*, "to weave."

tittle

See TO A T.

to a T

The curious phrase *to a T* means "with minute exactness; to the smallest particular." For example, if something suits you to a T, it means that thing is just right for you down to the smallest detail. You might be tempted to assume that the "T" in question here is the T-square used by draughtsman and carpenters to draw lines perfectly at right angles to each other. Good guess, indeed, but not one that's supported by the etymological evidence, I'm afraid. The problem is that the first in-print use of *T-square* occurred in 1785, while the phrase *to a T* first shows up in written form in 1693. (Tantalizingly, a 1701 math textbook defines a "Tee" as "a double Square in the form of a T." Close, but still not the linguistic cigar we're looking for.) However, there's the older phrase *to a tittle* which, happily for our investigations, has the same meaning as *to a T* and first appeared in the language in 1607. Sweet! So, clearly, the phrase *to a T* is just a short form of *to a tittle*. Okay, but what about this curious word *tittle*? Beginning in the sixteenth century, people used that word to refer to the dot over the lowercase letter *i*, so *to a tittle* referred to the finest details of something, equivalent to dotting all the i's in a manuscript. *Tittle*, by the way, comes from the Latin *titulus*, which referred to an inscription written over something. It's the source of the word *title*, but the variant *tittle* came about because we "write" the dot over the letter *i*.

toady

The unattractive word *toady* refers to a person who shamelessly uses flattery and favors to gain approval with another. How is a tailless, froglike amphibian related to a shameless flatterer? Many years ago, certain quacks would set up shop in fairs and towns to sell supposedly medicinal potions. To demonstrate the healing powers of these "remedies," a young boy (secretly the charlatan's assistant) would swallow a toad, which in those days was thought to be poisonous. The lad would duly keel over, but a quick sip of the medicine would have him back on his feet. Clearly, an assistant like that would do just about anything to gain favor, so over time any such person became known as a *toadeater*, which was eventually shortened to *toady*.

tomacco

See PLUOT.

tomcat

If a certain type of man *tomcats* around, it means he spends much of his time seeking sexual partners (and succeeding in his quest). You might think that this term's origins are simple: it comes from the noun *tomcat*, a male cat, which when they're let outdoors will often chase after female cats when they're not torturing mice and doing their business in your garden. True enough, but the story's a bit more complex (and a bit more interesting) than that. Prior to about 1760, a male cat was known as a *he-cat*, a *gib-cat* (*gib* is short for *Gilbert*) a *ram-cat*, or even a *boar-cat*. (Rams and boars are the males of their respective species, so these last two terms make some sense, although they're a bit odd.) Sometimes people would even refer to cats using a generic name such as Tybert,

T

Rutterkin, Puss, or even Roger. So what happened in 1760? Ah, that was the year an anonymous scribe published a somewhat racy book called *The Life and Adventures of a Cat*. The subject of the book was a male (or "ram") cat named Tom, and our hero spent much of his time chasing after the ladies (which were often called *doe-cats* in those days). Within a few years *Tom* (or *tomcat*) had become the favorite generic name for a cat, and by the late 1800s *tomcat*, meaning "lecherous man," had entered the language (with the verb to follow in the 1920s). Can't get enough about cats? Then see TABBY, earlier in the book.

tomfoolery

This enjoyable word refers to foolish or silly behavior and it comes from the noun *tomfool*, "a half-wit; a remarkably foolish person," from which we also get *tomfool idea*, "an extremely stupid or foolish notion." The original spelling of tomfool was *Tom Fool*, and there's written evidence of the latter all the way back to the fourteenth century! Who was this Tom and why was he such a fool? The "Tom" part comes from the long-standing use of "Tom" as a generic name for an unknown person (as in *Tom, Dick, and Harry*). The "Fool" part comes from the strange fact that, in less enlightened times, people were often allowed to visit insane asylums as a form of "entertainment." If the audience saw someone who was deranged in a particularly amusing way, they would nickname him "Tom Fool," and the epithet was later used in nonasylum settings.

torpedo

If you stretch your imagination way, way out until it's just this side of the breaking point, you can see a torpedo as a kind of fish. After all, a torpedo is a self-propelled underwater weapon, and a fish is a self-propelled underwater nonweapon. However, you don't need any imagination at all to see a torpedo as a fish etymologically, because the word *torpedo* comes from the Latin word *torpedo*, "electric ray." In turn, that word came from the Latin *torpēre*, "numb," because the electric ray's sting causes a numbing sensation. (The Latin *torpēre* was also the source of the English word *torpid*, "benumbed; dormant.") For a while, the word *torpedo* in English meant "someone or something that has a numbing influence." Navy types must have applied *torpedo* to the weapon either because it "numbs" a ship by disabling (or sinking) it, or (perhaps more convincingly) because it "stings" a ship when it strikes.

Please Quit!

In modern workplace slang, a *torpedo* is an inept employee who quits (probably with more than a little encouragement) to work for a rival company.

towhead

We sometimes call a person with blond or pale yellow hair a *towhead* (or described that person as *towheaded*), but what on Earth does being blonde have to do with the word *tow*, "to pull something"? In a word, nothing! That's because the *tow* in question here isn't the "pull" sense, but a more ancient sense that in Old English was used as a prefix that meant "spinning; weaving." (For example, in Old English the art of spinning raw fibers was called *towcraeft*.) Later the word *tow* came to refer to the fibers themselves, particularly flax, which in its raw state is a light yellow color. That flax color is close enough to the hair color of some people, so those people were called *tow-heads*. (Etymological bonus: this is why a person with light or blonde hair is also sometimes described as *flaxen-haired*.)

tragus

The *tragus* (*TRAY·gus*) is the pointed flap of cartilage that rises just above the earlobe and partially covers the entrance to the inner ear. The history of the word *tragus* goes back to the Greek word *tragos*, "a male goat," which is a bit of a brow-furrower. The explanation is that the tragus area is also where ear hairs sprout, so the combination of the hairs and the tragus must have reminded the Greeks of a billy goat and the "beard" of hair that hangs under his chin. (As an aside, the male goat's beard is also the source of the word *goatee*, "a beard that covers only the chin.")

trapeze

Trapeze artists are amateur mathematicians of a sort, because they're always working out angles and other on-the-fly (literally) calculations to ward off death (or, at least, the ignominy of a fall into the net). The mathematical nature of the art is also reflected in the word *trapeze*, which flies back to the Latin term *trapezium*, which in turn came from the Greek *trapezion*, both of which are geometry terms that refer to a four-sided figure with two parallel sides. (The term *trapezion* is the diminutive of *trapeza*, "table.") I know, I know, no trapeze apparatus that *you* have ever seen looks like that. However, the original trapeze equipment was a lot different. The basic setup was a crossbar suspended by ropes from the roof or a longer beam. The bar and roof (or beam) were parallel to each other (so that's the parallel sides part) and the ropes holding the bar would form the other two sides. This apparatus was called a *trapeze* in French (from the Latin *trapezium*), and that term swung into English in the 1860s.

The Trapezoid/Trapezium Mess

If you live in North America, your geometry teacher told you that a *trapezoid* is a four-sided shape (she'd have called it a *quadrilateral*, bless her) where two of the sides are parallel to each other. If you live anywhere else, however, she'd have called this geometric figure a *trapezium*. Back in North America, the word *trapezium* is reserved for a four-sided shape where none of the sides are parallel, a geometric figure that the rest of the world calls a *trapezoid*. Confused? Of course!

travel

Do you hate to travel? I know I do. I mean, I enjoy being somewhere else, but I despise getting there. Lots of other people must have had the same feelings over the years, because the word *travel* is just a variation on the word *travail*, "suffering; painful effort or labor." Sounds about right! But wait, it gets better (or worse, depending on which side you're looking at). The noun *travail* comes from the verb *travail*, "to torment, distress." That verb, via a fairly circuitous route, goes back to the Latin *trepaliāre*, "to torture," a verb based on the noun *trepālium*, "an instrument or engine of torture"! In modern English, this is now called "an economy class seat."

treasure trove

> Treasure founde is when any money, gold, or silver, plate, or
> bolion, is found in any place, & no man knoweth to whom the
> property is, then the property thereof belongeth to the queene,
> and that is called treasure trove, that is to say treasure found.
> —*Exposition of the Terms of Law*, 1567

For English speakers, turning nouns into verbs is as natural as breath-
ing. The psycholinguist Steven Pinker has estimated that fully one third
of English verbs started off their careers as nouns. A far less common
process is turning adjectives into nouns, but that process was at work
to create *treasure-trove*, "a find or discovery of something of value or of
unclaimed wealth." The compound comes directly from the Old French
phrase *tresor trové*—via the Latin *thesaurus inventus*—both of which
literally mean "treasure found." The French and Latin phrases rattled
around English texts from the late 1100s to the early 1500s. Anglicized
versions such as *treasure trovey* and *treasure founde* started appearing in
the mid-sixteenth century. The compound *treasure-trove* is first recorded
in 1591 (as *treasar-trove*). Also in the mid-sixteenth century a specific
legal version of *treasure trove* arose. The English Crown began distin-
guishing between two varieties of treasure: for a small treasure that had
been voluntarily abandoned or an unclaimed treasure that had been lost,
a person finding that treasure could keep it; for a treasure that had been
deliberately hidden (and so was presumed to be valuable), a person finding that treasure would have to give it to the Crown (with some compensation, of course). The latter was called *treasure trove*.

trillion

See BILLION.

triumph

See TRUMP.

trivia

Right about now I can see you with your arm raised as far as it will go,
and you're saying "Ooh, ooh, I know this one!" What with the game
Trivial Pursuit, TV shows such as *Who Wants to Be a Millionaire?*, and all

manner of tipplers taking part in pub trivia tournaments, we've all been awash in *trivia*, "useless or trifling information." And we've all heard the story that the word *trivia* comes from the Latin phrase *tri via*, "three roads," because back in Roman times the chattering classes would gather at the intersections where three roads came together to exchange gossip and other conversational TIDBITS of little importance. Unfortunately, that's all it is: a mere story. First, it seems likely that Roman intersections would mostly be where *two* roads came together, not three. Second, *trivia* is actually the plural of the Latin *trivium*, "three ways," which in the Middle Ages was the name given to the lower division of the seven liberal arts. The Trivium consisted of introductory courses in grammar, rhetoric, and logic, and back in the fifteenth century the adjective *trivial* was used to describe anything related to the Trivium. The higher division was the Quadrivium (from the Latin *quadrivium*, "four ways"), and it consisted of advanced courses in arithmetic, geometry, astronomy, and music. Most people thought that the more artsy Trivium was considerably easier than the more mathematical Quadrivium, and over time *trivial* came to mean anything trifling or unimportant.

trophy

When the winner of a tournament receives the trophy, he may be able to look back and discern a turning point in the action that led to his victory. That's apropos because there's a lot of turning in a trophy, at least linguistically. The story begins with the Greek word *tropē*, "turning," from which we get terms such as *trope*, "a figure (or 'turn') of speech," *tropism*, "turning toward or away from a stimulus such as heat or light," and even *tropic*, which comes from the old belief that the sun turned back when it reached the Tropic of Cancer and the Tropic of Capricorn. The Greek term *tropē* also meant "putting to flight; defeating," and in that sense it referred to a turning point in a battle. This led to the Greek word *tropaion* and the Latin word *trophaeum*, both of which referred to a structure erected on a field of battle commemorating a victory. (It's said that these memorials were placed at a turning point in the battle.) This sense was how the word *trophe* entered English in the sixteenth century (from the French *trophée*). By the end of the sixteenth century, the word had generalized to refer to anything that served as a token of victory in any endeavor, although particularly in a sporting contest, and sometime in the seventeenth century we settled on the spelling *trophy*.

More Trophies

Speaking of trophies, you've no doubt heard of the *trophy wife*, "a young, attractive wife who is meant to impress other people or to enhance the status of an older man," which was first recorded in 1989. A similar phrase is *trophy child* (also seen as *trophy kid*), which first appeared in 1990. These terms are part of a long series of phrases that use the word *trophy* as an adjective to mean "something used to impress others and enhance one's status." The series also includes *trophy house* (first seen in 1981), *trophy girlfriend* (1990), *trophy tree* (1991), *trophy car* (1992), and *trophy job* (1995). I'm still looking for *trophy trophy*.

trump

When you're playing bridge or euchre, if you play a trump card to take a trick, you've won a minor victory of sorts, and that's appropriate because the word *trump* is (as the *OED* harshly puts it) a corruption of the word *triumph*. Speaking of which, *triumph* comes to us via the Latin *triumphus*, a ceremony where a victorious military commander would enter the gates of Rome followed by his army and the SPOILS taken during the war.

tulip

Would you wear a tulip on your head? Perhaps if an irresistible hippie vibe suddenly struck, you might be inclined to stick a tulip in your hair, but that's about it, I suspect. But at least etymologically tulips and headgear are intimately related because we get the name of that flower from the Persian word *dulband*, "turban." It seems a long journey from a turban to a tulip, and the first leg of that journey was undertaken in the sixteenth century by a fellow named Ogier Ghiselin de Busbecq, who was the ambassador for the Holy Roman Emperor Ferdinand I to the court of the Turkish sultan Suleiman the Magnificent. At the time it was fashionable for people to stick a tulip or two into their turbans, and Busbecq thought the word *dulband* was referring to the flower, not the headwear. (Some authorities insist that the name comes from the supposed fact that a tulip looks like a turban, but that seems a bit of a stretch.) The Persian *Dulband* became *tuliband* in Turkish, which became *tulipan* in French, which became *tulipa* in English (which is still the Latin name for the plant's genus). The word *tulip* first appeared in print in 1615.

turducken

This German-looking word is actually a meat dish: a boneless turkey that's stuffed with a boneless duck that's stuffed with a boneless chicken. When an acquaintance first told me about the turducken, I thought he was kidding. Sure, his e-mail arrived in my inbox at 12:11 A.M. on April *2nd*, but he could have *sent* it on April Fool's Day. I suspected fowl play. However, some quick investigative journalism assured me that this Frankenbird was no canard and that, in fact, it was invented—I want to say "manufactured"—by none other than the famous chef Paul Prudhomme back in the early 1980s. Unfortunately, *why* he felt the need to construct a kind of Russian doll in meat remains a mystery. (At least Chef Paul isn't responsible for the *pigturducken*, which is—that's right—a turducken stuffed inside a pig, the resonant symbolism of which I won't get into here.)

Talking Turkey

The turducken is a kind of culinary mistake, which fits because the word *turkey* itself is based on a kind of ornithological mistake. Before the "discovery" of the New World, people in the Old World had been importing a type of guinea-fowl from Turkish colonies in Africa, and they called that bird a *turkey-cock*, or often just a *turkey*. The first settlers in North America noticed a native bird that they mistook for the African bird, so they called that bird a "turkey," as well. However, the American bird hailed from Mexico originally and wasn't even remotely the same bird as the African.

turmeric

Curry fans love turmeric since it's one of the main ingredients in curry powder (the others being cumin, coriander, chili, and ginger). It's clear that people have always enjoyed this aromatic and pungent root because it appears the name comes from the French phrase *terre mérite*, which was derived directly from the Latin phrase *terra merita*, both of which mean "worthy earth."

turnpike

The next time you traveling down a turnpike and have to pay yet another toll, you might be tempted to mutter "Okay, this means war!" under your breath. First, you might want to see someone about your anger issues. Second, pat yourself on the back for your perspicacity because yes, indeed, the word *turnpike* has its origins in war. Our story begins in the early fifteenth century when the warmongers of the day decided they needed some kind of portable barrier that would block a road, path, or other passageway to prevent the enemy hordes (particularly those on horseback) from attacking. The result was a nasty piece of work that used a long, horizontal piece of wood into which long, sharp spears had been inserted on all four sides. These spears were called *pikes* back in the day, and the fact that you could "turn" this defensive device out of the way to allow friends through the barrier led to the device being called a *turnpike*. A few hundred years later, profiteers started putting up road barriers not to prevent enemy attacks, but to halt traffic and demand a toll before allowing passage. They used a simple wooden bar to stop travelers in their tracks, but they were reminiscent enough of the old military devices that people started using the phrase *turnpike road* to describe these new toll roads. Within a few years, the word *turnpike* had cemented itself in the language.

tutu

The standard tutu is an extremely short skirt made up of layers of frills so that it basically sticks out straight from the body. (Actually, that's what ballet types call a "classic" tutu. There's also a version called a "romantic" tutu, which reaches halfway between the knee and ankle. Just so you know.) The radical shortness of this skirt seems to have contributed more than a little to name *tutu*. It comes to us directly from the French *tutu*, which the *OED* describes as a "childish alteration" of *cucu*, which in turn is the diminutive form of *cul*, a person's rump or bottom. The allusion here, if it needs to be spelled out, is that the tutu barely (so to speak) conceals the dancer's backside. A child (certainly not an adult, no) watching a performance of *The Nutcracker Suite* (or whatever) might say something like "I can see her cucu!", the "cucu" would come out as "tutu," and the rest is ballet history.

More Bottom-Feeding

The *cul* = *bottom* formula is also seen in the phrase *cul-de-sac*, "a street closed at one end," which from the French translates literally as "sack-bottom."

tuxedo

It's a bit ironic that the tuxedo, a tailless formal dinner jacket, may have its linguistic origins in an animal that most definitely has a tail. Those origins lie in the word *p'tuksit* (you don't pronounce the *p*), which was the Algonquian Indian word for a wolf, and it means literally, "animal with a round foot" or "round-footed one." (Let me interrupt my own narrative here for a second by also mentioning a second possible path to take on the road to *tuxedo*. Some claim that the Algonquians used the word *tuksit*, "round foot," to refer to the rival Wolf tribe, imply-ing that they were easily toppled in battle. Either way.) When English speakers moved into the Algonquian territory, they used *p'tuksit* (or possibly just *tuksit*) to name a particular lake, and the anglicized ver-sion of the word went through several incarnations, including Tuxcito, Tucksito, Tucsedo, Texedo, and the finally Tuxedo. In the 1880s, a wealthy tobacco magnate named Pierre Lorillard purchased much of the land around Tuxedo Lake and eventually built a luxury resort named Tuxedo Park. This was home to many a lavish affair, and in those days the fashion for men was white tie and tails. Sick of being a slave to upper-crust fashion, Lorillard's son Griswold showed up at one do in 1886 wearing a formal jacket, but without the tails. Scandalous! However, the new look soon caught on, and the tailless jacket was christened the *tuxedo*.

twerp

If you really don't like someone and you want to hit that person with a verbal zinger, call him a *twerp*, "an objectionable or insignificant person; a nobody or NINCOMPOOP." The word *twerp* first appears in print in a 1925 glossary called *Soldier and Sailor Words*, where the authors define it as "an unpleasant person." As to the origins of the word, no less a literary light than J. R. R. Tolkien of *Lord of the Rings* fame provides us with an interesting insight in a letter he wrote in 1944:

> He lived in O[xford] at the time when we lived in Pusey Street (rooming with Walton, the composer, and going about with T. W. Earp, the original twerp).

Bolstering this claim is the poet Roy Campbell, who included the following in his 1957 book *Portugal:*

> T. W. Earp (who gave the English language the word twirp, really twearp, because of the Goering-like wrath he kindled in the hearts of the rugger-playing stalwarts at Oxford, when he was president of the Union, by being the last, most charming, and wittiest of the "decadents").

Was there really a T. W. Earp? Yup, in fact, there was, and he graduated from Exeter College, Oxford, in 1911. Was he *really* the inspiration for the word *twerp*? Alas, we can't say for sure, because if the word *twerp* (or *twirp*) already existed when these fellows went to Oxford, who could resist calling someone with the almost too-convenient name *T. W. Earp* a "twerp"?

two bits

T

Ever wonder why some slangsters use the phrase *two bits* to refer to a quarter? You have to go back to the old Spanish milled dollars that could be broken into eight pie-slice-like pieces to make change. (These were the famous "pieces of eight.") Since there were eight pieces or "bits" to a dollar, *two bits* were a quarter of a dollar.

tycoon

> Gen. Butler has sent an imploring request to the President to be
> allowed to bag the whole nest of traitorous Maryland Legislators.
> This the Tycoon ... forbade. —John Hay, *Diary*, April 25, 1861

Did you know that many of U.S. President Abraham Lincoln's cabinet
members and advisors referred to him using the nickname "Tycoon"?
It's a fact (as the above citation attests), but it's an odd one since we
normally associate the word *tycoon* with a powerful or wealthy business-
person, and that definition most definitely doesn't fit Lincoln. What
gives? The story goes back to the 1850s when the West was just learning about Japan. One of the first to negotiate with the Japanese was
Commodore Matthew Calbraith Perry, who dealt with the shogun (the
commander of the Japanese army and the de facto ruler of the country)
rather than the emperor (the titular head). The Japanese were crafty in
their dealings, and they knew that the title *shogun* wasn't very impressive to foreigners (it means "general"). So they borrowed the Chinese
word *takiun*, which combines *ta*, "great," and *kiun*, "prince," to create
a new title for the shogun: *taikun*. The word *tycoon* first appeared in
English texts in 1857, and *tycoon* a year later. At first the word meant
"great ruler," hence its application to Lincoln, who quite clearly fit that
description. The more general sense of a powerful or dominant business type first started appearing in the late nineteenth century.

ukulele

The ukulele seems like the quintessential Hawaiian musical instrument, but it's actually a variation on the *cavaquinho*, a small four-string instrument of Portuguese origin that was brought to the Islands around 1879. The Hawaiians took to the instrument right away and named it *pila li'ili'i*, "little fiddle." A few years later, a British army officer named Edward Purvis was stationed on the Islands and he, too, fell for the instrument and learned how to play it. Purvis had a small build and his playing was apparently quite lively. So much so that to the Hawaiians he resembled a jumping flea. "Flea" in Hawaiian is *uku* and "jumping" is *lele*, so they called him *ukulele*. That nickname eventually transferred to the instrument itself, and it's been known as the ukulele since the late 1890s.

umbrage

If you take umbrage at something someone says or does, it means the transgression has caused you to become displeased, offended, resentful, annoyed, or all of the above. You could also say that your relationship with that person has been cast into a shadow of sorts, and that fits nicely with the origins of the word *umbrage*. It came to us via the Old French *ombrage*, which in turn was based on the Latin term *umbrāticum*, which came from *umbra*, "shadow." When *umbrage* first showed up in the early 1400s, it meant "shade; shadow." The meaning gradually changed over time: from "a shadowy or faint appearance" to "a feeling of suspicion or doubt" to "being in disfavor" and then finally to the modern "annoyance or resentment" sense. I should point out in passing that the Latin term *umbra* is the source of quite a few English words, including *umbrella, penumbra, somber, adumbrate* ("foreshadow"), and even *sombrero*.

Really Taking Umbrage

I would be remiss in my duties if I didn't also pass along a story told by the author Robert Hendrickson of an editor at a small newspaper during World War II who came upon a wire service story stating that the Russians had "taken umbrage" at something or other. Apparently clueless to the meaning of the word *umbrage*, the editor headlined the story, "Russians Capture Umbrage." Of course, it's almost certainly not true, but it's a fun tale nonetheless.

underdog

The *underdog* is the person or team that is expected to lose a game or contest, but it can also refer to anyone at a disadvantage. The word comes from the world of canines, where in a dog fight the one who ends up underneath is at a distinct disadvantage. The *OED* has an earliest citation for *underdog* from 1887, but the following poem by David Barker called *The Under Dog In the Fight* was published in 1859:

> I know that the world, the great big world,
> From the peasant up to the king,
> Has a different tale from the tale I tell,
> And a different song to sing.
> But for me — and I care not a single fig
> If they say I am wrong or right,
> I shall always go for the *weaker* dog,
> For the under dog in the fight.

understand

A quick examination of the word *understand* reveals it to be a blend of the words *stand* and *under*. Okay, so how does this apparent idea of standing under something possibly produce the word's meaning: "comprehend; come to know"? That looks like a shoulder-shrugger for sure, but the mystery reveals itself when you understand (wink, wink) that the prefix *under-* doesn't always mean "below." Another sense is "between; amid," and this sense comes from the same root as the prefix *inter-*. In other words, *understand* could just as easily have been *interstand*. Now things begin to make a bit more sense, because to "stand between or amid" things is to get to know them, to see them from all sides, to become familiar with them. The same process is at work in the verb *undertake:* when you undertake something, you don't go under it, you go into it, so to speak.

unicorn

In his famous encyclopedia *Naturalis Historiae (Natural History)*, Pliny the Elder described the mythical unicorn as:

> An exceedingly wild beast ... which has a stag's head, elephant's feet, and a boar's tail, the rest of its body being like that of a horse. It makes a deep lowing noise, and one black horn two cubits long projects from the middle of its forehead.

He actually referred to it as a "Monoceros," but both that name and the word *unicorn* come from the same source: the Latin term *ūnicornis*, which combines *ūnus*, "one," and *cōrnu*, "horn."

universe

See VARSITY.

unkempt

The *unkempt* person is untidy, messy, or disorderly. Unkempt goes back to the Old English word *kemb*, "comb." So unkempt originally described someone who had uncombed hair. And, in case you're wondering, the word *kempt* is legitimate (if not all that common outside of allegedly humorous word lists on the Internet) and means, not surprisingly, "tidy, trim."

U

A Couth Etymology

Kempt is another example of a back-formation that I yammered on about earlier (see PEA). In this case, someone saw *unkempt* and assumed that *un-* prefix was optional, so coined *kempt* as the opposite. A similar process occurred with the word *couth*, "sophisticated, refined." The original word was *uncouth*, "ungraceful, ill-mannered," which sprang from the Old English term *uncuth*, "unknown." (From this relatively neutral beginning, the word later took on the meanings "unfamiliar," then "strange," then "awkward" and "uncultured.")

upholster

The sturdiness of an upholstered chair or sofa would seem to be the main element that prevents us from falling to the floor when we sit down on such furniture, but could it be the upholstery itself? Perhaps not physically, but a case can be made for this etymologically. We begin with the verb *uphold*, which means "to support physically; to keep from falling." However, at one time it also meant "to keep from falling into disrepair," and that sense of the verb led to the noun *upholder*, "a maker or repairer of small wares or furniture," which popped up in the early 1300s. However, later on some folks seemed to prefer the suffix *-ster* over *-er*, and so the noun *upholster* surfaced in the early 1400s. It seems we've nearly reached our goal, but we're not there yet. In one of those odd quirks of the English language, a couple hundred years after the perfectly good word *upholster* had become part of the language, folks added the redundant *-er* suffix to create the awkward word *upholsterer*. This noun referred to a tradesman or shopkeeper who made or repaired furniture, particularly the kind that used stuffing covered with fabric. That noun first appeared in 1611 and things settled down for about 250 years with one exception: around 1649, the stuffing and fabric used to cover such furniture got its own name: *upholstery*. Then in the mid-1800s, someone had the bright idea that if a person who worked with upholstery was an upholsterer, then the verb *upholster* must mean "to furnish or trim with upholstery." This back-formation finally ends this long and embroidered tale.

upshot

And let me speak to the yet unknowing world
How these things came about: so shall you hear
Of carnal, bloody, and unnatural acts,
Of accidental judgments, casual slaughters,
Of deaths put on by cunning and forced cause,
And, in this upshot, purposes mistook.

—William Shakespeare, *Hamlet*, 1604

The word *upshot*, "a result or conclusion," began its life in the early 1500s as an archery term, where it referred to the final shot in a match. The *OED* says that in this sense the "force of the *up-* is not clear." Too true! However, just for the heck of it we can surmise that it was the final chance for the archer to raise himself up in the standings or to put himself "over the top" and win the match. By the end of the sixteenth century the word had taken on the more general sense of a PARTING SHOT, and before long the modern sense of a result or conclusion had taken hold (and the Shakespeare citation above is the first recorded use of that sense of the word).

urchin

Could the antics of an *urchin*, "a mischievous child," cause a person to become *prickly*, "easily angered"? If so, that would be ironic because it's the urchin that was prickly originally. Our word *urchin* used to be the word *hurcheon*, which came from the Old Northern French term *herichon*, which was itself derived from the Latin term *hēricus*, all of which mean "hedgehog." The word *urchin* first appeared in the mid-1300s, and was soon used to describe all sorts of supposedly hedgehog-like folks, including hunchbacks, ugly people, and significantly for our purposes, elves and goblins because the folklore of the day assumed that these beings would occasionally take the form of a hedgehog. Elves and goblins are by nature mischievous, of course, so it was natural that the term *urchin* would also shift to mischievous children, which it did around the mid-sixteenth century.

U

vaccine

If you receive an inoculation against some disease, you have a cow to thank, both medically and linguistically. On the medical side, back in 1796 a doctor named Edward Jenner noticed that milkmaids seemed to be mostly immune to the dreaded disease smallpox. However, they *did* get cowpox (which is a much milder disease), and Jenner wondered whether the pus from the milkmaid's cowpox blisters was somehow preventing them from contracting smallpox. So he took a bit of the cowpox pus and injected it into the arm of an eight-year-old named James Phipps. Lo and behold the cowpox virus caused Phipps to become immune to smallpox. Eureka! Jenner called his new wonder drug the *vaccine virus*, from the Latin word *vacca*, "cow." By 1846, the word *vaccine* was in general use as any substance that inoculates against a disease. See also PECUNIARY.

varsity

> I have such faith in the old University (never use that horrid word 'varsity, my lad; don't vulgarise the old place). —Henry Kingsley, *Hornby Mills*, 1872

You can probably tell from the context of the above citation—not to mention the telltale apostrophe—that the word *varsity*, "a university sports team; relating to a university team," is an abbreviation of the word *university*. The *OED* lists a couple of seventeenth-century citations for the direct shortened form *versity*, but the now common (and, to some given the above citation, "horrid") word *varsity* first appeared in the mid-1800s. The apostrophe that signifies a shortening has taken place—*'varsity*—stuck around until well into the 1920s. (Speaking of the word *university*, it comes from the Latin term *ūniversitās*, which originally meant "the whole or the universe," but later referred to "a society, company, or community taken collectively." When the word graduated into English around 1300, it referred right away to "a place of higher learning.")

vaudeville

The old vaudeville shows included plenty of songs interspersed between comedy routines and other variety acts, but there was a time when the word *vaudeville* referred to just a particular type of song. The history of this word goes back to fifteenth-century France, specifically the Calvados region in Normandy. In that region is a valley named Vire, and the people there were said to be inordinately fond of songs (called *chansons* in French). They were particularly fond of the satirical songs composed by a local named Olivier Basselin. The French word for *valley* is *vau*, so such a song became known as a *chanson Vau de Vire* ("song of the Valley of Vire"), and later simply as a *vau de vire*. These songs later became popular in cities, so some French punster must have noted that *vire* is pronounced similar to *ville*, "city,"—*ville* is pronounced VEE, and *vire* is pronounced VEER—so the phrase became *vau de ville* and then eventually *vaudeville*. That word entered the English stage in 1739 and referred to "a light popular song." The "variety show" sense opened its run around 1827.

vegetable

Though the Earth be not animated with a Sensible Soul, yet it is possible that it may be a great Immortal Vegetable. —Sir Matthew Hale, *The Primitive Origination of Mankind*, 1676

They had no occasion to mark the lapse of time in their monotonous and vegetable existence. —Archibald H. Sayce, *The Principles of Comparative Philology*, 1874

These two citations illustrate the dual nature of the outwardly simple term *vegetable*. The word comes to us via the Old French term *vegetable*, which in turn came from the Latin *veget bilis*, "animating; life-giving." The root is the Latin *vegetus*, "lively; active," which is also the source

V

of our words *vigor, vigil,* and *velocity.* On the other hand, if we want to insult someone who is listless, dull, and inactive, we call that person a "vegetable" who does nothing but "vegetate" (or "veg") all day.

venom

You may be familiar with the song *Love Hurts* which, depending on your age and musical tastes, you may remember as either an Everly Brothers song or a Nazareth song. Either way, it would be an apropos theme song for the word *venom,* "the poisonous fluid secreted by snakes." The love connection, so to speak, is the Latin word *venus,* "love" (also, of course, the name of the goddess), which is the root of the Latin term *venenum,* "love potion." Combining the idea that love somewhat addles the mind (in a nice way, of course) and the idea that a potion can have harmful effects, *venenum* eventually came to be used to mean "poison." The word entered English as *venin,* and it later became *venom,* with the meaning that we associate with the word to this day.

verdict

See JUDGE.

vermicelli

See WORM (yes, I said *worm*).

victuals

> And Laura waited long, and wept a little,
> And thought of wearing weeds, as well she might;
> She almost lost all appetite for victual,
> And could not sleep with ease along at night.
>
> —Lord Byron, *Beppo,* 1817

The plural noun *victuals,* "food; provisions," is archaic, but not so much so that it can't be trotted out from time to time for comic effect. The weird thing about this word isn't so much its origins, which as you'll see were straightforward, but that it's spelling and pronunciation developed on separate linguistic tracks! First to the etymology: *victuals* comes from the Latin plural noun *victuālia*, which derived from *victus*, "food," and that background influenced how we spell the word. The Latin word entered Old French first as *victaille*, but at some point the "c" fell by the wayside and the word became *vitaille* or *vitaile*. That term would have been pronounced *vuh·TY* in French, but the anglicized version would have been said as *vuh·TAL*. Eventually the stress moved to the first syllable, and the pronunciation became *VIT·tul*. So, bizarrely, we ended up with the Latin-influenced spelling *victuals* and the French-influenced pronunciation *VIT·tuls*.

villain

Sometimes the SUPERCILIOUS snobs of the world dictate the origins of a word. A case in point is the word *villain*, which now refers to an evil or nefarious character in a story, particularly the story's antagonist, but once had a completely different meaning. The starting point is the Latin word *villa*, "country house," which gave rise to the medieval Latin term *villānus*, "farm hand." That word became *villein* in Anglo-French, and it referred to a feudal serf who would provide dues and services to a lord in exchange for land. The word eventually became *villain* in English, and those highbrow lords soon began using it to refer to not just their serfs, but to any, as the *OED* puts it, "low-born base-minded rustic." The meaning of the term degraded over time, next referring to those who were dishonorable or depraved, and finally to people with the most base criminal instincts. These senses developed in the fourteenth and fifteenth centuries, but the "main evil character in a story" sense didn't appear until the 1820s.

viral marketing

This recently coined phrase refers to the promotion of a service or product by using existing customers to pass along a marketing pitch to friends, family, and colleagues. Why "viral" marketing? Probably because a biological virus replicates itself by invading a host cell and then using the cell's machinery to create new copies of the virus. So, analogously, a customer acts like a kind of "host cell" for a company's marketing message, and that customer is used to create new "copies" of the viral marketing message. Creepy, no?

V

vocation

A *vocation* is a regular occupation, especially one to which a person is particularly well suited. This word goes back to the Latin verb *vocare*, "to call." An earlier (Middle English) version of the word was *vocacioun*, which meant "a divine calling to a religious life." The word took on a more general sense over the years, but the word *calling* is still a synonym. Don't confuse *vocation* with *avocation*, a hobby or side occupation pursued for enjoyment. In this case, the *a*- prefix mans "away from," so this word literally means "to call away from."

vodka

See the sidebar near WHISKEY.

volume

When you read a book, do you "wallow" in the plot or get "involved" in the story? These are the literary signs of a good read, but they're also the linguistic signs of the origins of the word *volume*, "book." It comes to us (via Old French) from the Latin term *volūmen*, "coil; roll," the source of which is the verb *volvēre*, "to roll." It's not hard to see how this verb is also the root of *wallow* (originally, "to roll in mud") and *involve* (figuratively, "to roll up in"), but the book sense of *volume* is a bit tougher to wrap one's head around (so to speak). That is, until you learn that the original "volumes" were sheets of parchment or papyrus rolled up or wrapped around a stick or rod. Aha!

wag

A *wag* is a witty or humorous person, but did some wag invent the word? Probably not. The *OED* speculates that it comes from the verb *wag*, one sense of which means "to gossip; to speak indiscreetly." This makes a bit more sense when you realize that the original meaning of the noun *wag* was "a mischievous boy," and someone who gossips is up to mischief. However, the *OED* leaves open a second etymological door: that *wag* might be derived from the term *waghalter*, "a person who is likely to swing in a halter" (that is, be hung from a gallows). The idea behind this theory is that waghalters were merry rogues whose tongues would one day get them in trouble.

war

It may be a truism that "an army travels on its stomach," but could it travel on sausages in particular? I ask because of the surprising fact that the words *war* and *wurst* (a sausage such as bratwurst or liverwurst) share a common history. War goes way back to the root *wers-*, "to confuse; to mix up." This became *weera*, "confusion, strife," in Old High German, and then the "strife" part took over and eventually became our word *war*. Meanwhile, *wers-* also became *wurst*, "sausage," because a sausage is "mixed-up meat." Confused? Exactly.

wardriving

Wardriving is a hacking technique that involves driving through a neighborhood with a wireless-enabled notebook computer and mapping "hotspots"—houses and businesses that have wireless access points,

particularly unsecured ones. (This is also called *drive-by hacking*.)
Wardriving is a play on the older term *wardialing*, "using a software
program to automatically call thousands of telephone numbers to look
for any that have a modem attached." This term comes from the 1983
movie *War Games*, now a classic in hacking circles. In the movie a
young hacker (Matthew Broderick) uses wardialing to look for games
and bulletin board systems. However, he inadvertently ends up with
a direct connection to a high-level military computer that gives him
control over the U.S. nuclear arsenal. Chaos, of course, ensues. A variation on the wardriving theme is *warwalking* which, as the name implies,
involves a more pedestrian search for insecure wireless networks. (This
is also called, not surprisingly, *walk-by hacking*.) The usual activity of
the warwalker is *warchalking*, marking a special symbol on a sidewalk or
other surface that indicates a nearby wireless network, especially one
that offers Internet access. Warchalkers are also called *wibos*, "wireless
hobos," because the idea of marking hotspots was inspired by the old
"hobo language": the marks used by actual hobos during the Depression
of the 1930s to indicate houses and establishments that had available
food or work.

warmonger

A *warmonger* is a person who is eager to start a war. You know the origins of the word WAR from an earlier entry, but what about the suffix
-*monger*? That term goes back to the Old Saxon term *mongari*, which
came from the Latin word *mango*, "trader; dealer," so a warmonger
was originally one who traffics in or makes a profit from war. (In case
you're wondering, the Latin term *mango* has nothing to do with the
fruit named *mango*. That word comes from the Tamil term *mankay*.)
The suffix -*monger* shows up in all kinds of trading situations. You
probably know the words *fashionmonger*, *fishmonger*, *ironmonger*, *news-
monger*, and *scaremonger*. But over the years we've also seen the *cheese-
monger*, *cornmonger*, *fleshmonger*, *moneymonger*, and *muttonmonger*, to
name just a few.

water-cooler moment

A TV programmer's goal is to generate buzz about their show (show-buzz?), particularly at work, so they'll often include a controversial or exciting segment designed to get people's chins a-wagging. If successful, such a segment is called a *water-cooler moment*. To understand why, think of a classic workplace scene: two or three co-workers arrive at the office water cooler more or less simultaneously and, people being the social creatures that they are, a brief—and ideally non-work-related—conversation ensues. Nowadays, these confabs are just as likely to break out in the coffee room, alongside the photocopier, or while waiting to use the fax machine. But the water cooler was long ago chosen as the symbolic location for spontaneous workplace chit-chatting. That's the idea underlying *water-cooler moment*. Insert some gratuitously controversial or titillating content into a show, and the next day the water cooler conversations will begin with the phrase "Did you see last night's episode of *X*?"

we don't need no stinking X!

If you use this SNOWCLONE (a common variation is "X? We don't need no stinking X!"), you're showing utter contempt for X (albeit usually in a mocking way). This cliché's origins go back to the 1935 book *The Treasure of the Sierra Madre*, which includes the following lines:

> Badges …! We have no badges. In fact, we don't need badges. I don't have to show you any stinking badges!

When the book was made into a movie starring Humphrey Bogart in 1948, those lines made it in more or less intact:

> Badges? We ain't got no badges. We don't need no badges. I don't have to show you any stinking badges!

Then, in Mel Brooks's 1974 comedy *Blazing Saddles*, he included the following lines as a winking homage to the Bogart film:

> Badges? We don't need no stinking badges!

In modern contexts, "badges" gets replaced by whatever is bugging the writer: banks, laws, politicians, rules, you name it.

W

weblog

> After talking a lot about Frontier and Scripting News (www.
> scripting.com), I decided to start my own webpage logging the
> best stuff I find as I surf, on a daily basis:
>
> http://www.mcs.net/~jorn/html/weblog.html
>
> This will cover any [sic] and everything that interests me, from
> net culture to politics to literature etc. —Jorn Barger, "Lively new
> webpage," December 23, 1997

This post to the Usenet newsgroup alt.society.neutopia announces
the creation of Robot Wisdom, first-ever *weblog*, "a web page consisting of frequently updated, chronological entries on a particular topic."
Everybody calls them *blogs* now, of course, but it's easy to forget the
longer term, which combines the word *web*, short for World Wide Web,
and *log*, in the sense that the *OED* defines as "any record in which facts
about the progress or performance of something are entered in the
order in which they become known."

wedlock

The ever-so-slightly old-fashioned word *wedlock* means "the state of
being married." The presence of the word *lock* makes this seem like
someone has joined two people with some sort of latch or fastener and
thrown away the key. It's the whole "ball and chain" thing, isn't it? Not
so fast, pal. The word *wedlock* comes from the Old English term *wedlác*,
which is a combination of *wed*, "a pledge," and the suffix *-lác*, which was
once used to form nouns of action. So *wedlác* literally means "pledge-
making" or "the act of pledging." Old English was riddled with words
that used the *-lác* suffix, but only *wedlác* stood the test of time, and in
modern times the *-lock* suffix appears only in the word *wedlock*.

weird

If you think it's your fate to have something weird happen to you, your
friendly neighborhood etymologist will tell you that's true! In fact, he
or she would say that's true for absolutely everyone. That's because the
Old English term *wyrd* meant "fate, destiny," and by medieval times

people were referring to the Fates—the goddess trio that supposedly determines the course of each person's life—as the *Weirds* and later as the *Weird Sisters*. How on Earth did we get from the Fates to the modern sense of "strange, odd"? That, my friend, is all thanks to a fellow you may have heard of, William Shakespeare, whose love of wordplay caused the shift. In Shakespeare's original manuscript for *Macbeth*, he included the following lines:

> The weyward Sisters, hand in hand,
> Posters of the Sea and Land,
> Thus doe goe, about, about,
> Thrice to thine, and thrice to mine,
> And thrice againe, to make up nine.

Note Will's use of *weyward* instead of *weird*. Language was a more flexible thing back in those days, so Shakespeare thought nothing of spelling a word in different ways in the same play! In this case, we later see the following in *Macbeth*:

MACBETH	Saw you the Weyard Sisters?
LENNOX	No my Lord
MACBETH	Came they not by you?
LENNOX	No indeed my Lord
MACBETH	Infected be the Ayre whereon they ride, And damn'd all those that trust them.

So here he uses *Weyard*, which is at least a bit closer to *weird*. What happened, though, was that people saw Shakespeare using both *weyward* and *weyard* for *weird*, and since *weyward* is awfully close to *wayward* (which was almost certainly Shakespeare's intent), the "erratic" sense of waywardness infected the word *weird*, and by the mid-nineteenth century the old "fate, the Fates" sense was mostly forgotten and the new "odd, unusual" sense had taken over. Weird!

welcome our new X overlords

This SNOWCLONE (which is usually preceded by "I, for one") is most often used ironically to indicate that one really isn't all that pleased that

X has so much power, but is resigned to the fact because nothing can be done about it. The original is "I, for one, welcome our new insect overlords," the now immortal words of *The Simpsons* cartoon character Homer Simpson, which occurred in the episode *Deep Space Homer*, first broadcast on February 24, 1994. Here are just a few examples of this snowclone from recent newspapers and magazine:

> I, for one, welcome our new robot overlords.
> —*National Public Radio*, November 6, 2007

> I, for one, welcome our new Microsoft overlords.
> —*eWEEK*, October 26, 2007

> I, for one, welcome our new wireless overlords.
> —*PC Magazine*, September 4, 2007

> I, for one, welcome our new Googly overlords.
> —*Government Computer News*, July 30, 2007

well-heeled

If you're *well-heeled* it doesn't mean you have lots of shoes or that you have shoes with exceptionally high heels. Instead, it just means that you're wealthy. You might think that *well-heeled* is therefore the opposite of the expression *down-at-heel*, "shabby; rundown," which has been in the language since the early eighteenth century, and which comes from the idea of worn-down heels being a kind of symbol of a destitute state. Actually, the two phrases don't have anything to do with each other. Instead, the adjective *well-heeled* comes from the earlier adjective *heeled*, "armed with a weapon." That in turn comes from the earlier word *heel*, a verb from the seedy world of cock-fighting, where it meant "to attach sharp spurs to a bird," which, presumably, the bird would use as a kind of weapon.

Weltanschauung

A *Weltanschauung* (pronounced with your best German accent as *VELT·ahn·SHAW·ung*) refers to a comprehensive outlook or philosophy of the world or of human life. It's a German term (duh!) that combines *welt*, "world," and *anschauung*, "perception; view." So a *Weltanschauung* is literally a "world view." A similar term we get from the Germans is

Weltschmerz (*VELT-shmurts*), which refers to a mood of sentimental sadness or romantic pessimism caused by comparing the apparently poor state of the real world with an idealized view of what the world could or should be. It's a blend of *welt*, "world," and *schmerz*, "pain."

I Feel Your Consonants

Weltschmerz is famous in linguistic circles for its remarkable run of no fewer than six consecutive consonants!

whippersnapper

This word refers to an insignificant but impertinent person, especially a young person. The *OED* describes this word, pleasingly, as "a jingling extension of whip-snapper." A whip-snapper, it turns out, was a seventeenth-century layabout who would pass the time by hanging around on street corners and snapping a whip (kids those days!). Back then, a *snipper-snapper* was a "young insignificant or conceited fellow," so I'm sure it didn't take long for some wag to merge *whip-snapper* and *snipper-snapper* to make *whippersnapper*.

whipping boy

A person who's a *whipping boy* is one who (male or female) gets singled out for the blame or punishment associated with the mistakes made by someone more important. There's rarely a whipping involved these days, but there used to be. The phrase's origins go back to sixteenth-century Britain when the Divine Right of Kings held sway. This was the belief that all legitimate British kings were "God's lieutenants upon Earth" who "sat upon God's throne." These kings were answerable only to God, so no mere mortal could punish or censure them. The Divine Right of Kings also applied to any child of the king who could one day ascend to the throne. This meant that when the prince misbehaved, no one was to touch him, much less punish him. In the case of King Henry VIII's son Edward (who later became King Edward VI), a novel idea (but one that's almost comically bizarre to modern sensibilities) was created: of the noble youths with whom Edward was being educated, pick out one of them to be his "proxy for correction." That's a

W

gentrified way of saying that this poor sap would be punished each time Edward did something wrong. The "lucky" fellow in this case was one Barnaby Fitzpatrick, the son of an Irish baron. The practice took hold in other royal households, and the fellow who took the prince's punishment became known as the *whipping boy*. This all began in the mid-sixteenth century, and about a hundred years later the sense of *whipping boy* as someone who takes the blame for someone higher up had taken hold.

whiskey

Whiskey is a strong—typically 40 to 50 percent alcohol by volume—liquor distilled from a fermented mash of grain such as barley, corn, or rye. (*Mash* is crushed malt or grain meal steeped and stirred in hot water so it can ferment.) The word whiskey comes to us from the Gaelic word *usquebea*, which in turn comes from the phrase *usque beatha*, which means "water of life," a trope that whiskey-lovers will no doubt appreciate. (They're less likely to appreciate that the Comanche Indians called whiskey "stupid water," because of its none-too-flattering effects on the brain of the average drinker.) Note that, generally speaking, the spelling is "whiskey" in the United States and "whisky" in Britain.

The Booze/Water Connection

Whiskey isn't the only liquor with an etymological connection to water. The word *vodka* has Russian roots, not surprisingly, and it comes from the word *voda*, "water." The word *aquavit* is based on the Scandinavian term *akvavit*, which, like whiskey, means "water of life."

white-collar

It is a fact with which every union workingman is familiar, that his most bitter despisers are the petty underlings of the business world, the poor office-clerks, who are often the worst exploited of proletarians, but who, because they are allowed to wear a white collar and to work in the office with the boss, regard themselves as members of the capitalist class. —Upton Sinclair, *The Brass Check*, 1919

This citation from Upton Sinclair's book *The Brass Check*, his self-published critique of American journalism, shows that at the time the wearing of a white collar signified that one was engaged in nonmanual labor. This association led to the development of the adjective *white-collar*, "of or relating to nonmanual work," which first appeared in print in 1921. The white-collar worker's opposite, in a sense, is the manual laborer, who would often wear a blue work shirt, hence the term *blue-collar*, "of or relating to manual labor," an adjective that, surprisingly, didn't appear in print until 1950.

Other X-Collar Workers

Terms such as *white-collar* and *blue-collar* are relatively serious and earnest, but fortunately for us they've spawned a number of more whimsical variants:

Black-and-blue-collar	Football players
Black-collar	Miners (especially coal miners) and oil workers
Brown-collar	UPS employees
Dog-collar	Graphic artists or designers
Frayed-collar	Workers having trouble making ends meet
Gold-collar	Professionals or those with in-demand skills; employees over 55
Gray-collar	Skilled technicians; employees whose job descriptions combine some white- and some blue-collar
Green-collar	Environmentalists
Open-collar	People who work at home
Pink-collar	Secretaries and clerical staff
Scarlet-collar	Female porn-shop operators
Steel-collar	Robots

W

whole kit and caboodle

See KIT AND CABOODLE.

widget

See GADGET.

widow's peak

A *widow's peak* occurs when the hairline curves down to a point in the middle of the forehead. (If you're of a certain age, picture Eddie Munster's hairline; if you have no idea who that is, Google the name and you'll see.) The "peak" part comes from the sense of the word that means "a projecting or tapering point." What about the "widow" part? The *OED* also defines *peak* as "the projecting front of a headdress, esp. of a widow's hood," so that's one possibility about where the "widow" in *widow's peak* comes from. The other possibility (and the two could have been working in tandem here) is that, according to the folklore of the nineteenth century (and probably earlier), this tapered hairline was a sign that a woman would become a widow at an early age. A similar (but much older) superstition was the *widow's lock*, a tuft of hair sprouting out of the head in some nonstandard place, supposedly another sign of early widowhood.

wiki

This word comes from the Hawaiian word *wiki*, which means "quick or fast." Programmer Ward Cunningham first used the term in a software context back in the mid-'90s, when he created a collaborative site called WikiWikiWeb. Since then, we use the word *wiki* (the Hawaiian is pronounced *WEE-kee*, but most folks say it as *WIK-ee*) to refer to either a collaborative website that allows users to add, edit, and delete the site's content, or to the software that enables such collaboration. Feel free to also use it as a verb or an adjective. Wikipedia is by far the most famous wiki.

Wikiality

In the summer of 2006, *The Colbert Report* host Stephen Colbert introduced the world to a new word: *wikiality*, which means reality as defined by a consensus (it's a blend of *Wikipedia* and *reality*). He told his viewers to "apply [Wikipedia] principles to all information. All we need to do is convince a majority of people that some factoid is true." I should mention, too, that Stephen Colbert has some expertise in the coining of new words and getting them to stick in the culture. On October 17, 2005, in his very first show, Colbert coined the word *truthiness*, "truth without regard to facts, evidence, or logic," and by January 2006, the American Dialect Society had crowned *truthiness* as its Word of the Year!

willy-nilly

One of my favorite expressions (I'm quite certain I've used it in every book I've written) is the adjectival phrase *willy-nilly*, which means "haphazardly; in a disorganized or unplanned way; whether desired or not." The like-it-or-not-here-it-comes sense of this word was the original meaning, and it comes from the seventeenth-century phrase *will ye, nill ye*, a shortened form of *be ye willing, be ye unwilling*. Both of these mean "whether you like it or you don't like it" (*ye* is an archaic form of "you"). There's also a Latin version of this that comes up now and again: *nolens volen*, "unwilling, willing," that some people think might have been the true origin of *willy-nilly*, but no one knows for sure.

windfall

Whether you spy a quarter on the sidewalk, find a five-dollar bill in a coat pocket, or win the lottery, in each case you could legitimately describe the unexpected acquisition as a *windfall*. All of these things just seem to "fall" into your lap, perhaps at least metaphorically blown by some kind of favorable wind. So is that the origin of the word *windfall?* Nope, but fortunately the real story is even better. Back when Britannia ruled the waves, the powers-that-were decreed that no one could cut down a tree, because Britain's Royal Navy needed to control the lumber trade so that its ships would always have timber. Understandable, given

W

the circumstances. However, the Royal Navy did make a single exception: if a tree or branch was felled by a strong wind, the laid-low lumber was free to anyone who happened along. This idea of the wind producing an unexpected gain also applied to fruit knocked off trees and, by 1542, the word *windfall* (or *wyndefall* as they would have written it back then) had taken on its more general meaning.

window

In ancient times, long before glass was in common use, people would build their homes with holes in the walls to let in air and light. Because such a hole allowed the people to see out and allowed air in, it was called in Medieval English a *windoge*, a term that came from the Old Norse *vindauga*, which combines *vindr*, "wind," and *auga*, "eye." The holes were "wind eyes," which is a rather poetic way of looking at them. Interestingly, Old English already had a term for such a wall opening: an *eyethurl*, literally "eye hole," but for some reason the Scandinavian invader won this particular lexical skirmish.

windrow

A *windrow* is the pile of snow that a snowplow leaves at the end of a driveway. This comes from the older word *windrow*, "a row of hay raked up to dry before being rolled."

wiseacre

A *wiseacre* is a foolish person who thinks himself wise or worldly. His self-deception is vast, indeed, but is it an acre's worth? Nope, because although the "wise" half of *wiseacre* means just what you think it does, the "acre" half of the word has not a jot to do with the land measure. Instead, the origin of the word goes back to the Dutch term *wijsseggher*, "soothsayer" (it combines *wijs*, "wise," and *seggher*, "sayer"), used to describe a person who speaks the truth (*sooth* is an archaic word for "truth"). Even though your average Dutch wijsseggher was an upright, truth-telling dude, when English speakers borrowed the word they not only used it sarcastically, but they also decided that "wiseacre" was an easier way to spell it (and, sooth be told, I can't help but agree).

wisteria

You've seen a few times in this book that words are often formed because people make mistakes (see BUTTONHOLE, HANGNAIL, and PEA, to name just three). The name *wisteria* provides another example, this time what may have been a simple slip of the quill from the man who invented the word in the first place! I'm talking about Thomas Nuttall, an English botanist. In 1818, the American physician and anatomist Caspar Wistar died, and Nuttall named a newly discovered climbing vine after him: *wistaria*. In the dedication, however, Nuttall made his error: even though he spelled the name *Wistar* correctly, he spelled the vine as *wisteria!* He later tried to correct the error, but to no avail, and the plant has been called *wisteria* ever since.

witticism

> I wish I could produce any one example of excellent imaging in all this poem. Perhaps I cannot; but that which comes nearest it, is in these four lines, which have been sufficiently canvassed by my well-natured censors:
>
> > Seraph and cherub, careless of their charge,
> > And wanton, in full ease now live at large:
> > Unguarded leave the passes of the sky,
> > And all dissolved in hallelujahs lie.
>
> I have heard (says one of them) of anchovies *dissolved* in sauce; but never of an angel *in hallelujahs*. A mighty Wittycism! (if you will pardon a new word), but there is some difference between a Laugher and a Critic. —John Dryden, *The Author's Apology for Heroic Poetry*, 1677

When you search for the origins of words, 999 times out of a thousand the best you get is a rather vague sense of when and how a word or phrase was coined. So it's a true etymological thrill to find not only the when and how, but also the who, what, and where of a word's origins, and that's what we have here with the word *witticism*. In the above cita-tion (which I've quoted at length so you can get a better sense of the wordplay involved), the great English poet and dramatist John Dryden coins the word (as "Wittycism") as a pun on the word *criticism*. Nice!

W

Dryden used the word again in a 1683 play called *The Duke of Guise*. In that same year, a fellow named Edward Hooker used the word in a book preface ("What shal wee … think of Cramp-words, or Criticisms, Jocs, or Witticisms, Railleries and Drolleries"), and the future of Dryden's coinage was assured.

wizard

> ALBIUS   I have read in a book, that to play the fool
>   wisely, is high wisdom.
>
> GALLUS   How now, Vulcan! Will you be the first wizard?
>
> —Ben Jonson, *The Poetaster*, 1601

A *wizard* is a male witch, but it's more often used these days to refer to a person who is highly skilled in or knowledgeable about something. (The great inventor Thomas Edison's nickname was "The Wizard of Menlo Park.") It's high praise indeed to call someone a wizard, but that wasn't always the case. The word *wizard* comes from the Middle English word *wysard*, which combined the word *wys*, "wise," which sounds good so far, but also the suffix *-ard*, which has a negative connotation that indicates either sarcasm or excess. It's seen in lots of English insults, including *canard*, *coward*, *drunkard*, *laggard*, *sluggard*, and, of course, CELEBUTARD. For *wizard*, the original sense was probably something like "so-called wise man."

woebegone

> Welcome to Lake Wobegon, where all the women are strong, all the men are good-looking, and all the children are above average.
> —Garrison Keillor, *Lake Wobegon Days*, 1985

The name of Garrison Keillor's fictional town of Lake Wobegon, Minnesota, seems to be a misspelling of *woebegone* but, as you'll soon see, it's actually closer to the original spelling of the term. Since *woebegone* means "oppressed with sorrow, misfortune, or distress," you might think that the "begone" part is a kind of wishful or hopeful thinking ("be gone, woe"). Nope. Back in the 1300s, the original phrase was *woe bigon* (or *wo bigon*), where the word *bigon* meant "beset" (from the Old

English verb *bego*, "to go about") so the phrase meant "beset with woe." By the 1500s, this oft-used phrase had melded into the single word *woebegone*.

We're All Above Average Now

Garrison Keillor's fictional Minnesota town inspired the term *Lake Wobegon effect*, the tendency to treat all members of a group as above average, particularly with respect to numerical values such as test scores or executive salaries. It also refers to the tendency for most people in a survey to describe themselves or their abilities as above average. This effect is most often seen in educational test scores, where some teachers, schools, or school districts claim that all of their students score above average, a mathematical impossibility.

woolgathering

Shearing a sheep for its wool is hard work, but the old practice of woolgathering was a rather more laid back affair. In the sixteenth century, rural types would roam the countryside where sheep were kept to look for bits of wool that had snagged on bushes and hedges. Their plan was to gather enough wool to weave something they could sell for a bit of extra cash. As you can imagine, this involved a lot of wandering around and a lot of time, and to some it seemed that the resulting compensation wasn't enough to justify all that meandering. So around the middle of the sixteenth century, the phrase *to go woolgathering* meant "to indulge in idle fancies" and was being used to refer to indulging in daydreaming or a state of absent-mindedness. Eventually the phrase was shortened to just *woolgathering*.

work cut out for you

> Old Fezziwig stood out to dance with Mrs. Fezziwig. Top couple too; with a good stiff piece of work cut out for them. —Charles Dickens, *A Christmas Carol*, 1843

This citation shows that to have your *work cut out for you* means that you have a fairly arduous task ahead of you because you have about as much as you can handle (even if all you're doing is dancing). Did you

W

think the phrase had the opposite meaning, that having your work cut out for you was a good thing? After all, if some kind soul has gone and cut out your work for you, then that's one less chore you have to do, right? It's surprising how many people think this, but having your *work cut out for you* has had its "hands full" connotation since at least the early seventeenth century. The phrase comes from tailoring, as you might imagine. The idea behind it is that a tailor would have an assistant or apprentice who would do the actual cutting of the material, and the tailor himself would do the stitching. If the assistant got too far ahead of the tailor, he would end up with many pieces of cloth to stitch. Yes, his work is cut out for him, but that's not a good thing because the tailor now has to sort through the pile of material to get the right piece, which slows him down.

worm

And therewith began
A fearful battle betwixt worm and man.

—William Morris, *The Life and Death of Jason*, 1867

"A fearful battle betwixt worm and man"? What's up with *that?* Ah, the rub here is that the poet was speaking not of the tiny, harmless invertebrate that the *OED* wonderfully describes as a "slender, creeping, naked, limbless animal." Instead, he was using the older sense of the word *worm*, "a dragon or serpent," which came from the Old English *wyrm*, "serpent." That term's origin was the Latin *vermis*, "worm." (That Latin word is also, a bit disgustingly, the source of the pasta named *vermicelli*.)

worry

Excessive worrying can cause all kinds of harm, but can it kill a person? It's a possibility, but back in the day it was a certainty because when the word first entered the language in the eighth century it meant "to kill by strangling." Back then, the Old English term was *wyrgan*, which came from *wergia*, "to kill." (This comes from an old Indo-European root term meaning "to twist," which was also the source of twist-related terms such as *warp, wrangle, wrap, wreath, wrestle, wriggle,* and *writhe*.)

Over time the meaning of the word gradually became less violent. By the 1300s, it meant "to choke with a mouthful of food"; by the 1500s, it meant "to say something with closed teeth" and later "to harass physically or with hostile speech"; by the 1600s, it meant "to distress by inconsiderate behavior; to plague with repeated demands"; finally, by the mid-1800s, it took on the modern meaning of "to be anxious or troubled about something."

wunderkind

A *wunderkind* (officially pronounced as *VOON·dur·kint*) is a person who shows extraordinary talent or who has great success at a young age; it is, in short, a child prodigy. The literal meaning of this German word is "wonder child." *Kind* (pronounced *kint*) is German for "child," and it's where we get the word *kindergarten* (literal meaning: "children's garden").

W

XYZ

X and Y and Z, oh my!

This SNOWCLONE comes from *The Wizard of Oz*, where at one point in the action Dorothy, Tin Man, and Scarecrow say "Lions and tigers and bears, oh my!" Computer book authors seem to love the *X and Y and Z, oh my!* snowclone, and examples aren't hard to come by:

> Collaboration and Wikis and Blogs, Oh My!
> Lines and Transfers and Bits, Oh My!
> Backgrounds and Colors and Moving Text, Oh My!

X is the new Y

The idea behind this SNOWCLONE is the belief that some new thing "X" has become more popular than or has replaced some older thing "Y." The origins of this cliché go back to the 1950s, when *Vogue* editor Diana Vreeland commissioned the fashion photographer Norman Parkinson to do a shoot. In one picture, Parkinson shows a model in a pink coat beside a pink elephant. Vreeland's comment was "How clever of you, Mr. Parkinson, also to know that pink is the navy blue of India." This more complex "X is the Y of Z" formula gave way in the late 1970s to "X is the new neutral," which was very common for a time. That paved the way for "X is the new black," which dominated the fashion world in the 1980s. Now we see the general "X is the new Y" structure, and it's everywhere ("40 is the new 30," "Knitting is the new yoga," and on and on). You may recall that the tagline of the 2004 movie *Ocean's Twelve* (a sequel to *Ocean's Eleven*) was "Twelve is the new eleven." Apple marketed the iPod Shuffle by declaring that "Random is the new order." Not to be outdone, a Microsoft employee promoted the company's Zune media player with the phrase "Brown in the new black is the new white."

Xmas

When you shorten *Christmas* to *Xmas*, you may be struck by the apparent equation Christ = X, but do you ever wonder why in the name of you-know-who we do that? It comes from the Greek alphabet, of all things, which contains the letter chi—which is X as an uppercase letter and χ as a lowercase letter. Chi represents the sound we now associate with the letter K or a hard C. In Greek, *Christ* is spelled either as ΧΡΙΣΤΟΣ (uppercase) or χριστοσ (lowercase). Either way, the name begins with a letter that resembles the Roman X (that is, X or χ), so people have long used the letter *X* by itself as a short form of the word *Christ*. So *Christmas* becomes *Xmas*.

yacht

I'm always surprised at the number of yachts I see that fly pirate flags or have pirate-related names ("The Jollier Roger," "Pirates of the Hamptons," "Jack Sparrow's Nest"). Looking at things etymologically (as I like to do), these pirate pretensions are not surprising at all given the origins of the word *yacht*. It comes to us from the Dutch term *jaght*, short for *jaghtschip*, which referred to a "fast pirate ship"! (The literal meaning is "chase ship.") The term entered English in the mid-sixteenth century and, probably because no one could figure out the correct pronunciation of *jaght*, went through a comical series of spellings—*yeaghe*, *yoathe*, *yolke*, *yaugh*, *yaught*, *yought*, *yatch*, even *zaught*—before finally settling on *yacht* in the late eighteenth century.

yadda yadda yadda

You use the reduplicative phrase *yadda yadda yadda* to indicate that there's no point in providing details for some previous statement because those details are trivial, obvious, or uninteresting. Variations on the theme are legion, and they include the two-word version *yadda yadda*, spelling variants such as *yada yada*, *yaddah yaddah*, and *yatta yatta*, and even single-word blends such as *yadeyahdah*. Older instances (from

Y

the 1940s and 1950s) had extra syllables: *yaddega-yaddega* and *yattata-yattata*. It's likely this is an onomatopoeic phrase that imitates human speech, much like the equivalent phrase *blah blah blah*. The *OED* notes the resemblance to the word *yatter*, "idle talk; incessant chatter or gossip."

yahoo

> For as to those filthy Yahoos, although there were few greater lovers of mankind, at that time, than myself, yet I confess I never saw any sensitive being so detestable on all accounts; and the more I came near them, the more hateful they grew, while I stayed in that country. —Jonathan Swift, *Gulliver's Travels*, 1726

Earlier I told you about a couple of adjectives inspired by Jonathan Swift's great satire, *Gulliver's Travels*: BROBDINGNAGIAN and LILLIPUTIAN. Now we come to yet another Swiftian coinage: *yahoo*. Youngsters in the crowd may only be familiar with the name of the Internet company Yahoo!, but that has nothing to do with the word *yahoo*. (The company name is actually an acronym of the not-all-that-comprehensible phrase Yet Another Hierarchical Officious Oracle.) Swift used the term to refer to an imaginary race of brutish men, and within a few decades of the publication of *Gulliver's Travels* people were using *yahoo* to refer to any person lacking sophistication or cultivation, and later to your average lout or hooligan.

yellow journalism

The phrase *yellow journalism* refers to a sensational form of newspaper journalism that exaggerates or distorts the news to create publicity and increase circulation. The origin of yellow journalism goes back to a newspaper called the *New York World*, in which a cartoon strip titled *The Yellow Kid* featured a child in a yellow dress. This was in the late 1800s, so it was one of the first times color had been used in a newspaper. At the time, the paper was also printing sensational and exaggerated stories about Spanish atrocities against rebels who were fighting Spanish rule in Cuba. It was these stories combined with the yellow-print gimmick that produced the term *yellow journalism*.

yettie

When the dot-com boom was in full swing in the second half of the 1990s, young upstarts who reeked of arrogance and self-importance were written off as "dot snots." In fact the whole demographic was dismissed as a collection of *yetties*, young, entrepreneurial twenty-somethings. This is a play on YUPPIE, of course, but it also contains deliberate echoes of *yeti*, a hypothetical apelike creature that's supposed to inhabit the Himalayan Mountains. The yeti is a close cousin of North America's abominable snowman, so you often see the adjective "abomi-nable" and the noun "yettie" in the same sentence (or else shooting's-too-good-for-'em puns such as "the abominable showman").

yo

Linguists trot out the term *polysemic* when they come across a word that has many different meanings. The word *set*, for example, has 58 mean-ings as a noun, 126 as a verb, and 10 as an adjective! In hip-hop lingo, the polysemic champ is probably *yo*, which, depending on the context, can mean "hey," "what?," "check this out," "wow," "you," or "your," or it can act in a general way as an accompaniment or to add emphasis to a gesture or action. The word *yo* feels new, but versions of it have been in the language since the early fifteenth century, when it was originally used a kind of warning or a call to attention. (This sense gave us the famous nautical cry "yoho!")

yuppie

How a new word becomes part of the mainstream lexicon is a complex and mysterious bit of business. I've always maintained that it helps a lot if the word appears in print, particularly in a publication with a large readership, such as a big-city daily newspaper. That process seems to have worked to enshrine the word *yuppie* in the English language Hall of Fame. According to one account, Bob Greene, a syndicated colum-nist for *The Chicago Tribune*, overheard someone in a bar use the word *yuppie*. In a March 1983 column, Greene sprang the word on his exten-sive readership:

Y

While [Gerry Rubin] and Abby Hoffman once led the Yippies—
the Youth International Party—one social commentator has ven-
tured that Rubin is now attempting to become the leader of the
Yuppies—Young Urban Professionals.

The word *yuppie* subsequently appeared in dozens of articles over the
next few months, and it has never looked back. For a similar creature,
see YETTIE.

zaftig

All right, just between us guys: Does the sight of a full-figured woman
make you drool? Yes? Okay, first, you might want to have that problem
looked at. Second, this makes some linguistic sense in a male-chauvinist-
pig sort of way. You see the word *zaftig* (pronounced *ZAWF-tig*), "full-
figured," comes to us via Yiddish, which borrowed the Middle High
German word *saftec*, "juicy" (from *saft*, "juice").

M. Chauvin

You mostly see the term *chauvinist* nowadays as part of the phrase *male
chauvinist pig*, which entered English around 1970. However, the word
chauvinist had been part of the language for 100 years prior to that
with the more general meaning of "a person with an excessive sense of
superiority" or "a person who displays exaggerated loyalty." The latter
sense was the original, and it comes from a French soldier named
Nicolas Chauvin, who was ridiculed in his day for his excessive loyalty
to Napoleon.

zany

Do you know someone named John who is amusingly unusual or even
comically ridiculous? If so, call that person up right now and tell him
that he's "zany." Why? Because the source of our word *zany* is the
Italian given name *Giovanni*, "John," a form of which is *Gianni*. In
Italian commedia dell'arte (see also PANTS), one stock character was the
buffoonish servant who caused no end of trouble trying to imitate his
master, a professional clown. The foolish servant character was usually
named Gianni, and in certain locations (such as Venice), that name was

rendered as *Zanni*. In the late sixteenth century, the word *zani* (or *zanie*) made its English debut and had the same meaning as the Italian word. Witness the following bit from Shakespeare's 1588 play *Love's Labour's Lost:*

> Some carry-tale, some please-man, some slight zany,
> Some mumble-news, some trencher-knight, some Dick,
> That smiles his cheek in years and knows the trick
> To make my lady laugh

The noun soon generalized into any person who played the fool for amusement, and the adjectival form that we know today first made its appearance in 1616.

zeitgeist

> It is what we call the Time-Spirit that is sapping the proof from miracles,—it is the "Zeit-Geist" itself. —Matthew Arnold, *Literature and Dogma*, 1873

The *Zeitgeist* (it's almost always written with a capital "Z") refers to, as the *OED* quite thoroughly puts it, the "spirit or genius which marks the thought or feeling of a period or age." It's the sum total of the ideas— particularly those of culture, science, and religion—that are prevalent in a particular place at a particular time. The poet and critic Matthew Arnold brought the term *Zeitgeist* into English (he first used it in a letter written in 1848), and he imported it directly from German where, as the above citation shows, it blends the words *zeit*, "time," and *geist*, "spirit."

zenzizenzizenzic

For reasons known only to the chipmunks toiling away inside my brain, I desperately wanted to include in this book one of the craziest words I know: *zenzizenzizenzic*. It's an obsolete (no wonder!) term for the eighth power of a number. It comes from another dead word, *zenzic*, which meant "the square of a number." Put three "zenzics" in a row (with some adjustments), and you get the eighth power, just like that (since 2 times 2 times 2 equals 8). *Zenzic* comes from the Latin *zenzicus*, which

Z

is the root of our word *census*. How are a square of a number and a census even remotely related? A long time ago, mathematicians thought of a squared number as being the mathematical representation of a square area of land, and a person's land contains that person's possessions. The word *census* originally referred to the registration not only of the citizens of a country, but also each person's property, which included his possessions.

zilch

The history of the word zilch ("zero; nothing") is murky indeed, but one intriguing line of thought takes us back to a 1930s humor magazine called *Ballyhoo*, which featured a comic strip that included an unseen character named Mr. Zilch. What you *did* see was a bunch of near-naked, suggestively posed young women who would exclaim "Oh, Mr. Zilch" in reaction to something or other our hidden hero had done. Since there was nothing to see of Mr. Zilch, it's possible that his name came to mean "nothing." Another angle is that in the 1920s, slang slingers referred to an ordinary or nondescript person as *Joe Zilsch*, which is similar to more recent names for nobodies such as *Joe Average*, *Joe Blow*, *Joe Citizen*, *Joe Lunchpail*, *Joe Schmo*, and *Joe Six-pack*. No one knows where the word *Zilsch* came from, but an issue of *Literary Digest* magazine published in 1925 claims, unhelpfully, that the word "seems to have been coined at first as an imaginary instrument in an orchestra vaguely resembling the big bass horn."

zwieback

> Hope gave Nicky a zwieback and he stopped crying. —John Irving, *The World According to Garp*, 1978

The name of this crisp, dry bread comes from the way it's made: first you bake the loaf, then you slice it and bake (or toast) the slices to get them good and crispy. The loaf is literally "twice-baked," and that's also the literal translation of the German word *zwieback*, which combines *zwie*, "twice" (from *zwei*, "two") and *backen*, "baked." The word *zwieback* first showed up in English texts in 1894.

zydeco

The exuberant, toe-tapping Cajun music known as *zydeco* gets its name from an unlikely source: the humble bean. Early Cajun music would often include the line *Les haricots sont pas salés*. Here's an example with my translation:

> O Mam, mais donnez-moi les haricots.
> O yé yaie, les haricots sont pas salés.
> Oh Mama, give me the beans.
> O yé yaie, the beans are not salty.

"The beans are not salty" is a kind of code phrase that means there isn't any salted meat to go along with the beans, which is itself yet another code that refers to a person or family being too poor to afford meat. The key for our purposes is the French phrase *les haricots*, "the beans," which is pronounced *lay·ZAH·ree·coh*. Ideally, you want to have a little flutter of the tongue on the roof of the mouth when pronouncing the *r*, so the pronunciation sounds closer to *lay·ZAH·dee·coh*. Thanks to this pronunciation, over time, Cajun-English speakers replaced the French phrase *les haricots* with the Cajun word *zydeco*. The popularity of the term was assured when the most famous early Cajun singer Clifton Chenier recorded a song called "Zydeco Sont Pas Salé":

> O Mama! Quoi elle va faire avec le nègre?
> Zydeco est pas salé, zydeco est pas salé.
> Oh Mama! What's she going to do with the man?
> The beans aren't salty, the beans aren't salty.

The new word *zydeco* eventually transferred to the music itself, and an authentically American music genre had its own name.

Z

Appendix A

Resources to Further Your Etymological Education

This book gives you the origins of nearly 600 words and phrases. That sounds like a lot, but it's actually only about one tenth of 1 percent of all the words in the English language! In other words, if you're up for an extra dose of etymology, there's plenty more where all this came from. If you're not sure where to go from here, this appendix lists my favorite resources, both old-fashioned (books) and new-fangled (websites). Happy hunting!

Page Turners: Books on Word Origins

Here are a few tomes on word origins that I've enjoyed over the years:

Ayto, John. *20th Century Words*. Oxford University Press, 1999.

———. *Dictionary of Word Origins*. Arcade Publishing, 1990.

Chantrell, Glynnis, ed. *The Oxford Dictionary of Word Histories*. Oxford University Press, 2004.

Claiborne, Robert. *The Roots of English: A Reader's Handbook of Word Origins*. Times Books, 1989.

Farkas, Anna. *The Oxford Dictionary of Catchphrases*. Oxford University Press, 2003.

Hendrickson, Robert. *The Facts on File Encyclopedia of Word and Phrase Origins*. Checkmark Books, 2004.

Liberman, Anatoly. *Word Origins … and How We Know Them*. Oxford University Press, 2005.

McQuain, Jeffrey, and Stanley Malless. *Coined by Shakespeare: Words and Meanings First Penned by the Bard*. Merriam-Webster, 1998.

Merriam-Webster's New Book of Word Histories: Fascinating Stories About Our Living, Growing Language. Merriam-Webster, 1991.

Metcalf, Allan, and David K. Barnhart. *America in So Many Words: Words That Have Shaped America*. Houghton Mifflin Company, 1997.

Morris, Evan. *The Word Detective: Solving the Mysteries Behind Those Pesky Words and Phrases*. Plume Publishing, 2001.

Onions, C. T., ed. *The Oxford Dictionary of English Etymology*. Oxford University Press, 1966.

Quinion, Michael. *Ballyhoo, Buckaroo, and Spuds: Ingenious Tales of Words and Their Origins*. Collins Publishing, 2006.

Word Mysteries and Histories: From Quiche to Humble Pie. The Editors of American Heritage Dictionaries, Houghton Mifflin Company, 1986.

And of course, I would be remiss if I didn't mention the following two books, both written by a certain fellow who shall not remain nameless:

McFedries, Paul. *The Complete Idiot's Guide to a Smart Vocabulary*. Alpha Books, 2001.

————. *Word Spy: The Word Lover's Guide to Modern Culture.* Broadway Publishing, 2004.

Online Etymology: Some Websites to Check Out

Prefer to get your word origins on the web? Looking to kill some time at work? Wondering when this incessant questioning will end? Here's a bunch of fun websites that'll give your clicking finger a workout:

Behind the Name   www.behindthename.com

Etymologically Speaking   www.westegg.com/etymology/

Online Etymology Dictionary   www.etymonline.com

Oxford English Dictionary   http://oed.com

The Phrase Finder   www.phrases.org.uk

Take Our Word for It   www.takeourword.com

Wordorigins.org   www.wordorigins.org

The Word Detective   www.word-detective.com

Word Spy   www.wordspy.com

World Wide Words   www.worldwidewords.org

Appendix B

Glossary: Some Etymology Words You Should Know

acronym A pronounceable word created by using the first one (or sometimes two) letters of each word in a phrase. For example, see NIMBY. Other examples include UNICEF from United Nations International Children's Emergency Fund, and NATO from North Atlantic Treaty Organization.

aphaeresis The process of creating a new word by chopping off the initial letter or syllable of an existing word, as in the origins of NICK-NAME and *apron* (which I also discuss in the NICKNAME entry).

back-formation A word-coining process where a person sees an existing word, falsely places it in a particular grammatical category, and then modifies the word based on that false assumption. See, for example, PEA and UNKEMPT.

blending A linguistic process that creates a new word by combining the first part of one word with the last part of another word. For example, "brunch" is a blend of "breakfast" and "lunch." In this book there are dozens of blends, including CELEBUTARD ("celebrity" plus "retard") and FRIENEMY ("friend" plus "enemy").

borrowing   A linguistic process that creates new English words by bringing in words from other languages.

clipping   A kind of linguistic laziness that creates new words by lopping off great chunks of existing words. Usually the victims are unstressed syllables or nonprimary stress syllables. For a couple of examples, see BOGUS and PANTS.

Cockney rhyming slang   See *rhyming slang*.

compounding   Creating a new word by bolting two existing words together. See, for example, UNDERSTAND and WEBLOG.

echoism   This is the same as *onomatopoeia*.

elision   A linguistic process that creates a new word from a phrase by tacking on the last letter or syllable from the first word to the beginning of the second word. See, for example, TAWDRY (which comes from "St. Audrey").

etymology   The history of a word. For example, the etymology of *etymology* is that it comes from the Greek word *etumologia*, which combines *etumon*, "the true sense of a word," with *logia*, "the study of."

ex nihilo   The creation of a new word without reference to any existing word or phrase (literally, "from nothing"). See, for example, GOOGOL.

false analogy   This is the same as *back-formation*.

Indo-European   An ancient proto-language that linguists believe is the source of approximately one third of the world's languages, including Latin, the Romance languages (such as French, Italian, and Spanish), the Slavic languages (Czech, Polish, Russian, and others), the Indo-Iranian languages (Sanskrit, Persian, and others), Greek, Celtic, and the Germanic languages, which include English.

initialism   An unpronounceable word created by using the first one (or sometimes two) letters of each word in a phrase. For example, NHL from National Hockey League and NYPD from New York Police Department.

lexicon   The entire list of words in a particular language, subject, or profession, or the words that are known by a person.

loanword   An English word borrowed from another language. This book has too many loanwords to count, but PAPARAZZI and ZEITGEIST are two good examples.

onomatopoeia   This term means, literally, "name-making," but it refers to the specific process of creating words from the sounds associated with things. Check out FLIBBERTIGIBBIT and YADDA YADDA YADDA.

portmanteau   A word formed by *blending* the parts of two words.

reduplication   A word-forging process that creates a new word by doubling all or part of an existing word. See RIFF-RAFF.

rhyming reduplication   A form or *reduplication* where two words that rhyme are combined, as in HEEBIE-JEEBIES and HODGEPODGE.

rhyming slang   This is a form of slang that replaces a word with a phrase where the last word rhymes with the original word. (It's also called Cockney rhyming slang because it emerged from the Cockney population of London's East End.) See, for example, RASPBERRY and GET DOWN TO BRASS TACKS.

semantic shift   A linguistic process where the meaning of a word changes over time. For example, the word "nice" once meant "foolish or stupid" and people originally used "silly" to mean "deserving of pity." See also SHAMBLES and SURLY (to name just two of the many semantic shifts recorded in the book).

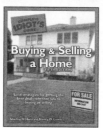

Great gifts for *any* occasion!